OUT OF THE SHADOWS

Canada in the Second World War

OUT OF THE SHADOWS

Canada in the Second World War

W.A.B. Douglas
and
Brereton Greenhous

REVISED EDITION

Dundurn Press
Toronto • Oxford

Design: Ron & Ron Design and Photography
Printed and bound in Canada by Metrolitho Inc.
First edition published in 1977 by Oxford University Press

The publisher wishes to acknowledge the generous assistance and ongoing support of the Canada Council, the Book Publishing Industry Development Program of the Department of Canadian Heritage, the Ontario Arts Council, the Ontario Publishing Centre of the Ministry of Culture, Tourism and Recreation, and the Ontario Heritage Foundation.

Care has been taken to trace the ownership of copyright material used in the text (including the illustrations). The author and publisher welcome any information enabling them to rectify any reference or credit in subsequent editions.

J. Kirk Howard, Publisher

Canadian Cataloguing in Publication Data

Douglas , W.A.B. (William Alexander Binny), 1929-
    Out of the shadows : Canada in the Second World War

Rev. ed.
Includes bibliographical references and index.
ISBN 1-55002-151-6

1. Canada. Canadian Armed Forces – History – World War, 1939-1945. 2. World War, 1939-1945 – Canada. 3. World War, 1939-1945 – History – 1939-1945. I. Greenhous, Brereton, 1929-   . II. Title.

D768.15.D69 1995   940.53'71   C94-932521-X

Dundurn Press Limited
2181 Queen Street East
Suite 301
Toronto, Canada
M4E 1E5

Dundurn Distribution
73 Lime Walk
Headington, Oxford
England
0X3 7AD

Dundurn Press Limited
1823 Maryland Avenue
P.O. Box 1000
Niagara Falls, N.Y.
U.S.A. 14302-1000

CONTENTS

MAPS

PREFACE FOR THE REVISED EDITION

Since the first edition of this book appeared, in 1977, there have been many books and articles published, many films and television programs produced, about all aspects of the Second World War. Canadian academic journals, some of them only established in recent years, have published interesting and often important new interpretations of the 1939-45 period. It is no longer true to say, as we did in the preface to the first edition, that there is no adequate account of Canada's part in the war. Why then bring out a revised edition?

The answer to that question lies in the nature and purposes of history. It was our intention to provide a popular overview of events so that the general reader could form a balanced view of this period in the country's history. There is still no other general and popular overview of that kind, while the need to understand those crucial years in the development of Canada is perhaps greater than ever. The discovery of new information about the Second World War, particularly in the realms of intelligence and cipher, and about individuals who have either written their reminiscences or been the subject of biographies, has led to new interpretations of key policies and operations. Consequently, our judgements on some matters have changed, and we would like to put those changes on record.

The task of revising the first edition has been a pleasant one. It is encouraging to find that, in spite of the many revisionist accounts of the war, and the raging controversies, we can still stand largely by the account we wrote eighteen years ago. Moreover, after a number of vigorous discussions the authors can still reach a consensus and are still speaking to each other. We hope the reader will enjoy reading this revised edition as much as we have enjoyed writing it.

ACKNOWLEDGEMENTS

We have many people to thank, especially the late General J.A. Dextraze, CBE, CMM, DSO, CD, chief of the Defence Staff, who encouraged us in this project at its inception. Critical comment and valuable information from our colleagues in the Directorate of History, National Defence Headquarters, is gratefully acknowledged, especially on the part of Norman Hillmer, the late Fred Hatch, and William McAndrew. Previous official historians, notably C.P. Stacey and G.W.L. Nicholson, have paved the way for all scholars in this field. S.F. Wise gave us moral support, which we both appreciated. J.L. Granatstein, who also was an official historian at one time, is one of the most prolific scholars now working on this period and we have frequently consulted his writings; we are further in his debt because he read the entire manuscript, making invaluable suggestions. Peter Robertson of the Public Archives of Canada gave particular help in selecting photographs. Jacquie Stevens of the Vancouver Public Library, John Chown of the Canadian War Museum, and Robert Crawford and his staff at the Imperial War Museum also provided useful assistance in this task. William Toye, Richard Teleky, and Martha Dzioba of Oxford University Press (Canada) gave valuable editorial help in the preparation of the first edition, as did Judith Turnbull of Dundurn Press with the revised edition.

WABD & BG

Quoted Material

Excerpts from the following books have been reprinted with the kind permission of the copyright holders.

Earle Birney, *Turvey* (The Canadian Publishers, McClelland and Stewart Limited, Toronto). Barry Broadfoot, *Six War Years: 1939-1945,* Copyright © 1974 by Barry Broadfoot (Doubleday & Company, Inc.). Barry Broadfoot, *Ten Lost Years: 1929-1939.* Copyright © 1973 by Barry Broadfoot (Doubleday & Company, Inc.). Humphrey Carver, *Compassionate Landscape* (University of Toronto Press). Lucien Dumais, *Un Canadien français à Dieppe* (Editions France-Empire). Alan Easton, *50 North: An Atlantic Battleground* (McGraw-Hill Ryerson Limited). Martha Gellhorn, *The Face of War* (Sphere Books Ltd). ©1936, 1937, 1938, 1939, 1940, 1941, 1942, 1943, 1944, 1945, 1959, 1967 by Martha Gellhorn. By permission of Elaine Greene Ltd, Literary Agency. Richard Gentil, *Trained to Intrude* (Bachman & Turner Publishers). J.E. Johnson, *Wing Leader* (Chatto & Windus Ltd and Ballantine Books, a Division of Random House, Inc.). Alexander McKee, *Caen: Anvil of Victory* (Souvenir Press Ltd). Daphne Marlatt, *Steveston Recollected* (Aural History, Provincial Archives, Victoria, B.C.). Jerrold Morris, *Canadian Artists and Airmen 1940-45.* By permission of the author. Donald Pearce, *Journal of a War* (The Macmillan Company of Canada Limited). L.B. Pearson, *Mike: The Memoirs of the Rt. Hon. Lester B. Pearson, Vol I: 1897-1948* (University of Toronto Press). Charles Ritchie, *The Siren Years: A Canadian Diplomat Abroad 1937-1945* (The Macmillan Company of Canada Limited). Gabrielle Roy, *The Tin Flute* translated by Hannah Josephson (The Canadian Publishers, McClelland and Stewart Limited, Toronto). Hans Rumpf, *The Bombing of Germany* (White Lion Publishers). Warren Tute, *D-Day* (Sidgwick & Jackson Ltd). John Windsor (ed.), *Blind Date* (Gray's Publishing Ltd). John Winton (ed.), *The War at Sea 1939-1945* (A.D. Peters & Co. Ltd, London).

Illustration Credits

Atomic Energy of Canada: 131. Department of National Defence: 2, 11, 12, 13, 14, 16, 17, 23, 29, 30, 31, 32, 33, 34, 35, 36, 37, 38, 39, 40, 41, 42, 43, 44, 45, 46, 47, 48, 49, 50, 52, 53, 54, 55, 56, 57, 59, 60, 61, 62, 63, 64, 65, 66, 67, 68, 69, 70, 71, 72, 73, 74, 75, 76, 77, 79, 80, 81, 82, 83, 84, 85, 86, 87, 88, 89, 91, 92, 93, 94, 95, 96, 97, 98, 100, 101, 102, 103, 104, 106, 108, 109, 110, 111, 112, 114, 115, 116, 118, 119, 120, 121, 122, 123, 124, 125, 126, 127, 128, 129, 133, 135, 146, 147, 148, 149, 150. *Herbie,* Bing Coughlin (Thomas Nelson & Sons Limited): 78. Imperial War Museum: 90, 99. Metropolitan Toronto Library Board: 24, 28, 58, 140, 141, 142, 144. *Normandy and On* by Lieut. Les Callan (Longmans, Green and Co.): 113, 117. The National Archives of Canada (National Photography Collection): 1, 4, 5, 6, 18, 19, 20, 21, 22, 25, 26, 27, 51, 130, 132, 136, 137, 138, 139, 151. The National Archives of Canada (Montreal *Gazette*): 7, 9, 10, 134, 145. The National Archives of Canada (Historical Photo): 15. Copyright© *Toronto Sun:* 143. Ullstein Bilderdienst, Berlin: 105, 107. Vancouver Public Library: 3, 8.

1 Young Canadians
awaiting the appearance
of the King and Queen,
June 1939.

Chapter 1

The Eve of War

Beneath a clear blue sky the Canadian Pacific liner *Empress of Australia* sailed under the ramparts of the Citadel of Quebec on Wednesday morning, May 17, 1939, watched by thousands of people in a holiday mood. King George VI and Queen Elizabeth had come to Canada, and the excitement surrounding the royal visit had reached a high pitch. It was the first-ever visit to Canada by a reigning sovereign, and only the third time a British monarch had left Europe. Red Ensigns, Union Jacks, and tricolours flew from the buildings in Quebec's Lower Town; girl guides, boy scouts, and Papal Zouaves lined the streets; and twenty-five thousand schoolchildren gathered on the Plains of Abraham, waiting to sing 'God Save the King' in French.

William Lyon Mackenzie King, Liberal prime minister of Canada, headed the official welcoming party at Wolfe's Cove. The tour was something of a coup for him, planned while he visited London for the Coronation and the Imperial Conference in 1937. Besides certain political advantages (it would prove that loyalty to the Crown in Canada was not confined to the Tories), there were good diplomatic reasons for the visit. After the virtual collapse of the League of Nations over the Ethiopian crisis of 1935, Europe seemed to be drifting to war and, in an unstable world, it was surely desirable to strengthen the emotional ties of Canadians to Britain and the Commonwealth.

At the Imperial Conference of 1937, Mackenzie King had successfully campaigned against those who would entangle him in an imperial foreign and defence policy; he gave his support, however, to a policy of economic and political appeasement to prevent conflict. His personal response to the threats against world peace that Hitler portended was a somewhat quixotic one: he resolved to try bringing Britain and Germany together himself. After the Conference was over he visited the German dictator, with whom he felt he shared a sympathetic concern for the workingman, and endeavoured to explain the peaceful intent of the British Empire. As he told a later British High Commissioner to Canada, Malcolm MacDonald, he warned Hitler "that if Germany should ever turn her mind from constructive to destructive efforts against the United Kingdom all the Dominions would come to her aid and that there would be great numbers of Canadians anxious to swim the Atlantic."[1] He came out of the interview, as so many had done before him, just as blissfully unaware of the real Hitler as when he went in. On his return, he told a Canadian

2 Adolf Hitler: "To His Excellency the Canadian Prime Minister Dr W.L. Mackenzie King as a friendly reminder of his visit on 29 June 1937."

radio audience that the Führer's charm had persuaded him of his host's "great sincerity."

The European situation worsened. In 1938 – "Hitler's Year" in the words of one historian – came the Nazi takeover of Austria and Hitler's demand to incorporate the Sudeten Germans of Czechoslovakia into the Third Reich. At Munich, in September, he persuaded Prime Minister Neville Chamberlain of Great Britain and Premier Edouard Daladier of France to accept his promise that he would ask for no more territory, and he was allowed to occupy the Sudetenland. But in March 1939, without any warning, his troops occupied the rest of Czechoslovakia. Although King still hoped for appeasement, he had now come to believe that war was inevitable, and envisaged "bombers raining death on London." There, the British Cabinet nearly advised King George VI to cancel his Canadian visit. The monarch was in a difficult position. He wanted to be in Britain if war broke out, yet he believed a visit to Canada would strengthen its ties to the mother country at a crucial moment in his-

The Eve of War

tory. In addition to this, he was most anxious to strengthen Anglo-American relations by means of personal diplomacy in the United States – a desire that President Roosevelt shared. A decision was made that the visit should go ahead.

The enthusiastic and harmonious reception that greeted the royal couple in Quebec City belied a complex set of feelings in Canada. As a member of the British Empire – or the British Commonwealth of Nations, as it was now called – the country had taken part in the Great War of 1914-18, sharing the common belief that future world peace depended upon the defeat of Britain's enemies. Canada had been deeply affected by that war, in which the slaughter had been so great that "never again" became a frequent isolationist cry in the 1920s and 1930s. Readily identifiable segments of the population rejected the idea of becoming involved in any more European quarrels. Even after Hitler had seized power in Germany in 1933, and peace again became a fragile thing, their isolationism prevailed.

However, the Great War had also reinforced a sentimental attachment to the imperial connection in a politically significant cross-section of the country whose views were made known in the press through political activists led by C.G. McCullagh, publisher of the Toronto *Globe and Mail* and organizer of the short-lived but nationally influential Leadership League. The European crisis that developed with Hitler's ascendancy brought out their deep-seated conviction that Britain must be supported in a war. But it was not as simple as that. The well-known editor of the *Winnipeg Free Press*, John W. Dafoe, had written in 1937 that, in a crisis, "the people of Canada will begin to get on one side or another of a line which will run through every province, every township, and through a good many homes as well."[2]

It was not only the European crisis that created divisions in Canada. The economic depression that Canada and the United States had been suffering for nearly ten years had brought about hardships and privations that produced strong feelings of resentment towards government – federal, provincial, and municipal. These in turn spawned active political discontent – especially on the Prairies, which had undergone unusually severe droughts and dust storms. The Co-operative Commonwealth Federation (CCF), a democratic socialist party, was formed by farm and labour groups in Calgary in 1932, and the Social Credit party took power in Alberta in 1935 under Premier William Aberhart, who preached an 'easy money' doctrine that would bring production and consumption into balance to overcome the paradox of plentiful goods and scarce money. Like some other provincial premiers, Aberhart opposed the assumption of additional powers by the federal government.

Widespread unemployment was epitomized by the "On-to-Ottawa" march of June 1935, when a thousand unemployed men, commandeering freight trains, headed east from Vancouver to protest

13   *The Eve of War*

3 Depression malaise: RCMP and Vancouver police clear out the post office after the sit-down strike by Relief Camp workers in June 1938.

their situation. When they entered Regina a week later, their numbers had doubled. However, the trek ended in abortive meetings and a riot, with no solution to their problems. Strikes continued across Canada. A peaceful 'sit-in' by relief camp workers in the Vancouver Post Office and other public buildings was broken up by the Royal Canadian Mounted Police on 'Bloody Sunday' (June 19, 1938) when thirty-five strikers were injured. The Liberal premier of the province, T. Dufferin Pattullo, responded to the protest by deporting unemployed non-residents of British Columbia back to their homes on the Prairies.

The difficulties in Canada worried the British. Sir Maurice Hankey, the secretary of the Committee of Imperial Defence, was asked in 1934 to assess the attitudes of Canada towards the imperial connection, especially in case of a European war. Finding that the Depression had intensified an isolationist spirit in Canada, he observed that French Canadians were "bitterly hostile to co-operation in Imperial Defence," along with "great blocks of unabsorbed aliens" – Ukrainians, Russians, Poles, etc. – and that "a number of people on the prairies and in the west of British or American origin, who have fallen on hard times, are in a bitter, resentful frame of mind."

The Eve of War

To these adverse forces, which count for much in an election year, must be added the 'highbrows' who meet in places like the Institute of International Affairs and, judged by what I heard and read of their proceedings, talk a lot of dreadful 'slop.' The kind of idea they ventilate is that Canadian territory is secured by the Monro [*sic*] doctrine; that Canada ought to remain neutral in an Empire war; that Japan and Germany are so well aware of this sentiment, that they would be careful to avoid any action against Canada; but that it would be preferable to put up with insult and aggression, the sinking of Canadian ships and cargoes, and the loss of most of her overseas trade, rather than to fight.[3]

In his report, Hankey made the point that Britain would be drawn into a European war only through extreme provocation. Under those circumstances, he felt, Canadians would come to Britain's aid; but he also believed, correctly, that pressures from "the old country" would not suffice to win Canadian support. It was essential for Canadian leaders to educate their public about British motives. There was none of the fervid imperialism he had found in Australia and New Zealand. He eventually concluded that, in the event of Britain's becoming involved in a war against Germany, "Canada would respond," just as it had done in 1914. In that statement he echoed the words of Mackenzie King at the time of the Imperial Conference of 1923. At the same time, he found in the Canada of 1934, and especially in Ottawa – which had gained autonomy over the nation's foreign policy with the Statute of Westminster of 1931 – a "calculating aloofness" that made assumptions about Canadian attitudes difficult.[4] Yet assumptions soon became necessary. Remembering that Canada had made a significant industrial contribution to the Imperial cause in the First World War, Whitehall asked, in 1935, for information concerning the potential of Canadian industry in the production of munitions.

Responding to this initiative, the Canadian Army, Navy, and Air Supply Committee embarked on a continuing survey of industrial firms. By the end of 1938 reports of 1,227 enterprises indicated that Ontario was the largest single source, with 673; Quebec followed with 219. Their potential contribution to the war effort was followed by that of British Columbia, which had managed to preserve a strong industrial base in spite of the Depression. The industrial contribution of the Maritimes would be insignificant. By their geographic position they were deprived of much of the trade going to central Canada, which moved through Montreal rather than through Atlantic ports. As a result, the hinterlands of Halifax and Saint John had not developed widespread industry.

Limited Canadian rearmament began in 1935 – the year Mackenzie King became prime minister for the third time – but it did not reflect a sudden change of heart. Rather it represented the concern of the Cabinet, which had been warned by the Canadian service chiefs of unprepared armed forces, and it was pushed by a vocal and influential section of the populace that considered any dereliction in Canada's contribution to Imperial defence tantamount to pulling out of the Commonwealth. Rationalizing his decision to rearm, in January 1937, King observed that "Meighen [the Conservative ex-prime minister] would do so much more – at least so he says – and Woodsworth [leader of the CCF] would do nothing at all. The safe policy is the middle course between these two views – the safe policy is a rational policy of domestic defence."[5]

King was an experienced politician who had been at the forefront of Canadian politics for more than fifteen years by 1937, and he was probably right. But in the spring of 1939 thoughts of war were far from the minds of those who thronged to see the King and Queen. Enthusiasm for the Imperial connection seemed to be everywhere, even in Quebec City. The old French-Canadian capital had been a critical choice for the start of the tour. The conscription crisis of 1917 had had a divisive effect on the nation and Quebec isolationists and nationalists, such as Henri Bourassa, had attacked British policies then, arguing that Britain was an imperialist power engaged in a war for territory.

Similar arguments had reappeared in the 1930s, and might still be expected to arouse strong feelings against participation in a British war, yet the monarch arrived in Quebec to find a scene of apparent harmony and content. Loyal sentiments in the province had been stirred up by politicians, veterans' organizations, and church leaders. There were other ingredients of loyalty that were of particular significance in the shadow of war. They were well represented by the Royal 22ᵉ Régiment du Canada (colloquially called the 'Van Doos') whose colonel-in-chief was the King himself. The proud military tradition with which the Van Doos were associated contributed to the festive and loyal mood.

Ernest Lapointe, Mackenzie King's Quebec lieutenant and his minister of justice, was an extremely powerful figure in Quebec and one Québécois who recognized that Canada would have to participate in a major British war. Thus he was anxious to secure an enthusiastic reception in French Canada for the royal couple. On his advice, presumably, Senator Raoul Dandurand was selected to greet them, a choice that seemed to acknowledge the existence of isolationist feelings in the province, for it was Dandurand who had coined the famous isolationist phrase, "We live in a fireproof house far from inflammable materials," in a speech to the League of Nations in Geneva in 1924.

Dandurand still opposed commitments to Imperial and European defence and he was inclined to blame Britain, the United States, Italy, and Germany, all more or less equally, for the threatened

4 The King and Queen sign the visitors' book at the Montreal City Hall, with Mayor Camillien Houde in attendance and Prime Minister Mackenzie King seated in the background, May 18, 1939.

demise of the League and the impending approach of war. But above all, he was a patriot, a *Canadien tout court*, and in many ways he was typical of French Canada. His demonstrated attachment to the Crown must have carried much weight in the province. When the King responded to Dandurand's welcome in French, the onlookers were delighted; Queen Elizabeth's easy use of the language also made a favourable impression.

As the tour proceeded through Quebec, the royal couple scored more political points. Mayor Camillien Houde of Montreal was allowed the place of honour in the royal procession through the city, taking precedence over Mackenzie King and all other dignitaries. When a hundred thousand people massed outside the Windsor Hotel in Montreal on May 18, Houde revelled in the reflected glory. A wily politician, he was happy to demonstrate friendship with such a popular monarch.

By the time the King and Queen reached Ontario – they arrived in Ottawa on May 19 – they had caught the imagination of hundreds of thousands of Canadians. Wherever crowds gathered, allegiance to the monarchy was underscored by the presence of war veterans. Ten thousand of them gathered at the unveiling of the National War Memorial in Ottawa, where the King and Queen walked among them. Wherever the royals went, political leaders hastened to go too. Mackenzie King became their constant shadow, eager to implant the idea that he was closely associated with the Crown; and in the presence of the Sovereign the inherent political disunity of the country tended to be forgotten.

Toronto was a traditional cradle of loyalism. Yet even there, isolationist sentiment was strong. Frank Underhill, the distinguished historian, and a First World War veteran, was perhaps most outspoken in his views. He had written in the *Canadian Forum* that "all these European troubles are not worth the bones of a Toronto grenadier." His views, of course, were those of a minority. As Bruce Hutchison observed in *The Unknown Country* (1942), it was in Toronto that "the Colonial Mind, that vestigial organ which no longer functions but often can ache, still manages to exist without nourishment." Indeed, by the time the royal couple left on May 23, there was no question of the city's overwhelming loyalty.

From a British perspective, their tour was already a grand success. Two years later, in the spring of 1941 and the midst of the war, Charles Ritchie, the second secretary at the Canadian High Commission in London, was to reflect, somewhat cynically, upon its impact.

> The Royal Tour in Canada was the occasion for an overpowering manifestation on the part at any rate of some Canadians of a deep yearning towards the *mother* country. (England never thinks of herself as a mother country nor is the phrase ever heard here.) Above all the whole Tour was an example of the English genius for making use of people – a genius so highly developed in both their political and private lives.[6]

When the King and Queen proceeded westward to the Prairie provinces, they faced a major test. Here were to be found "the great blocks of unabsorbed aliens" reported by Hankey in 1934, and here

18   *The Eve of War*

was the worst Depression-induced poverty in the land. But here, also, were political leaders who showed unambivalent feelings towards the British connection. William Aberhart, for instance – later an opponent of the strong Anglo-American ties in the Atlantic Charter – had proclaimed, in his popular daily religious broadcasts, that the British Commonwealth and the United States were "God's battle axe."

George VI seemed to confirm this belief in the Commonwealth as a force for good while speaking in Winnipeg on May 24. "Hold fast to all that is just and of good report in the heritage which your fathers have left you...." The message would have fallen on deaf ears if Hankey's assessment of 1934 had been entirely correct. Yet again and again the King and Queen found the same welcome and the same enthusiasm they had encountered in the two central provinces. Although Manitoba, Saskatchewan, and Alberta were unable to match Ontario and Quebec in population or industry, their reception of the monarch was no less enthusiastic.

On the other side of the Rockies, the response did not quite follow the pattern of the other provinces. According to Margaret Ormsby, the historian of British Columbia, cheers for the royal couple "were less spontaneous" than those for the Prince of Wales (later Duke of Windsor) had been in the 1920s. When the King and Queen appeared, accompanied both by the prime minister and the premier of British Columbia, Duff Pattullo, the crowds must have found it difficult to put out of their minds their smouldering resentment towards Patullo for his handling of the Vancouver Post Office riots only a year before.

They not only were still bitter about his harsh treatment of unemployed Canadians, but compared it unfavourably with his disregard of so-called subversive elements and fifth columnists in the province – spectres in the public imagination that had been created by war scares in both Asia and Europe. The substance of loyalty was undoubtedly there – the response to the Great War by British Columbians, many of whom were English-born, had been exemplary – but the appearance was somewhat muted.

After making a return journey across Canada, which brought a succession of enthusiastic demonstrations, the King and Queen visited the United States from June 7 to 10. They went to Washington and attended the World's Fair in New York – the city's mayor, Fiorello La Guardia, claimed that their visit "did more good than the sending of a dozen ambassadors or the interchange of fifty diplomatic notes" – on their way to the Roosevelt home at Hyde Park, New York, where Eleanor Roosevelt gave her famous hot-dogs-and-beer picnic.

The royal couple re-entered Canada from Vermont and continued east to the Maritimes. Although New Brunswick, Prince Edward Island, and Nova Scotia had Liberal governments, their ties with

Ottawa were weak. Anti-confederation feeling inherited from a past generation still ran strong, while suspicion of 'Upper Canada' was greater there than in any other region of the Dominion. But in the Maritimes generally, and particularly in Nova Scotia, there had always been a strong Imperial sentiment, and there could be no doubt of the affection for Britain. That spirit was reinforced by the military and naval presence in the old garrison town of Halifax, the port from which the King and Queen sailed on June 16, and the port from which, three months later to the day, the first wartime convoy would sail for England.

Not even the prime minister had expected the royal visit to be so successful. In his diary King paraphrased his farewell words to Their Majesties:

> I hoped they would go away feeling that they had helped to unite Canada and different parts of the Empire and to consolidate a continent in friendly feelings. That I honestly believed that they had done a service to the world at a time of the world's greatest need, and in a manner which only they could possibly have performed that service.[7]

One provincial premier had told the King's private secretary: "You can go home and tell the old country that any talk they may hear about Canada being isolationist after today is just nonsense."[8] That was undoubtedly exaggerated but isolationist feeling had, indeed, been dulled. Other causes of disagreement and even discontent remained, however. Canada still lacked cohesion. Provincial governments still contended against federal authority. There was still massive unemployment. The youth of the land resented their lack of opportunity. The government, in its response to the Depression, had shown extreme caution – 'stand pat-ism' had substituted for social reform. But it is probably true to say that the royal visit diverted attention from these problems and did so at an opportune moment.

When Hitler marched into Poland on September 1, 1939, and Europe prepared for war, Canada responded – but without the wave of enthusiasm that had characterized 1914. Instead the Cabinet laid its contingency plans rather timidly, preparing not for total war but for a war of limited liability – and one in which Canada's stake was certainly not that of a principal power. The prime minister recognized that there had been some change in national sentiment as a result of the royal tour, but he – and, he believed, the country – had no desire to plunge heavily into military commitments. Georges Héon, a Tory MP from Quebec, urged "co-operation but was against the sending of an expeditionary force and against conscription" – an attitude that vast numbers of French Canadians shared.

O.D. Skelton, the under-secretary of state for external affairs and King's most trusted adviser, counselled his chief to concentrate on air

6 The departure of the King and Queen from Halifax in the *Empress of Canada*, June 17, 1939. The sea and air escorts represented virtually all Canada's naval and air forces on the Atlantic coast.

rather than land commitments, so that military activity overseas and manpower problems at home would be kept to the minimum. And more important than any military effort, Skelton stressed, was the provision of munitions, raw materials, and foodstuffs. That would help Britain and help beat the Depression, too.

At the end of August, shortly after Hitler had stunned the world by successfully concluding a non-aggression pact with the Soviet Union, the Cabinet had declared a state of apprehended war by Order in Council, thus enabling the armed forces to go to a war footing. On September 3, Britain and France declared war, but Canada did not immediately follow suit. Mackenzie King had always maintained that "Parliament will decide," and he meant what he had said. An emergency session was summoned to meet on September 7, but while MPs began to converge on Ottawa the government maintained its posture of apparent non-involvement. In the quarter-century since 1914 (when Canada had gone to war without any say of its own people) the

21

Statute of Westminster had given Canada autonomy, if not independence, in foreign policy. Now Canadians themselves, through their elected representatives in Ottawa, would decide whether or not to go to war.

CHAPTER 2

An Unmilitary I

German tanks crossed the Polish border on the *1939* and *Luftwaffe Stukas* began their relentless dive-bombing attacks on enemy communications that became identified with the *Blitzkrieg,* terrorizing all of Europe. Britain, honouring defence agreements with Poland, declared war on Germany two days later and France immediately followed suit. Though Canada preserved the appearance of neutrality by waiting for the authority of Parliament to declare war, the Cabinet went ahead with creating the machinery for wartime government. On August 30 the Emergency Council – consisting of the prime minister, the ministers of defence, fisheries, finance, mines and resources, and the Senate government leader – had come into being. It set in motion the mobilization of the armed forces on September 1.

On that day Mackenzie King also cabled London for advice about Britain's expectations of Canada. Anthony Eden, the newly appointed Dominions secretary, responded on September 6. "It is hoped that Canada would exert her full national effort as in the last war," he wrote, "even to the extent of the eventual dispatch of an expeditionary force." Meanwhile, the Admiralty wanted operational control of Royal Canadian Navy ships; recruits were needed for the Royal Naval Reserve and the Volunteer Reserve; and the Air Ministry asked the Royal Canadian Air Force to recruit for the Royal Air Force, promising a Royal Canadian Air Force contingent when sufficient men had been found. The mother country looked to the Canadian army for support as well, although the British government realized that "no statement of policy on these lines is likely to be possible for the moment."[1]

Mackenzie King was still opposed to embarking on adventures abroad and was surprised to discover that his chiefs of staff were thinking in terms of sending the army overseas. In London, there was now a sound strategic basis for dispatching a British Expeditionary Force to the continent, something that had not seemed likely only a year before, and to exclude a Canadian component from such a force was unthinkable to Canadian military planners and the pro-British segments of the population. But the prime minister, who was not well versed in the strategic (or tactical) implications of war, did not believe that this was the real reason for the proposal to send troops overseas. He looked upon it as though it were a deliberate conspiracy to undermine his determination to restrict demands on manpower and to avoid conscription.

An Unmilitary People

The British World Digest
THE WORLDS BEST DIGEST BOOK
THE WORLDS BEST DIGEST BOOK
ON SALE
Star Subscriptions Taken Here
Newspapers from your Home Town
Send a Funny Postcard home
SPECIAL EXTRAS AT 9:30 — ON THE TONIGHT!
FRANCE
SPECIAL EXTRA AT 9:30 — TONIGHT!

By the time the Cabinet met, on September 6, the war situation in Poland seemed grim, yet King was surprised to find that some of his ministers were showing more support for an expeditionary force than he had imagined they would. He was even more taken aback when he detected pro-conscription sympathies among some members of Parliament. He sided with Ernest Lapointe and opposed conscription for overseas service, though he did not rule out the possibility of calling up men to defend Canada.

Parliament met in an emergency session on September 7. Though J.S. Woodsworth, the CCF leader, opposed the decision to go to war on pacifist grounds, and Liguori Lacombe, a Quebec Liberal, opposed it in isolationist terms, there were few other voices of protest. The Conservative opposition not only supported the government but, back in March, had already adopted an identical attitude towards conscription. Not all Conservatives agreed, but Dr R.J. Manion, the party's leader, had committed himself to the position that Canadian youth should not be conscripted to fight outside Canada's borders.

There is ample evidence to show that this emergency session accurately reflected a lukewarm response of the electorate. Canadians

An Unmilitary People

generally supported the government with various reservations. Major-General W.A. Griesbach, a Conservative senator and veteran of two wars, represented the opinion of thousands with similar backgrounds who believed the country should participate but were worried that the youth of the nation – discontented as they were with their lot – would not react favourably. O.D. Skelton, like others of his essentially nationalistic and liberal persuasion, accepted the war partly as a blow dealt by fate, partly as a result of British bungling. In French Canada only André Laurendeau's *Le Devoir* showed any overt opposition to King's policy; the other newspapers in the province gave it their cautious support.

Throughout the country the strong pacifist beliefs of many clergy held sway, but these were countered by a differing view of 'the church militant' held by many others. Perhaps the decisive factor was a realization that staying neutral would create unacceptable anomalies in relations with Britain and the rest of the Commonwealth. Neutrality might tend to destroy the indivisibility of the British Crown with the Dominion of Canada – a principle successfully brought home by the royal visit only a few months before.[2]

Overt opposition to Canada's participation in the war seemed equally half-hearted. As Bourassa's disciple, André Laurendeau, admitted later, "I was a militant anti-participationist, but there was little evidence that I was followed by the majority of my compatriots."[3] On the face of the evidence it is possible to argue, and indeed it has been argued, that most Canadians believed this was to be a war of limited liability, in which the principal contribution would be economic rather than military.

So on September 9, the Canadian Parliament approved the policy of declaring war against Germany. The following day Canada cabled the draft text of a declaration of war to Vincent Massey, the

8   The Militia in June 1937. Reflecting a grandiose paper organization of eleven divisions and four cavalry divisions, this small unit on church parade in Vancouver was called the 11th Divisional Signals.

An Unmilitary People

Canadian high commissioner in London, who would relay the final version to George VI for signature. It was a momentous occasion – the first time Canada had declared war on its own behalf – and proper form had to be observed. Lester Pearson, who was a member of Canada's diplomatic corps in London, later wrote in his memoirs:

> We had no experience in declaring war ... [I] wrote out the proper words on a plain sheet of paper. Then I telephoned my friend, Tommy Lascelles, at the palace, to ask whether I could show him the draft document for approval or amendment. He told me to come along, and in a few minute I was in his office.... Since the king was in the office next door, he would 'pop in' and get royal confirmation. He returned in a few minutes to say that His Majesty had not only approved the text but had indicated this by signing it. This was satisfactory but somewhat startling, as it was only a draft for consideration.... The written, formal submission which was to follow the cabled one did not arrive for some weeks. This was indeed reprehensible delay because the earlier informal document, a cabled message, obviously could not have on it the Prime Minister's written signature. A legal purist could claim, indeed, that without such a written signature the submission had no legal effect and that Canada was not, technically, at war until the formal submission signed in his own handwriting by the Prime Minister was received and approved by His Majesty. Therefore, on 24 October Mr. Massey had to telegraph Ottawa: "Buckingham Palace enquiring when they may expect formal submission in writing."[4]

A formal submission – signed by Mackenzie King and ante-dated September 10 – finally reached the King for signature on November 27, eleven weeks after Canada had declared war. The prime minister took much satisfaction in the way he had brought the country into the conflict, "with a quietude and peace almost comparable to that of a vessel sailing over a smooth and sunlit lake; ... we had kept down all passion and faction, and now were a united country."[5]

Political consensus for a declaration of war was one thing; the military and industrial capability to back it up was another. Much effort was necessary before Canada would be able to make more than a token contribution. It would be an understatement to say that the country was not prepared for the scale of conflict about to be experienced.

The pre-war army – the service most noticeably affected by mobilization – was based on a Permanent Force of only four thousand trained soldiers, buttressed by a Non-Permanent Active Militia (as one regimental historian has observed, "Canadian governments are partial to cumbersome euphemisms to describe their military forces") that included another fifty thousand partly trained men at the begin-

9 The somewhat remote aspect of the war in this Montreal *Gazette* photograph of September 12, 1939, is reflected by the 18-pounder gun, a relic of the Great War; by the uniforms of similar vintage; and by the self-conscious pose of the recruiters.

ning of 1939. According to the war plans of Defence Scheme No. 3, first drafted in 1930 with amendments as late as July 10, 1939, the army would form a Mobile Force for the direct defence of Canada. Some ten thousand men had been called out as a preparatory measure on August 25, two days after the Russo-German non-aggression pact was signed, and a flood of volunteers arrived when mobilization began on September 1 – so many that the chiefs of staff received orders by September 5 not to stimulate recruiting, "as it is probable that more men are now available than can be conveniently handled."

The militia had been so badly neglected that mobilization often took on the appearance of comic opera. As an example of peacetime penury, in June 1939 forty pairs of boots were issued (for the first time) to every hundred men of the Loyal Edmonton Regiment. Not until October 23 did five hundred recruits who had joined in early September receive their rifles – and even then they were the pre-First World War Rosses, which had been tried and found wanting in 1915-16.

The Royal Regiment of Canada, in Toronto, had to delay medical examinations for lack of medical forms, and recruits, wearing armbands instead of uniforms, lived in the International Pavilion of the Canadian National Exhibition, with no heat, no cleaning utensils, and inadequate toilet and washing facilities. The West Nova Scotia Regiment, in Bridgewater, moved into the main building of the Lunenburg County Exhibition, using the cattle and poultry sheds for cook houses and mess halls. Thomas Raddall wrote in the regimental history:

> It was common to see a burly lumberjack wearing a flat-topped army hat, a mackinaw shirt, a khaki web belt, a pair of bulls-wool trousers (cut off at the calf, woods fashion and

An Unmilitary People

showing a length of gray woollen stocking) and shod in anything from a pair of battered shoe-packs to a pair of patent
leather shoes lately purchased in a local shop.[6]

That sort of thing was repeated across the country, forcing soldiers to
improvise in all kinds of situations. Most problems had their origin in
pre-war budget cuts. As late as December 1938 the government had
slashed $8 million from a $28-million budget proposed for the army
in order to meet expenses for air force and naval expansion.

There were equally severe shortages of armour (only sixteen light
tanks) and light machine guns; there were no more than twenty-three
anti-tank rifles, four two-pounder anti-tank guns, and four modern
anti-aircraft guns, making defence against armour and aircraft virtually non-existent. Even the Permanent Force was not fit to go to war,
although it was qualified to organize and supervise the basic training
needed to create soldiers and preserve an army tradition with a certain
Canadian flavour. Though inter-war apathy had not furthered efficiency, the professional soldiers of 1939 – who included many with
experience of combat in the Great War – had devoted most of their
energies to the training of the Non-Permanent Militia. Those skills
could easily be deployed to deal with the immediate influx of many
new volunteers.

The greatest inter-war problems had arisen from restricted regimental strengths and lack of equipment – this had made it difficult to
experiment and to develop military thought, so important to a peacetime army. There was another detriment in peace: restrictions on pro-
motion. Captain J.N. Edgar, who had commanded A Company,
Princess Patricia's Canadian Light Infantry, with great distinction in
the Battle of Tilloy in 1918, was still in command of the same company seventeen years later.

Almost all the general and senior officers were products of the
Royal Military College of Canada, at Kingston, Ontario, which combined the educational objectives of West Point Military Academy in
the United States with the military ideals of the British Army. Major-
General T.V. Anderson, chief of the General Staff, was a fair representative of this small élite. A graduate of RMC in 1900 who joined the
Permanent Force in 1905, he had had a distinguished career, losing an
arm in the First World War and receiving the DSO. Major-General
A.G.L. McNaughton was another. One of the few regular officers
who was not a graduate of RMC – he had a degree in electrical engineering from McGill – he had been a brilliant artillery and staff officer with the Canadian Corps in the First World War, had risen to be
chief of the General Staff in 1929, and then had been seconded to the
National Research Council as its president in 1935. McNaughton's
scientific accomplishments (he was joint inventor of the cathode-ray
direction finder in 1926) had extended his horizons far beyond his

An Unmilitary People

10   September 17, 1939: the Black Watch (Royal Highland Regiment) of Canada on its first wartime church parade. The men are more or less in step, with quite respectable bearing, but are wearing a curious miscellany of clothing.

military career, but when war came he was considered by Mackenzie King the best choice to command Canadian troops in the field.

Canadian public opinion seemed to focus on the army where matters relating to the armed forces were concerned. The distinguished record of the Canadian Corps in the First World War was a matter of national pride, while much less was known about the other two services. So the public, when thinking of a Canadian contribution to the war, probably thought more in terms of ground troops than of ships or aircraft. Cabinet decisions in September 1939 certainly seemed to recognize such a feeling, especially in the acceptance of General Anderson's statement on September 28 that army programs must not be cut back, even to satisfy the needs of the air force expansion that then appeared to be in the wind.

In fact, despite Mackenzie King's reluctance, Anderson and the professionals on his staff had little difficulty convincing the government that an expeditionary force should be dispatched overseas.

An Unmilitary People

Asked to make recommendations on the best response to Eden's cable of September 6, they advised sending a Mobile Force overseas. Anderson proposed that Canada should immediately offer to send and maintain one division – about 23,000 men, including support personnel – as well as some technical units that the British had specifically requested. He thought the country should aim at having nothing less than a corps of two or more divisions in the field.

On September 19 the government announced its decision to dispatch one division "to be available as an expeditionary force, if and when desired." British reaction was prompt. "The reputation Canadians earned in the last war has not been forgotten," reported Colonel G.P. Loggie, the Canadian officer who, together with Lieutenant-Colonel E.L.M. Burns, had discussed the offer with the Imperial General Staff. "Except for regulars and one or two territorial divisions, there are no troops whom the C[ommander] in C[hief of the British Expeditionary Force] would rather have with him."[7] So the die was cast, and on October 17 A.G.L. McNaughton assumed command of the 1st Canadian Infantry Division.

The army had a tradition based on the outstanding performance of the Canadian Expeditionary Force in the First World War. But the navy had no such tradition. There is some truth in the popular view that in 1939 the Royal Canadian Navy, which barely survived as an independent service between 1924 and 1925, was little more than a small offshoot of the Royal Navy. Pre-war personnel derived not only their ships and weapons but also their British customs and professional standards from the RN.

It would be wrong, however, to judge the RCN entirely on its derivative characteristics. Although the oceans exert an impersonal sway over men who follow a life at sea and national idiosyncrasies fade in the face of such relentless impartiality, nationality remains a powerful factor in motivating all armed forces. In 1939 the tightly knit ships' companies of the RCN were highly competitive groups determined to show that they were as good as Britain's best. A strong rivalry had grown up between east- and west-coast ships and with British vessels of the North America and West Indies squadrons.

Though the RCN had been formed by authority of the Naval Service Act of 1910, it was not until 1934 that one of its own, Percy Nelles, became the third director of the Naval Service. (His predecessors, Rear-Admiral C.E. Kingsmill and Commodore Walter Hose, came to Canada from the Royal Navy.) The officers serving in 1939 had a variety of backgrounds. Between the wars, some regular officers had gone to RMC for two years and then completed their training in the Royal Navy or the British Merchant Marine. Nelles himself had begun his naval career in the Canadian government ship *Canada* in 1908, even before the passing of the Naval Service Act. During the

An Unmilitary People

11 The navy goes to war. HMCS *Fraser* in the Panama Canal en route to Halifax from Esquimalt, September 1939. She would be the first ship lost by the RCN, June 25, 1940, when she was cut in half by the cruiser HMS *Calcutta* off the coast of France.

First World War he had served on Royal Navy cruisers and afterwards became flag lieutenant to Rear-Admiral Kingsmill.

After the war, Nelles again served mostly on British ships, but in 1931 he became the first captain of HMCS *Saguenay*. Following a year at the Imperial Defence College, in London, he was promoted to captain; and shortly after that he was made commodore and was later appointed the first chief of the Naval Staff, reaching the rank of rear-admiral in 1938. The pattern of his career was similar to that of other regular officers. All of them spent much too little time on Canadian ships, but there was not much that could be done about it because of the small size of the fleet.

In 1939 decisions concerning the navy did not have the political implications that manpower problems created for the army. With only six destroyers, Canada could not form an independent naval force, and there seemed little likelihood of a need for heavy reinforcements. There was no intention of satisfying the British Admiralty's request to recruit Canadians for the Royal Navy, and the only question at issue was whether Admiralty control of Canadian ships would be acceptable.

The answer, predictably enough, was that the Cabinet would hear of no such thing. Eventually a compromise permitted Canadian ships to co-operate with the British naval forces "to the fullest extent." British and Canadian naval forces would act as one and the senior officer present, from either service, would take command of sea operations: but ultimate control of Canadian ships would be exercised by Naval Service Headquarters in Ottawa. For the moment, the chief concern was to expand the naval forces sufficiently to meet the

An Unmilitary People

requirements of controlling and defending seaborne trade in Canadian waters.

In March 1939 the combined strength of the permanent and reserve naval forces numbered 3,276 personnel. Not all of these were immediately available – by the end of September less than three thousand had been mobilized. Yet the moment the RCN was placed on active service, wartime sea duties began on HMCS *Saguenay* and *Skeena* – the first warships to be built expressly for Canada – and on two minesweepers, from their base at Halifax. *Fraser* and *St Laurent*, C-Class destroyers acquired from the Royal Navy in 1937, sailed for the east coast from Vancouver on August 31, arriving at Halifax five days after Canada declared war. Their sister ships, *Ottawa* and *Restigouche*, remained on the west coast with three minesweepers based at Esquimalt.

On August 21 the Admiralty assumed control of British merchant shipping, and officers, both British and Canadian, earmarked as Naval Control Service Officers (NCSOs), received notice to take up their posts. Some were Volunteer Reserve personnel, some retired naval officers. On August 26 the Canadian government authorized

12 Mobilization. Fitting torpedo warheads in HMCS *Ottawa*, September 1, 1939 – the first step in preparing for war.

An Unmilitary People

the RCN to control the movements of all merchant ships in Canadian waters, and by September 10 the Canadian NCSOs at Halifax, Sydney, Saint John, and Montreal were in full operation. They reported to the North American intelligence centre for the Admiralty, which was established in Ottawa.

Some warships lacked Asdic, the submarine detection device eventually to be known as Sonar, and it had to be fitted as soon as the vessels arrived from the west coast. Furthermore, boom defence – the system of nets and controlled entrances or 'gates' that were necessary to keep enemy submarines out of Halifax and Esquimalt harbours – were not ready. Until they could be made available, these ports (especially Halifax) would not have the security expected of a naval base in time of war. The construction and salvage firm, Foundation Maritime, received a contract on September 6 to lay an anti-submarine net, and two old minesweepers were assigned as gate vessels. By the end of the month preparations for constructing the defences were in full swing, but some material was still only on order. Esquimalt, on the west coast, was rather more advanced than Halifax.

The war brought an influx of reserve naval personnel from a wide cross-section of the community. The Volunteer Reserve brought in large numbers of men with little maritime experience (some had never even seen the ocean); amateur sailors and retired naval personnel were also found in the organization. The Royal Canadian Naval Reserve was formed from the Merchant Service, which brought valuable professional experience into the wartime navy. Finally, there was a Fishermen's Reserve on the west coast that manned ten patrol vessels by the end of September 1939.

The Royal Canadian Air Force was the smallest of the three services in 1939. Founded in 1924, it had functioned as a subordinate arm of the Militia until 1938. Since 1935 considerable efforts had gone into expansion and rearmament, but the results were pathetic. The Permanent Active Air Force (as it was called after 1938) had increased from 569 to 1,031 personnel, a number totally inadequate for the needs of war. There was a desperate shortage of equipment. At the time of the Munich crisis in September 1938, the Cabinet had authorized an expenditure of over $6 million for aircraft and equipment from the United States; on October 7, when the crisis was apparently over, the government rescinded its authorization, however. In August 1939, much too late, it approved the purchase of twenty bombers and fifteen training aircraft, which, by then, had to be smuggled across the border because of American neutrality laws.

Apart from sixteen Hawker Hurricane fighters, ten Fairey Battle light bombers, eight Supermarine Stranraer flying-boats, and some training machines, all available military aircraft were obsolete. Even the Battles and Stranraers were obsolescent. In spite of these shortcomings, Ian Mackenzie, minister of national defence, argued in June

An Unmilitary People

13   RCAF recruits drilling. Ottawa, September 1939.

1939 that the air force had a "tremendous advantage over the other two services." Canada was a "natural flying country" – an allusion to its dependence on aviation to cover its vast distances. Aviation had taken firm root in Canada between 1915 and 1918 and a number of the experienced pilots available were Canadian veterans of the First World War in the British flying services. An aircraft industry had been established and the growth of civil aviation had created a reserve of experienced pilots.

The senior officers of the RCAF often had markedly different backgrounds from those in the army and navy. Air Vice-Marshal G.M. Croil, for instance, chief of the Air Staff since December 1939, had moved to Scotland with his family before the First World War, become a civil engineer, and later managed a tea and rubber planta-tion in Ceylon. In 1915 he returned to Britain as a captain in the Gordon Highlanders, joined the Royal Flying Corps in 1916, and served the remainder of the war in the Middle Eastern theatre, where he sometimes acted as pilot for Lawrence of Arabia. He returned to Canada in 1920, as a squadron leader, to join the newly formed Canadian Air Board, and transferred to the RCAF on its formation in 1924, becoming senior air officer in 1934. This was not a typical career, but there could be no such thing among the senior ranks of a force whose origins were so recent.

Except for veterans of the First World War, Permanent Force offi-cers on the RCAF's General List – that is, all those who were aircrew –

34   *An Unmilitary People*

were graduates of the Royal Military College or a civilian university. Only in 1938 had the air force begun to offer 'short service' commissions of five years' duration to selected high school graduates. Before 1935 there was little professional military training for air force officers. Some had attended staff courses given by the Royal Air Force, some had served as exchange officers with that service. There were in Canada a few desultory courses and exercises in army co-operation, and some emphasis was given to precision flying in two aerobatic teams formed between the wars.

RCAF personnel had been used primarily to foster civil aviation, to engage in air surveying, or to co-operate with the RCMP in contraband patrols. As a result the RCAF was manned with highly skilled flyers who lacked training in modern air warfare. Like the navy, however, the air force suggested a means of contributing to the war effort without having to find excessive numbers of men as reinforcements. The RCAF claimed to need fighter squadrons to defend key ports, especially Halifax and Esquimalt, from aerial bombing – though where the bombers were to come from was unclear, since Canada lay far beyond the range of European-based bombers and Germany had no aircraft carriers. More reasonably, bombing and reconnaissance squadrons were expected to patrol and protect the sea approaches to Canada from maritime threats, while army co-operation squadrons would provide air observation for coastal defence against enemy surface raiders.

Overseas requirements would be minimal. On September 12, 1939, the prime minister offered Canadian squadrons for loan to the RAF, to be equipped by Britain at Canadian expense. Earlier in the year, Canada had also offered Britain some training facilities, although in 1936 and 1938 the prime minister, supported by his advisers and the Cabinet, had turned down suggestions to train RAF pilots in Canada. It had been argued then that the RCAF was planning its own schools and wanted no competition for facilities, equipment, or personnel; but the real fears were that the nation would give up some of its autonomy if British training took place in Canada, and that Britain intended to recruit Canadian manpower for the RAF.[8]

The Conservative opposition got hold of the issue and eventually forced Mackenzie King to alter his policy of catering only to Canada's needs: in April 1939 the agreement had therefore been amended to train fifty RAF as well as seventy-five RCAF pilots in Canada every year.

Mobilization revealed the inadequacy of pre-war preparations. At the outbreak of war there were seven RCAF bomber and reconnaissance squadrons available for service on the east and west coasts. Two squadrons were on the west coast; two fighter, one army co-operation, and two bomber and reconnaissance squadrons were either on, or assigned to, the east coast. On August 25 all leave was cancelled in the Permanent Active Air Force and, two days later, designated squadrons

14 Soldiers entraining for overseas. One man has a suitcase and is carrying a civilian raincoat; another has his bayonet – still in its scabbard – fixed to his rifle; many are wearing Great War ammunition pouches on their web equipment.

– only one of which was equipped with any completely up-to-date aircraft (the Hurricane fighters) – began to move to their war stations.

An example of the condition of these units is provided by No. 3 Squadron as it began to stage through a series of airports with its seven obsolete Westland Wapitis on August 26. These ancient machines gave no end of trouble as the squadron literally staggered across the country. Two came down with engine trouble at Millinocket, Maine, and nearly found themselves interned in the United States because the weather closed in. They were finally able to leave the day after Britain declared war, and arrived at their destination two days later after another delay caused by weather at Blissville, New Brunswick.

On September 3 the three wing headquarters and eleven of the twelve squadrons of the Auxiliary Active Air Force went on full-time duty. In the following two weeks authority was given to call out reserve personnel and a Special Reserve came into being for wartime recruits.

In spite of these modest beginnings the role played by the air force in the Second World War eventually transcended anything the Canadian government had foreseen. Although King had first rebuffed RAF requests for training facilities in Canada, and reached the agree-

An Unmilitary People

ment of April 1939 with the greatest reluctance, forces beyond his control were at work. As in the First World War – when a British air training scheme had been established in Canada – the British Air Ministry knew that it would need training facilities beyond those available in the British Isles. Canada was by far the most suitable location. Not only were the flying conditions ideal, but Canada already had a great deal of the expertise and the facilities necessary to mount a large training program.

The British training programs of the First World War had produced thousands of Canadian pilots for the British flying services, many of whom were still active airmen and important supporters of aviation in Canada. Encouraged by the RCAF and supported by the government's civil aviation department, numbers of them were running private flying clubs scattered across the country; these clubs were intended to provide elementary training for the RCAF in time of war. In addition, some of the airfields and buildings built in 1917 were still in use, and more fields had been constructed by Relief Camp workers in the 1930s.

Once more Britain looked to Canada for air training assistance, even though there were other training areas in the British Commonwealth – Australia and Southern Africa, for instance. Canada was the closest training area to Britain, connected by the one lifeline that had to be kept open at all costs if Britain was to survive a European war: the North Atlantic.

Responding to an initiative emanating from the Australian and Canadian high commissioners in London, in consultation with the British Cabinet, the chief of Air Staff in Ottawa proposed on 15 September to train 12,000 men a year – including 8,000 ground crew – for the RAF. This would require a training force of 600 officers and 6,500 other ranks. Following an Emergency Council meeting of 28 September, the prime minister accepted this proposal in principle. It came to be called the British Commonwealth Air Training Plan (although for a long time the British persisted in calling it the Empire Air Training Scheme). Mackenzie King saw it as "a form of military effort that likely would not lead to enormous casualties, a positive inducement for French Canada to admire the government's wise management of affairs." "The answer," commented the official historian of Canadian defence policy, "to any Canadian politician's prayer."[9]

By the end of September the government had brought Canada into the war with little fanfare. The war potential of the nation had hardly been scratched, but it was already clear that intentions to defend only Canadian territory (the principle that had previously guided planning) had been replaced by involvement in all military aspects of the war. These developments had profound implications for all Canadians, but the event which had the greatest impact was probably the formation of the 1st Canadian Division for service overseas.

An Unmilitary People

Men of the 1st Division were later labelled "breadliners" by men of the 2nd, because the war had offered countless unemployed men the chance to join the army. Put another way, unemployment was a form of conscription. However, more than half the men of the 1st Division were answering a call to duty as members of the Permanent or Non-Permanent Active Militia. The unemployed themselves acknowledged that they were by no means the only volunteers. Thirty-five years later, one soldier recalled joining up.

> There was every type. There was us, out of the [railroad] jungles. Lice on us, every one.... There were men in business suits and college kids, I guess, and kids who looked like they should have been in school behind their books. There was old guys just itching to get in, guys from the last war....
>
> I wasn't patriotic. None of my buddies were. I just wanted some good clothes and hot showers and three decent meals a day and a few dollars for tobacco and beer.... You found out later that the others wanted other things. One college kid wanted to impress his girl and he was the biggest fool of all. The high school kids wanted adventure, and ... that is probably what we was all looking for. Not adventure, maybe, but a new life. Same thing.[10]

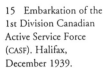

15 Embarkation of the 1st Division Canadian Active Service Force (CASF). Halifax, December 1939.

In 1939 the word 'adventure' had special meaning for the men who enlisted, the men who would build on what G.F.G. Stanley has

called "The Military History of an Unmilitary People."[11] About two years later, the architect and town planner Humphrey Carver – in the company, inexplicably, of a captured *Luftwaffe* pilot – witnessed from a nearby rooftop the mustering of recruits for a new armoured regiment at Windsor, Ontario.

> For about an hour we were together ... looking down at the raw recruits on the parade ground, an untidy rabble still without any soldier's discipline in their postures and outlook. They were the sons of Canadian immigrants and they had lived as teenagers through the years of the Depression that had knocked the stuffing out of Canada. They hadn't been roused by any kind of national zest for life. Their lives had been flat and uneventful like the boring voice of W.L. Mackenzie King, their leader.[12]

The Germans' impression of this motley crew can be imagined.

Whatever Canadians may have expected in 1939, a war of limited liability was impossible. Instead there would be pain and hardship and permanent tragedy for countless men and women; but, by the same token, there would be very few flat and uneventful lives. War would be the means of creating the national pride that young people had lost in the economic hardships and uncertain politics of the 1930s. In the purposeful atmosphere that the outbreak of war stimulated, even official Ottawa could no longer preserve the calculating aloofness that was evident to pre-war observers. Events were forcing Canada to step out of the shadows.

An Unmilitary People

CHAPTER 3

The Sinews of War

In the Second World War, as in the First, the North Atlantic Ocean played a vital strategic role, one that placed Canada in the forefront of planning considerations by the Allied nations. If Canada had not taken full advantage of its position at the western end of the Atlantic bridge, Britain (whose survival depended on North American supply) and the United States would have moved in to fill the vacuum.

Canada's eastern seaports, placed as they were on or near all the northern trade routes between North America and Britain, were obvious convoy routing centres and would become flourishing entrepôts of trade and shipping. The airfields at Dorval, Goose Bay, and Gander inevitably became vital links in the trans-ocean air ferry route that came into existence in 1940.

In 1939 Canada was the only dominion with the potential to produce and supply a wide range of raw materials and munitions, but it was by no means certain that the country – economically weakened by the Depression – could rise to the situation. There was every possibility of its remaining a client nation, exporting nothing more than relatively unsophisticated munitions, raw materials, natural resources, and men to the principal belligerents, as in the First World War. Initially there was a need to know the market potential for all the munitions Canada could manufacture; the exact British requirements in terms of tonnage and costs; the financial resources Canada needed to call upon in order to assist Britain; and the Dominion's industrial capacity. Whitehall's expectations of Canada in 1939 were summarized in Anthony Eden's telegram of September 6.

> Defence department would like to increase our normal food imports from Canada by a very large amount.... Ministry of Supply wish to purchase large supplies of raw materials, in particular, copper, aluminium, nickel, and perhaps timber. Moreover, Air Ministry in addition to their outstanding commitments, would like to place very substantial further orders for aircraft and accessories.... In the circumstances perhaps the most valuable immediate assistance which Canada could give in this field would be any steps which are possible to assist us in the financing of desired purchases.[1]

What responses there were to these enquiries proved tentative. A recent survey of industry had not given British leaders much confidence in Canada's industrial expertise. Furthermore, amazing as it may seem, Britain had no machinery for considering all her import demands together. This was not because she had no experience in

The Sinews of War

these matters – the First World War had given her ample – but because she had no idea that the inadequate utilization of shipping space would create desperate shortages as soon as the nation shifted from peacetime to wartime production requirements. Even after spending years preparing and issuing orders for the use and control of merchant ships in the event of war, British authorities were not adequately informed of the shipping capacity available to them from either British or foreign merchant fleets. Not until war broke out did the British government consult the experts in shipping controls, but even then there was serious competition between different departments for the use of space to import urgently needed food and other types of product, with the result that critical shortages developed in several vital industries. Only in May 1941 was the Ministry of Shipping allowed to dictate an equable distribution of shipping space to each government department.[2]

Under such circumstances Britain, in 1939, could not have planned a long-term program to justify Canadian industrial expansion, even if she had wanted to. The British decision to exploit what was immediately available from Canada explains the early emphasis on raw materials, finance, and the British Commonwealth Air Training Plan.

Canada was aware that British planners were not thinking ahead beyond three years. There could be little development of Canadian industry in that time, but Mackenzie King's Cabinet exerted every effort to maintain national control of the entrepôts and to ensure that they would be supplied as much as possible with Canadian products, expanding the national economy and its industrial base to meet the resulting demand. A few Canadian firms did have war contracts, but this was only because the Imperial Conference of 1937 had established the principle of fostering a Canadian war potential, not because an urgent need for help was envisaged. John Inglis Ltd, Toronto, had an order for seven thousand Bren light machine-guns; Marine Industries Ltd, Sorel, and the National Steel Car Corporation, Malton, were manufacturing 25-pounder field guns and 3.7-inch shells; Canadian Industries Ltd was producing TNT explosive; a central contracting company called Canadian Associated Aircraft had an order for Hampden bombers; De Havilland of Toronto had an Air Ministry contract for four hundred Tiger Moths; and Canadian Car and Foundry of Fort William had received a separate order for forty Hurricanes.

If Canadian factories were ever to supplement British industry significantly, such 'educational' orders were essential, particularly in the field of aeronautics even though the cost of production in Canada was much greater than in Britain. Yet the program smacked of tokenism – of abiding by the principle established by the 1937 Imperial Conference. Until the summer of 1940 Britain's munitions production was adequate for her own needs, limited as they were by the desultory skirmishing on the Western Front, dubbed the 'phoney war,' that preceded the German spring offensive. Orders from Britain barely began to tap existing Canadian resources.

The British Commonwealth Air Training Plan was a different matter. It has been said of the BCATP that "In essence, the British had found an idea and they brought it to Ottawa looking for someone else to put up the cash."[3] There is some truth to this comment, though it was clear that the Air Ministry put a great deal of store in the scheme, and was prepared to give it extensive support as well as to respect Canadian sovereignty when setting up bases in Canada. But the BCATP had a difficult birth, marked by hard bargaining on the part of both British and Canadian members of the negotiating teams.

Discussions began in Ottawa on October 15, 1939. They dragged on for over two months, mostly as a result of Canadian refusals to accept British terms. Canada successfully insisted on having administrative responsibility for the plan; however, there were protracted arguments about the sharing of costs. At one point the government tried to make agreement conditional on a satisfactory wheat-purchasing arrangement. It was suggested that, if Britain would accept the Canadian price of $93^1/2$¢ a bushel – 20¢ more than the current depressed market price – Canada would be prepared to sign the BCATP agreement. It must have seemed to the British negotiators that blackmail was not very far from the minds of their hosts, although from the Canadian point of view such a hard bargain was justified to alleviate the distress of the Prairie farmers.

Eventually a price of $82^1/2$¢ was settled on through a negotiating team in London, independently of the BCATP negotiations. In the meantime, in Ottawa, Canada agreed to contribute $353 million of an estimated $607 million to the BCATP. There then followed several weeks' delay while Mackenzie King stubbornly insisted that, as one of the terms of the agreement, the plan must be accepted as Canada's first priority in the war effort, an acceptance which would enable him to show his electorate that the major Canadian contribution to the war was to be made by the air force, and not by what he called "great expeditionary forces of infantry."[4]

Undoubtedly the principal advantage of the BCATP to Canada and to the Liberal government was the chance to make a recognizable and significant contribution to the war effort at home rather than overseas. There would be economic benefits from the establishment of training bases and the requirement to manufacture training aircraft. And if the BCATP had priority over an expeditionary force, there would be less likelihood of a reinforcement crisis like that of 1917 demanding some form of conscription to satisfy manpower requirements for the army.

The plan also offered a means of furthering Canadian national autonomy. King demanded that it be written into the plan that Canadian graduates of the scheme be incorporated into RCAF units in

16 A drafting room at RCAF Headquarters, Ottawa, during the planning stage of the BCATP.

the field. This eventually produced the following wording in Article 15 of the Memorandum of Agreement:

> The United Kingdom Government undertakes that pupils of Canada, Australia and New Zealand shall, after training is completed, be identified with their respective Dominions, either by the method of organizing Dominion units and formations or in some other way, such methods to be agreed upon by the respective Dominion Governments concerned....[5]

After the negotiations were over, the principals on each side formed a jaundiced view of the motives and methods of their opposite numbers. When the agreement was signed, the British High Commissioner in Ottawa, Sir Gerald Campbell, commented testily that "the Canadian Government saw everything in terms of the advantage which might be secured for Canada and themselves." We certainly know that Mackenzie King thought the British "seemed to think that all they have to do is tell us what has to be done," and that British negotiators for their part took away unflattering opinions of the Canadian prime minister. Harold Balfour, the British Air Ministry representative, believed (incorrectly) that there was mutual distrust between King and his Cabinet, that King played off one section of opinion against the other, "thus cunningly holding the balance of power in his own hands."[6]

The BCATP was not only vitally significant but extremely complex in its organization. Fifty-one air-training schools were created between April 1940 and December 1941. Another great accomplishment was the intake of nearly forty thousand trainees – more than half as many again as originally planned for. Canada contributed over 80 per cent of all students until May 1942. Although the mechanics of the Plan were brilliantly formulated and effectively carried out, its full political and human implications were not immediately apparent. Both the air minister, C.G. Power, and his personal selection as chief of Air Staff, Air Marshal Lloyd Breadner, failed to insist on imple-

The Sinews of War

17 Students at No. 4 Elementary Flying Training School, Windsor Mills, Que., about to go up for instruction flights in Fleet Finch aircraft.

mentation of the posting of Canadians to RCAF squadrons. The outlook from Ottawa was somewhat blinkered, and it has to be recorded that Power's alcoholic lapses often interfered with his ability to make coherent decisions. In the end, as a result of their common inability to grasp the reality of RAF personnel policies, only some 40 per cent of Canadian aircrew ever got to serve in RCAF squadrons – the remainder being posted to units of other Commonwealth squadrons, principally those of the RAF.[7]

Demographically the most interesting feature of the Canadian contribution to the BCATP was the large proportion that came from Ontario. Numbering about a third of the total population, Ontarians accounted for almost half the aircrew applicants and a proportionate number of graduates, a percentage that helps to explain why the RCAF was sometimes called the Royal Ontario Air Force, only half in jest, by aircrew from that province. The other provinces with the exception of Quebec, were represented more or less in proportion to population.

When the BCATP agreement was renegotiated in 1942 the United Kingdom took responsibility for filling "not less than 40 per cent of the training capacity." It subsequently provided about 48 per cent of trainees over the rest of the Plan's life. Between 1942 and 1945 Canada found about 25 per cent, the other dominions another 25 per cent between them, and miscellaneous Allied countries the remaining 2 per cent. Canada's monthly contributions reached their highest – 3,379 – in August 1943 and during eight months of that year exceeded 2,000 per month. By the war's end the BCATP had produced 131,553 aircrew, of which 72,835 (51 per cent overall) were Canadians.

During the BCATP negotiations of 1939 Britain suffered her first food crisis owing to the shortage of shipping. In mid-November 1939 some flour mills actually stopped work for lack of grist. Because Canadian supplies were essential, ships were diverted from other des-

The Sinews of War

tinations in North America to the St Lawrence ports on an emergency basis to load up with wheat that had already been purchased by Britain in the form of futures in 1938. Not so urgent in 1939, but just as important, was the need for Canadian timber, because German control of the Baltic had severely restricted the supply from that source. By the end of the year, Canada, still Britain's major supplier of nickel and aluminum, had also increased exports of iron and steel, and manufactures thereof, by more than a third but, generally, Canadian productivity and business were not much affected by the torpor of the 'phoney war.'[8]

However, Hitler's electrifying campaigns in Scandinavia and France during the spring of 1940 brought a sudden end to the stagnation. After the fall of France in June and the successful evacuation of the British Expeditionary Force from Dunkirk, Britain and her few allies (essentially the white dominions) found themselves confronted by a predominant enemy. So long as that near and powerful menace to the United Kingdom could be resisted, they could call upon badly needed shipping not available before, some diverted from service to France, some acquired from German-occupied countries. British leaders, therefore, no longer obliged to support a full-scale military effort on the European continent, were free to exploit maritime strengths against the enemy while whittling away at his Mediterranean and North African outposts, and at his aerial defences. There was now total dependence on maritime forces and lines of communication, and North American supplies became even more necessary than before.

As soon as war had been declared a British Purchasing Mission had come to North America and acquired a temporary home in Ottawa. When the United States Congress agreed to alterations in the Neutrality Act late in 1939, so that American war supplies could go to Britain, the Purchasing Mission moved to New York, leaving behind a small British Supply Board in Ottawa. It soon became evident that British authorities preferred to shop south of the border – and for very good reasons. In the first place, Roosevelt had always assured Britain of his eagerness to support the Allied cause. Even before the war, in July 1939, he had told the British ambassador he favoured establishing an American naval patrol in the western Atlantic to prevent the "warlike operations of belligerents," and the changes in the Neutrality Act constituted further proof of the transition to something more than benevolent neutrality; to something, in fact, that was more like non-neutral belligerency.

In the second place, the United States was believed to be a reliable source of supply and Canada was not – at least not until its industrial potential could be assessed properly. When Britain abandoned all caution in the expenditure of dollars in June 1940, there was no financial reason for choosing doubtful Canadian sources rather than proven American ones, and the British Supply Board was distinctly lethargic in creating orders for Canadian firms.

A number of events brought about a change in this attitude. The British government had earlier refused to let Canada supply its Army Overseas with equipment from Canadian sources but insisted that the letter of a 1939 agreement be adhered to, and that orders be placed through the British Ministry of Supply. In April 1940, however, as a result of Canadian pressure, the British agreed to place such orders in Canada – mainly for political reasons because, in British eyes, there was no requirement to go outside Great Britain. The fall of France had shattered this preconception: soon after Dunkirk, the Ministry of Supply allocated to Canada about a third of its orders for re-equipping the British army.

Canada was now on its way to finding an international market for its war products, and it was essential to organize a massive program for industrial expansion. Under these circumstances the war turned up men of outstanding ability who made great efforts, often at considerable personal sacrifice, to serve the cause. It is not an exaggeration to say that C.D. Howe, minister of munitions and supply, changed the country from a very small producing nation to a respectable industrial power. But even the dynamic Howe could never have done this had not international events created the essential framework for expansion. For example, Dunkirk – where the British army lost so much equipment, particularly vehicles, that British factories could not meet the demand for replacements – created a need that Canada could help to fill because it already had a small but flourishing automobile industry.

The international framework also imposed limitations on the nature of Canadian production. In the case of the automobile industry, American domination was so complete that engines – whether for land vehicles or aircraft – were never produced in Canada during the Second World War. Furthermore, it was necessary to resolve two crucial financial problems, exchange barriers with the United States and the British dollar deficits in Canada, before Canada could exploit the urgent demands for goods created by the events of 1940.

Finally, Canada had to come to terms with the United States concerning the defence relationships of the two countries. In August 1940 Mackenzie King accepted Roosevelt's invitation to visit him near Ogdensburg, New York, where the president and prime minister signed an agreement recognizing joint American and Canadian responsibilities for the defence of North America, to be spelled out in decisions recommended by the Permanent Joint Board of Defence (PJBD).

Although the creation of the PJBD did not have specific implications for the munitions industry, it provided the machinery for negotiation between the two countries in time of war. Ogdensburg marked an important step in Canada's growing independence of Britain, as

18   A machinist pauses for a snack before he finishes a gun barrel on the lathe at Sorel Industries Limited, Que., December 1940.

well as in its new relationship with the United States, and it heralded Canadian attempts to obtain a voice in international decisions for countries that were not Great Powers.

Eventually the PJBD made thirty-three formal recommendations concerning North American defence, and all except two were approved by the Canadian and American governments. The Board also conducted a great deal of important informal discussion, and worked out the vitally important Basic Defence Plans for North America. A bitter debate over the strategic direction of forces on Canadian territory reached its climax in Washington, at the end of May 1941, with the temperature at 94° Fahrenheit and the air-conditioning cut off. "Every so often the American section would break off into a huddle to concert some fresh assault," recalled General Maurice Pope, "but we poor Canadians seemed to have nothing to huddle about, save our determination not to give in."[9]

The Canadians won their points, however. By Joint Basic Defence Plan No. 2, American commanders did not have authority over the administration and discipline of Canadians: each nation maintained strategic direction and command of its own forces, although tactical command against an enemy threat would be given to one supreme commander.

Roosevelt and Mackenzie King may have established a friendly relationship, but Canadian representatives had to employ some deftness in protecting Canadian interests at meetings of the PJBD and other similar boards, to avoid military, political, and economic domination of Canada by the United States in decisions affecting both countries.

The Sinews of War

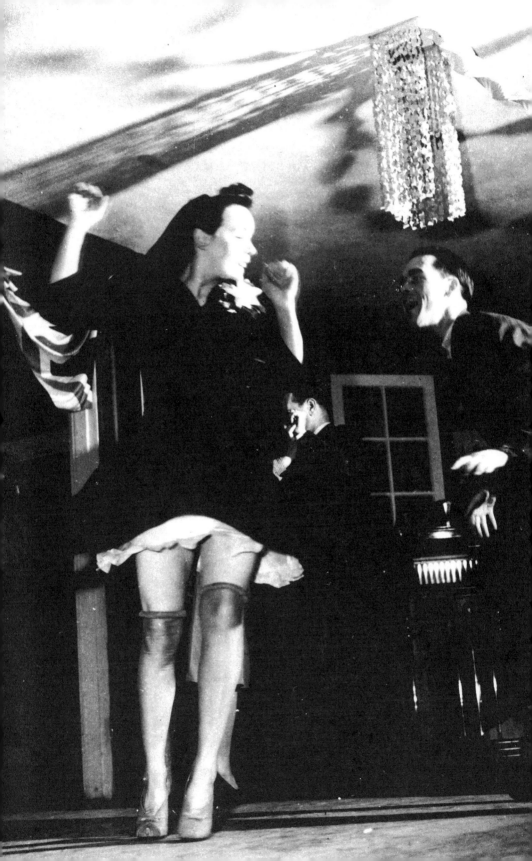

19, 20   In these two photographs Veronica Foster, named the 'Bren gun girl,' is shown jitter-bugging at the Glen Eagle Country Club near Toronto and posing for the photographer at the John Inglis plant, Toronto, where she worked. May 1941.

In March 1941 the United States government made the momentous decision to provide war materials to Britain on a 'lend and lease' basis, which allowed American war supplies to reach Britain in exchange for a theoretical deferred payment. This raised difficulties for Canada, which itself had a severe balance-of-payments deficit in the United States. How could Canada pay for American-made components needed to complete existing British orders without accepting lend-lease itself? To do so might have resulted in the liquidation of Canadian investments in the United States, and in a poor bargaining position for Canada after the war. For that matter, why should Britain pay cash for Canadian products when she could have American ones on credit – a most attractive proposition to a country with a dollar deficit in Canada.

The Canadian government, helped by the great goodwill towards both Canada and the Allied cause that was prevalent in the United States, solved both problems in an imaginative and practical way. Mackenzie King went to Washington and, after negotiating with Cordell Hull, the secretary of state, and Henry Morgenthau, secretary of the treasury, he visited Roosevelt at his Hyde Park estate, pressing the argument that if the United States "insisted upon taking from Canada what few possessions she had in the U.S. [by liquidating investments in order to make American aid possible], it would only give voice to anti-U.S. sentiment in this country." He proposed, therefore, that the Americans should buy from Canada as much as Canada was buying from the United States. "On a grand Sunday, April 20, 1941," in Roosevelt's words, he and King signed the Hyde Park Declaration, which provided for a virtual barter in war materials, the United States paying in dollars for Canadian manufactures and Canada using the proceeds to purchase American goods. "Roosevelt thought this was a swell idea," Mackenzie King told the Canadian journalist Grant Dexter.[10]

The Sinews of War

21 The first Valentine tank produced at the Montreal Locomotive Works inspected by C.D. Howe, minister of munitions and supply. May 27, 1941.

The necessary raw materials, machine tools, and spare parts for the fulfilment of British orders could be considered as lend-lease items and would not affect Canada's balance of payments position. In no time, large American defence orders began to flow into Canada and, by 1942, that problem had been overcome.

British dollar deficits in Canada were met initially by the repatriation of British securities, acceptance of payment in sterling, and payment for as much as possible in gold, which Britain was still obtaining in limited quantities from South Africa. In July 1941, however, as it became clear that British dollar deficits would restrict the continuing purchase of Canadian products, C.D. Howe pressed the Cabinet to take radical financial measures to help Britain. "The time to be generous with Britain is now," he said, "rather than in the post-war period when our people will be in a less generous mood."[11] When Canadian sterling balances in London became unacceptably large, they were converted into an interest-free loan to Britain of $700 million, and in January 1942 munitions and war supplies, including food, were contributed as an outright gift to the extent of one billion dollars – a far greater sum, relatively speaking, then than now.

In 1943, when the credit ran out, an arrangement was made whereby Canada would donate its surplus production to the Allies through a Canadian Mutual Aid Board. (Although aid went to other Allied countries, the bulk went to the United Kingdom, to the value of more than one-and-a-quarter billion dollars.) On learning of this proposal for mutual aid, an official in the Dominions Office commented that Canada's gift would cost, in terms of its population, "about five times what lend-lease cost the United States."

The Sinews of War

It would be true, if cynical, to say that Canadians, having produced the goods, gave them away because no one could afford to buy them. But not to have put to use the output of Canadian industry would have made no sense at all when the demands of war were at their height, and when a reduction of output would have brought back unemployment and prejudiced the chances of establishing a strong post-war market. It was, none the less, a remarkable gift, representing the true spirit of Canadian policy; it embodied the heartfelt concern and support in the nation for the survival of Britain and liberation from Nazi conquest of Europe.

The industrial growth that accompanied these developments could not have occurred without the imaginative use of organizational and technical talent. Howe's Department of Munitions and Supply, which came into being on April 9, 1940, became the force behind the acceleration, control, and co-ordination of Canadian industry. For Canadian products to meet the exacting standards necessary for munitions production, British expertise was called upon in the form of naval and air technical missions and the Anglo-Canadian Inter-Government Inspection Board. Renamed the Inspection Board of the United Kingdom and Canada in January 1941, it made Canada an acceptable alternate source of supply to Britain in many critical areas. But not only to Britain. Canadian fighting services now had to fall back on Canadian sources of supply where they had previously relied on British. In fact all the Allied armed forces overseas would come to use Canadian industrial exports.

The Wartime Industries Control Board, created on June 24, 1940, regulated raw materials and services needed by industry. Crown Companies, which involved a large cross-section of industrial and business leaders, were formed to solve production problems beyond the capabilities of existing industry and to overcome difficulties in supply, purchasing, and administration raised by the special circumstances of the time.

One such enterprise, Citadel Merchandising Co. Ltd, based in Ottawa, was created to procure some forty to fifty thousand machine tools urgently required for munitions production. Another company, War Supplies Ltd, created in May 1941 under the formidable direction of E.P. Taylor, drummed up sales for Canadian products in the United States. In less than three months, contracts worth about $200 million had been obtained. Altogether twenty-eight Crown Companies were incorporated: eleven operated production facilities and the remainder carried out supervisory, administrative, and purchasing functions.

Large-scale production began in July 1940. This was when the new minister of national defence, J.L. Ralston, received Cabinet approval to order for the Canadian army three hundred 25-pounder field guns, nine hundred 2-inch mortars, forty 40-mm guns, and nearly five hundred Valentine tanks complete with armament. It was

22 Lieutenant-General A.G.L. McNaughton, commander of First Canadian Corps, examines a 25-pounder field gun at Sorel, Que., during a visit to Canada on February 9, 1942.

no fault of the Canadians that the mortars and tanks, constructed to British specifications, were to prove quite inadequate on the battle-field. From this modest beginning Howe's ubiquitous department oversaw such growth that, by 1945, Canada had supplied more than 815,000 transport and combat vehicles to our allies. This degree of expansion naturally demanded continual additions to existing plants.

The pattern of such growth is graphically demonstrated by the development of ammunition production between 1939 and 1943. In 1939 the only vestige of Canada's enormous output of ammunition in the First World War was the Dominion Arsenal at Quebec, which had been kept in existence. By re-activating old equipment, it raised its production from 750,000 rounds a month to 12,500,000. In addition, another creation of the First World War, the Dominion Arsenal at Lindsay, Ontario, was opened up again. These plants were found particularly useful in 1941 because they were the only ones capable of rolling steel used in the production of shells and cartridges to the tolerances required by the Small Arms and Ammunition Branch, so they were given responsibility for supplying this product to other plants that were by then in existence.

A small plant at Valcartier, a branch of the Dominion Arsenal at Quebec, had been the only one capable of filling shells with explosives at the beginning of the war. When more output was needed, this highly skilled and dangerous work was undertaken by firms that were mostly under the direction of Defence Industries Ltd, a subsidiary of Canadian Industries Ltd: the Cherrier plant at Saint-Paul l'Hermite and the Bouchard plant at Saint-Thérèse, Quebec. A new government factory, York Arsenals Ltd, began production in February 1942 under the management of the Canadian Acme Screw and Gear Company Ltd of Toronto.

When orders began to exceed the capacity of government plants, Defence Industries Ltd again took up most of the overflow. A factory was constructed at Brownsburg, Quebec, which started large-scale production in August 1941; and urgent orders for 9-mm Sten gun ammunition arrived in 1942 at yet another new plant, the Montreal Works. In February 1943 it became clear that a shortage of satisfactory tools might lead to large rejections of ammunition made at such plants, so Defence Industries Ltd set up the Westmount Tool Works. At about the same time new sources of supply were created in a Toronto plant operated by Industrial Associates (Canada) Ltd and by Dominion Rubber Munitions Ltd.

Other areas of production followed similar patterns, each overcoming its special problems. The National Research Council – always an innovative force in Canadian technology – achieved a modest contribution in the development and design of weaponry for land warfare. It developed a method for the large-scale production of the new explosive RDX using radically new techniques, and produced another new explosive called DINA from which it was possible to develop the flashless propellant Albanite for the U.S. Navy.

The 'Ram' tank, consisting of an American chassis and a Canadian-designed cast-steel superstructure, attempted to combine the best features of American and British tank design in late 1940 but was soon superseded by the American 'General Sherman' – the most successful Allied tank of the war – which had in turn been influenced by an early mock-up model of the Ram. Canadian developers were more successful when, using the Sherman chassis, they produced a number of self-propelled guns of which the 25-pounder, or 'Sexton,' proved to be the most successful.

By the end of the war, equipment produced in Canada for use in land warfare included several weapons for which it was the only reliable alternate source to Britain: Bren light machine-guns, 25-pounder guns, Boys anti-tank rifles and 2-pounder anti-tank guns (until they were superseded by the 6-pounder in 1942), as well as 3.7-inch anti-aircraft guns. These were all British-designed weapons made to British standards under British tutelage. To have adapted highly developed American industry for these products would have been impractical: thus Canada turned its industrial backwardness to advantage.

The shipbuilding industry had the most startling impact on Canada in its effect on the distribution of Canadian manpower and in its total contribution to the war effort. Canada had built a number of vessels in the First World War and there were fifteen yards scattered throughout the country capable of producing a variety of ship types. But all of them together employed no more than four thousand men in 1939. Four companies had the capacity to build ships of 10,000 tons deadweight; five others had berths for building ships up to 4,700 tons.

The RCN alone stated requirements for 104 new vessels of all types, and even after the Cabinet reduced this figure for financial reasons, an authorized program received approval in February 1940 for 92 British-designed corvettes and Bangor-class minesweepers. In April 1940 the Naval Shipbuilding Branch came into existence and started placing contracts. By the end of the year 14 new corvettes were commissioned – 8 of them into the Royal Navy (although manned by Canadians) and 6 into the Royal Canadian Navy. Britain placed orders for 26 merchant ships of 10,000 tons deadweight in December 1940, but work did not start on them until April 1941, when Wartime Merchant Shipping Ltd came into being as a Crown Company.

Since Canada did not have a code of standards for the construction of warships, the British Admiralty Technical Mission, aided by technical officers of the RCN, had to establish British dockyard standards. The task was enormous. Yards in the Great Lakes and Quebec, where trawlers and corvettes were built, were unbelievably primitive

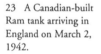

23   A Canadian-built Ram tank arriving in England on March 2, 1942.

The Sinews of War

GET YOUR TEETH
INTO THE
JOB

24　A poster issued by
the Wartime Information
Board about 1942.

to naval officers accustomed to Admiralty standards. "In one," observed a member of the mission, "there was no drawing office at all; the percentage of skilled labour was very small throughout; and the Lakes' yards tended naturally to follow Great Lakes' practice which specialized in the reduction of costs.... [The process of education] was explosive at times."[12]

Procuring the fittings and weapons for ships posed a special problem because most large engineering firms, by July 1940, were committed to orders for the army and air force. The mission was able to surmount this difficulty by sending members of its staff – which in 1943 reached a peak of nearly two thousand people – across the country to find plants capable of producing the equipment required for the shipbuilding program. For instance, the CPR Locomotive Repair Shops in Calgary became a prime source of naval guns and the Parker

The Sinews of War

Pen Company of Toronto manufactured primers for naval ammunition.

Such things as magnetic compasses, hydraulic steering gears, tachometers, and large diesel engines, never before made in Canada, were contracted out to Canadian firms wherever possible; but they often came from the United States because only a limited number of firms in the Canadian electrical industry were able to handle the entire process of design, production, engineering, and manufacture. Steel plates of the size and quality needed for shipbuilding had to be imported until 1942, when the Steel Company of Canada completed a new rolling mill.

By 1946 the industry had gone through a rapid apprenticeship, solved problems by extensive improvisation, and found new sources of equipment by persistent searching and a willingness to rely on untried manufacturing plants. The results were modest by British or American standards, but considering that the Canadian industry had been moribund in 1939, the final accomplishment in the space of five years was striking. Canada had built 410 merchant ships, 487 escorts and minesweepers, 254 naval tugs, and 3,302 landing craft. At its peak in 1943 the shipbuilding industry employed 126,000 men and women. It was the second-largest employer in the country after the manufacturers of industrial equipment and materials.

25 A merchant ship begins to take shape at the Dominion Bridge Company, Montreal, probably in 1943.

26 Delicate fingers were an asset in assembling instruments. This woman is working on airspeed indicators in Winnipeg. May 16, 1942.

27 Canada produced its own version of the famous Consolidated 'Catalina' flying boat, the Canso 'A' amphibian, shown here in production at Canadian Vickers, Montreal.

Like shipbuilding, aircraft production grew out of small beginnings in 1939. There had been some manufacture of aircraft in the First World War and, what was never achieved in the Second World War, a few engines. In the early 1920s orders from the Canadian Air Board sparked a small but fairly lively industry that soon ran into difficulties but managed to struggle through the Depression. The industry's fortunes improved in the late 1930s with the decision to spend most of the Canadian defence budget on air force expansion, and with the consequent show of interest by the mission sent out from Britain under Lord Weir in 1938 to investigate technical industrial potential in North America.

This mission resulted in orders likely to bring the aviation industry up to speed much faster than other branches of manufacturing. Requirements of the BCATP after December 1939 offered a further shot in the arm. In June 1940 the government provided the co-ordinating services to bring about the rapid expansion of aircraft production when the Department of Munitions and Supply created the Air Production Branch and incorporated the Crown Company of Federal Aircraft Ltd. When a second Crown Company – Victory Aircraft Ltd – was formed in 1942 to take over the National Steel Car Corporation at Malton, Ontario, Canadian aviation manufacturers were producing a large range of training and combat aircraft, including the 'wooden wonder,' twin-engined Mosquito and the very large (for its time) Lancaster bomber.

De Havilland Aircraft of Canada provides an excellent example of the Canadian experience in aircraft manufacturing during the war. Situated in Toronto, it grew rapidly in 1940 to fill orders not only for Tiger Moth biplane trainers but for about forty Fairey Battles and seven hundred twin-engined Avro Ansons to meet training requirements. In search of workers, the firm went beyond local technical schools to the labour market and recruited totally unskilled men and women who enrolled in crash courses with a token allowance of three to five dollars a week.

Their introduction to airframes was the fuselage of a First World War Curtiss JN-4 – nothing more than a skeleton strung with some remains of wire rigging. Nevertheless, they were taught to read a blueprint, to work with precise measurements, and how to work with metal. Those with mechanical aptitude went into skilled tasks such as tool-and-die jobs; the others went on to assembly lines. The training program was almost too successful because the plant was for a time in the embarrassing position of having too many trained employees for the available work. Some simply quit their jobs in disgust because there was nothing for them to do; others discreetly slipped out of sight of the foreman until new bays had been built and the plant had tooled up for the latest production requirements.

In September 1941 De Havilland (Canada) began to build Mosquito aircraft, which in spite of the gradual expansion of previous years created several problems – some of them anticipated but none the less awkward. Inevitably, both British and American parts were used, and since they had different measurements – for screw threads and wrenches, for instance – mechanics had to have two sets of tools.

Sub-contracts for fuselages, tail assemblies, flaps, and undercarriages went to the most unlikely places. Cockshutt Plow of Brantford became responsible for aircraft hydraulic parts and had to make considerable adjustments to meet the standards of cleanliness required. Otaco Ltd, of Orillia, Ontario, manufacturers of farm implements, carriages, and rural hardware, provided undercarriages. (This firm succeeded in building an exceptionally strong landing gear.) By hard work, ingenuity, and improvisation, De Havilland's first Mosquito was ready for its test flight on September 24, 1942. Production was disappointingly slow, however, and in 1943 C.D. Howe appointed J. Grant Glassco as controller of the firm, to shake up management and meet higher monthly quotas. At the war's end the plant had produced over a thousand Mosquito aircraft. By way of comparison, the De Havilland plant in Britain built 5,200, other firms there built 500, and another 212 came from Australia.

It has been calculated that in terms of weight – which allows for the much larger aircraft being produced late in the war – the last quarter of 1944 saw one hundred times the production achieved during the last quarter of 1939: over seven million pounds (the weight of the 905 aircraft produced in 1944) as opposed to seventy thousand pounds (the weight of the 31 aircraft produced in 1939). Employment in the industry reached its peak of 116,000 – something less than the figure for shipbuilding – in August 1944, after all other branches of production in Canada had started to fall off. The achievement of the industry was a triumph because it placed Canadian aircraft firms in an exceptionally strong position for post-war competition. However, even though the industry had the advantage of a head start with orders received in the late 1930s, and was able to police its own standards with the co-operation of the RCAF, it still had difficulty in meeting production goals, which took the edge off the triumph.

For Canadian industry as a whole, 1944 was the record year, when the effort reached its peak and the economy was fully committed to the needs of war. Men and women employed in industry numbered 1,239,327, a figure that was not reached again until 1947. The gross value of production was $8,725,350,000, an amount that increased only marginally in 1944 before falling off substantially in 1945 and 1946. The manufacturing production index, set at 100 in 1949, was 104.1 for 1943 and 106.1 in 1944, and this level was not matched until 1950.

The Canadian government had succeeded in exploiting its industrial potential, reserves of manpower, and geographic position not only to preserve national control of the economy but also to establish

a favourable position for competing with countries that had dominated world trade before 1939. There was still a military victory to win, however, and Canada was just as preoccupied with its military contribution as with the industrial efforts that supported it.

CHAPTER 4

The Atlantic Bridge

The sea and air lanes between North America and Europe formed a harsh and sometimes cruel setting for the battle that, in 1939, was about to be fought for Britain's lifeline. The best routes across the Atlantic were the northern ones because they were the shortest and the least accessible to German naval forces. Offsetting this advantage was the terrible climate. The North Atlantic, where it is not tempered by the Gulf Stream, is one of the most inhospitable places on the face of the earth. Fog settles down on the Newfoundland Banks and near the shores of Canada's Atlantic provinces like a cold blanket for weeks at a time, shutting out sight and distorting sound. Gales come almost as a relief because they break up the fog; then, however, the sea and swell often build up to heights of more than sixty feet and the danger of collision or grounding gives way to other perils.

In winter, the weather deteriorates for weeks on end into one massive storm system that stretches from North America to Europe. Winter temperatures turn spray and breaking seas into ice that builds up excessive topweight on the superstructure of ships and exposes even the most seaworthy vessels to the possibility of capsizing or foundering.

Such weather patterns spelled danger for airmen as well as seamen, since it caused the icing-up of aircraft in the air and the closing down of their bases. But unlike sailors, aircrew welcomed the respites that from time to time brought sunny skies, excellent visibility, and seas that were miraculously transformed to gentle waves or even flat calms. For seamen, especially after enemy submarines were able to extend their patrols well out into the Atlantic after 1940, good weather brought with it the ever-present danger of destruction by torpedo because such conditions favoured the submarine.

Bridging the Atlantic was the key to strategic supply. To transport as much as possible – merchant ships and their cargoes, troopships with their human freight – to Britain, and from there, if necessary, to various theatres of operations, it was vital for naval authorities to exercise complete control of ship movements. Loading and unloading had to be carried out with maximum efficiency and every effort had to be made to avoid congestion by large numbers of vessels in port at any one time.

Shipping companies and personnel, like the British population as a whole, remembered German unrestricted submarine warfare in the First World War. The answer to that had been the institution of a convoy system. In 1939, as then, naval doctrine was by no means wedded to the convoy principle, but the sinking of just one passenger liner was enough for the Admiralty to start sending ships across the ocean in convoy, in order to regulate their movements and the more easily to provide protection, both by sea and air.

This did not mean that protection was adequate: not until 1943 were convoys used to their best advantage as a system of mutual defence that offered the best statistical chance of survival. In the meantime, there were far too few naval vessels or maritime patrol aircraft available. The first convoys that formed up in Halifax with twenty to thirty ships in the fall of 1939 had no more than an escort of two Canadian destroyers and one flying boat for their first twenty-four hours at sea. For the rest of the way across, they were shepherded by an armed merchant cruiser or, perhaps, a battleship – useful against surface raiders, but with no anti-submarine capability. About five hundred miles from their destination in Britain, sea and air escorts of the Royal Navy and Royal Air Force began to provide a measure of anti-submarine protection. Ships with a speed of more than fifteen knots often steamed independently because they could outrun an attacking submarine.

Early Asdic (an acronym used by the Commonwealth navies until NATO navies standardized with the American term Sonar after the war) was largely ineffective against surfaced submarines at night. Thus, even when more ships and aircraft turned from distinctly unprofitable, so-called offensive operations against enemy submarines to escorting convoys, the system failed to prevent heavy losses in 1939 and 1940. Moreover, convoys caused problems in cargo handling through the congestion their arrival created in British ports.

As German capabilities improved and Allied fortunes in Europe waned, the rising losses at sea gave the Battle of the Atlantic a desperate character. In September 1939 there were fewer than fifty operational *Unterseeboote*, or U-boats; in subsequent months there were sometimes even fewer available, and numbers did not increase dramatically in the first eighteen months of the war. Yet by seeking out weak points in the naval defences of the Allies and concentrating their efforts there, they attacked merchantmen with devastating effect until the spring of 1943.

After May 1943, however, although the U-boat fleet grew rapidly, their successes dropped off dramatically in the face of better trained and equipped escorts, the formation of 'hunter-killer' groups, and improved surface-air co-operation. Enemy surface ships and aircraft were also used for attacks on shipping, but only the U-boat posed a deadly menace. "The only thing that ever really frightened me was the U-boat peril," Churchill wrote. "Never for one moment could we forget that everything happening elsewhere – on land, at sea and in the air – depended ultimately on its outcome, and amid all other cares, we viewed all its changing fortunes day by day with hope and apprehension."[1] By May 1945, Germany had produced 1,170 submarines.

At one time, the operational strength rose to about 450 but, by the end of the war, losses had reduced that number to 144.

The U-boat attacks began on September 3, 1939, the day Britain declared war, when a German submarine sank the British liner *Athenia* on her westward passage to New York and, by May 1943, 2,190 ships had been sunk in the Atlantic. With these disastrous losses the amount of tonnage available for cargo fell off rapidly and new construction did not begin to reverse the trend until late 1942; not until August 1943 did shipyards produce enough ships every month to outstrip sinkings.

Canada participated in almost every phase of the development of anti-submarine warfare, from the planning of convoys to the forming of hunter-killer groups. As our navy expanded in five years from 11 fighting ships and about 3,000 men to more than 370 ships and about 93,000 men and women, Canadian warships were not only concentrated on the supply lines to Europe. They served with the British fleet off Norway and with convoys to Russia; they went to the Mediterranean, Caribbean, and Pacific theatres; and they were employed extensively for coastal operations off the coast of northwest Europe in 1944 and 1945.

In the process of this rapid expansion there were severe problems of technical modernization, training, and morale, so that between 1939 and 1943, when the Battle of the Atlantic reached its climax, the Canadians often did not measure up to the needs of the convoy battles. But it must be added that, at a critical moment, the RCN shared the worst of hardships experienced in the war at sea; and, even though the Canadian contribution before 1943 was not so effective as that of Great Britain, it was both generous and strategically vital. Moreover, after 1943 Canadian ships and aircraft achieved results that compared favourably with those of other Allied forces.

The predominance of naval ships and personnel has preserved the memory of the Battle of the Atlantic as a naval achievement, but the parts played by airmen and merchant seamen were indispensable to defeating the enemy attack on shipping. Similarly, because more Canadian ships and naval personnel were involved in the Atlantic

29 Ships sailed from Halifax in relative safety in October 1940. It was when they approached Ireland that enemy submarines began to take their toll.

The Atlantic Bridge

30 Part of HMCS *Noranda,* a Bangor-class minesweeper, iced up from heavy seas breaking over the ship, December 1942.

than in any other theatre, the defence of convoys has been thought of as the real function of the Canadian navy in the Second World War. In fact, the RCN seized the opportunity to develop new roles, just as the Royal Canadian Air Force was forced to expand its maritime air role. The RCAF increased its squadrons for anti-submarine patrol from two to ten on the Canadian Atlantic seaboard by late 1943, detached one of them to operate under British control from Iceland in 1944, raised four squadrons for service with Coastal Command of the RAF (mostly in the Atlantic theatre), and sent many Canadians to serve with RAF squadrons.

In 1939 the superb natural harbour of Halifax, already the nation's principal naval base, was the scene of feverish activity as hundreds of ships from North American ports were marshalled there. By the summer of 1940 the number of merchant ships available for convoy had become so large that the harbour could no longer efficiently accommodate all the shipping present. The rule that ships must be capable

65   *The Atlantic Bridge*

31 The corvette HMCS *Chambly*, which had one of the best fighting records in the RCN, convoying in fog, 1941.

of speeds of nine knots to sail in convoy had to be bent when shipping needs became critical. Some pretty ancient vessels began to turn up and their masters, sometimes untruthfully or optimistically, claimed higher speeds than their ships could actually manage. The speed of the main body often had to be reduced to prevent these old crocks from becoming stragglers – prime targets for U-boats in the eastern Atlantic. In August 1940, therefore, slow convoys were instituted, and Sydney, Cape Breton, became their rendezvous so long as that harbour was free of ice. Letters allocated to convoys in the early years of the war indicated their destination or point of departure. Outward bound convoys had the label 'BO' or 'O'; homeward bound were 'H' ('HX' from North America and 'HG' from Gibraltar, for instance). Slow convoys from Sydney received the designation 'SC,' probably standing for 'Sydney-Clyde.' Troop convoys were given the special designation 'TC,' and it was on December 10, 1939, that TC-1, consisting of passenger liners turned troopships – the *Aquitania*, *Empress of Britain*, *Duchess of Bedford*, *Monarch of Bermuda*, and *Empress of Australia* – followed the destroyers HMCS *Ottawa*, *Restigouche*, *Fraser*, and *St Laurent* out of Halifax harbour, past Mauger's Beach, Chebucto Head, and the Sambro Lightship, into the broad reaches of the Atlantic. The Canadian escort parted company the next day, but with the protection of a strong covering force of the Royal Navy, the stately liners filled with men of the 1st Canadian

The Atlantic Bridge

Infantry Division delivered to Britain the first visible evidence that Canada was in the war.

Over the next three years Canada's pre-war fleet was joined by several new types of vessel to meet the requirements of the sea war. Of these, and of all the warships with which the RCN has been identified, the corvette is the most famous. It was adopted as the result of fortuitous circumstances and not, as it would be natural to assume, on the direct recommendation of British naval advisers. In August 1939 a mission of the Canadian Manufacturers' Association had brought home from England plans of several new types of ships being developed by the Admiralty. Among them were those for the 'Smith's Dock Patrol Vessel – Whaler Type,' which had been approved by the Admiralty in June as the best anti-submarine vessel for rapid production. The shipbuilding representative of the Canadian mission, when he returned to Canada, deposited the plans with the National Research Council in Ottawa. Somebody at NRC phoned Naval Service Headquarters to see whether the navy would be interested in having them and was told it would.[2]

The RCN immediately adopted the design for the patrol vessel because it was easier and cheaper to build than the ships that had previously been under consideration for the anti-submarine role. The corvette, as it was called by the Admiralty, was 190 feet long, carried a 4-inch gun and an Asdic set, and was equipped with depth charges for attacking submarines. It had a maximum speed of sixteen knots. At the same time the navy also selected the Bangor-class minesweeper for construction in shipyards across the country. The Bangor could double as an anti-submarine escort, was 162 feet long, armed with a 4-inch gun, could readily be fitted with Asdic, and was fractionally faster. In February 1940 the decision was made to build sixty-four corvettes, and orders were also placed for fourteen Bangors, while another fourteen were ordered before the end of August 1940. By the end of the year the first fourteen corvettes were in service, and by December 1941 all except one of the original order had been completed.

The corvette has rightly been lauded for its ability to turn on a dime and outmanoeuvre a submarine. With its long endurance (particularly true of later versions) and its ability to bounce in the water like a cork rather than pound into heavy seas, it made an ideal escort and was an important asset to the Canadian and British navies. However, living conditions on board were terrible. Corvettes were what is known as wet ships. Seas breaking over them would result in water seeping in through hatches, ventilators, and leaky seams. For weeks on end their crews lived in a state of continual dampness, usually having to tolerate sea water mixed with food (and sometimes vomit) sloshing about on the deck. The atmosphere below became progressively more foul from day to day.

There'd be about 30 men in our quarters. Once we picked up 12 guys in a lifeboat and most of them came in with us. You could say it was crowded, a room hardly big enough to swing a small cat by the tail. Hammocks everywhere, messing table in the centre, and guys off watch sleeping, guys playing cards, writing letters, just staring at nothing, and half the time the whole goddamned Atlantic was trying to get in at us. That's a mess deck for you. If you opened the portholes any time but a nice summer day you'd freeze, and you couldn't open them at night. Blackouts. God! Just so you wouldn't get fished, torpedoed.

Say, 15 or 20 days across, Halifax, to Londonderry – 20 days if you had a few old tubbers doing 8 knots – and the smell just got worse and worse. No showers, you see. The navy rule, no showers on ships at sea. Not even for officers and P.O.s. You could shave, but some never did and some kids were so young they never had to. Oh, I tell you, it was a grand life, great to be a sailor. The ship was a floating pigpen of stink. You couldn't get away from it. The butter tasted of it. The cooks used to bake bread every night and the bread smelled of feet and armpits. There must be something about eggs. They'd pick up the smell. Everything did, and that goes for meat too.[3]

Until naval construction provided sufficient escorts, armed yachts helped to fill the gap: but since they had little or no anti-submarine capacity they provided only the appearance of a defence

The Atlantic Bridge

against submarine attack, although the experience their crews received was good training.

In October 1940, as part of the 'destroyers for bases' deal negotiated between Britain and the United States, six of the fifty ancient destroyers involved came to the RCN as a gift from Britain. A seventh was added, several months later. Known, because of their four funnels, as 'four-stackers,' they were unstable in heavy seas, as difficult to manoeuvre as battleships and extremely uncomfortable. The ship's wheel, recalled the captain of HMCS *St. Croix*, was "as large as a normal cart wheel – what you might expect to find in a Mississippi paddle boat." Rather than the hydraulic lines by which more modern ships transmitted helm movements to the steering engine, the four-stackers had wires "which ran right along the deck ... and were liable to be stuck by ice or even a fender rolling against them." Ships' captains and engineers lived in a perpetual nightmare because so many things could go wrong but, as sailors so often do, they developed a perverse affection for their difficult charges.

The American destroyers did not join the fleet until December 1940. By that time Canada's seven original destroyers had all sailed for British waters, to assist in the evacuation of forces from France and the protection of convoys in the eastern Atlantic. Canada suffered its first naval loss on June 25 when HMCS *Fraser* was cut in two by the cruiser HMS *Calcutta* while manoeuvring at close quarters by night. Four months later HMCS *Margaree*, a destroyer newly commissioned into the RCN, was sliced in half on October 23 by a merchant ship when a convoy was altering course at night.

On November 6, HMCS *Ottawa*, whose captain was Commander E. Rollo Mainguy, RCN, in company with the British destroyer, HMS *Harvester*, responded to the distress call of the merchantman *Melrose Abbey*, west of Ireland. The two destroyers successfully hunted the attacking submarine to destruction, and by participating in this sinking of the Italian *Faa di Bruno*, *Ottawa* achieved the first Canadian success of this kind during the war. Regrettably, the sinking was not confirmed until more than forty years later, when new evidence came to light.

Less than a month later, on the night of December 1, HMCS *Saguenay* – which, with two Royal Navy destroyers, was defending a Britain-bound convoy from Gibraltar against continuous U-boat attack – surprised another Italian submarine, the *Argo*, on the surface. A torpedo blew off forty or fifty feet of *Saguenay*'s bow as a reward for her efforts, and caused a major fire on board, so that she was compelled to limp back to port without damaging the *Argo*. By the time 1940 drew to a close, therefore, the RCN had been thoroughly tested in combat.

Enemy submarines were attacking merchant ships much further west by this time, with new, long-range U-boats working from bases in the Bay of Biscay, following on the fall of France. For the most part,

The Atlantic Bridge

The Atlantic Bridge

33 (FACING PAGE) This photograph, taken on the bridge of HMCS *Barrie* in the North Atlantic in June 1945 (with the war just over in Europe), shows what conditions were like on a relatively calm day. The man on the left holds a cup of hot, sweet cocoa ('ki'). The staple remedy for cold, weariness, hunger, and thirst, it revived the energy and spirit of men on watch.

34 (ABOVE) On board the corvette HMCS *Kamsack* in August 1942. Men slung their hammocks over the tables in the messdecks of British- and Canadian-built warships.

The Atlantic Bridge

their victims were ships steaming independently, stragglers from convoys, and slow convoys either with inadequate escort or beyond the
endurance limits of warships and aircraft based in Britain and
Northern Ireland. Escorts could not detect surfaced submarines
because their Asdic worked only under water; thus surfaced U-boats
could move rapidly into the paths of convoys at night and attack
before they could be discovered, creating extreme confusion as they
picked off their targets and then escaped in the darkness. Until new
tactics could be developed, little could be done about this.

The loss of ships from westbound convoys that had been dis-
persed because their escorts had reached the limits of their endurance
and had to turn back, was partly solved by establishing new bases for
ships and aircraft in Iceland and Newfoundland early in 1941. The
Newfoundland bases, after considerable negotiation, became a
Canadian responsibility, and the Newfoundland Escort Force – or, as
it was later called, the Mid-Ocean Escort Force – was placed under
the command of a Canadian officer, Commodore L.W. Murray, who
reported to the British commander-in-chief, Western Approaches, in
Liverpool. The first seven RCN corvettes arrived at St John's on May
27, 1941 and, in June, all Canadian destroyers were withdrawn from
British home waters for service with the Newfoundland Force.

The navy had been preceded in Newfoundland by the RCAF.
Canadian aircraft had been flying patrols from Gander since 1939,
and the first detachment of No. 10 (Bomber Reconnaissance)
Squadron – the jargon used for maritime patrol squadrons – had been
stationed at Gander since June 1940. By June 1941 the squadron,
with its sixteen Douglas Digbys, provided a limited adjunct to the
Newfoundland Escort Force. In July, four Catalina flying boats of No.
116 Squadron began operations from Botwood, the seaplane base
near Gander.

By this time, naval and air staffs in Britain had devised tactics for
both ships and aircraft to deal with night attacks by surfaced submarines, Canadians had received briefings on the new developments,
and the likelihood of Canada's making a major and autonomous
Canadian military contribution to the Battle of the Atlantic had suddenly become very strong.

Both the navy and air force had to lean heavily on a small nucleus of trained personnel, especially the few who now had first-hand
experience of anti-submarine warfare. Destroying submarines was not
a pastime for novices. It demanded instinct and foresight based on
familiarity with the prey, and had to be done in all kinds of sea and
weather conditions. The vast majority of ships' companies were totally inexperienced – innocents abroad. The captain of one corvette has
written:

> With more than three-quarters of the [ship's] complement as
> fresh to the sea as the ship herself, it was hard to perform our

simple task; hard to keep steam up, avoid the shoals or even steer a straight course. Had anything warlike occurred there would have been a shambles.[4]

The RCAF had somewhat less difficulty because flying operations, although no less demanding mentally than their naval equivalents, did not involve the fundamental readjustments necessary to living and working at sea. Unlike the navy, however, the ranks of airmen flying with Eastern Air Command of the RCAF had not been bolstered by men who were familiar with the war against U-boats in the eastern Atlantic. British officers from Coastal Command of the RAF, as well as Canadian naval officers, had visited Canadian squadrons and lectured on the newest anti-submarine tactics, but Canadian airmen had no direct experience or opportunity to experiment with them until a U-boat ventured into one of their patrol areas, within six hundred miles of the east coast of Newfoundland.

The first such pioneer was detected by shore-based radio-direction-finding stations on May 21, 1941, but neither ships nor aircraft were able to locate it. In the following months there was an increasing number of contacts in the northwest Atlantic, but not one U-boat was destroyed. Sometimes sheer bad luck robbed the Canadians of success; more often, unfamiliarity with their duties and inexperience in identifying targets were the cause of failure.

On September 11, however, the corvettes *Chambly* and *Moosejaw* abandoned a training cruise in order to defend SC-42, a convoy of sixty-four ships and four escorts attacked by eight submarines off the east coast of Greenland. This led to the second successful Canadian attack on an enemy submarine, U-501 (which was on her first operational cruise), the result of wise decisions by the senior officer present, Commander J.S.D. Prentice, pinpoint navigation by an officer brought up in the merchant service, efficient classification of the underwater contact by a well-trained Asdic team, and a measure of luck. When U-501 blew her tanks and surfaced, *Moosejaw* fired only one round with her 4-inch gun because the next shell jammed in the breech. Attempting to ram her enemy, the corvette ran close alongside the U-boat, at which point the captain of U-501, to everybody's astonishment, stepped on to the corvette's upper deck. The first lieutenant of *Chambly* then led a group that attempted to retrieve the U-boat's papers, but the sea cocks had been opened and the vessel quickly sank, one Canadian stoker in the boarding party being drowned. Prentice, who had come out of retirement in the Cariboo country after twenty years' service in the Royal Navy, was reported to have stood nonchalantly on the bridge of *Chambly*, issuing the appropriate orders throughout this strange incident, his monocle at the right angle. "Not once did it fall out," an officer commented. "It looked as if it were part of his face."[5]

37 Commander J.S.D. Prentice, well known for the monocle he wore even at the height of battle, engineered the first submarine kill entirely by Canadian forces.

In October 1941, Canadian naval forces were put under American "co-ordinating supervision," as it was politely described, even though the United States was still officially neutral. This arrangement made tactical sense, in so far as it replaced control by the British commander-in-chief, Western Approaches, based in England, with an American commander in Argentia (one of the Newfoundland bases exchanged for destroyers) who would be much closer to the situation. But Canada was not consulted. Murray was most unhappy about the decision. He believed that the British were prepared, in his words, "to sell us down the river" in order to keep the Americans active on the western side of the Atlantic by giving them full responsibility in Newfoundland.[6]

American warships of both the navy and Coast Guard now began to escort shipping from American ports and sometimes found themselves in combat with U-boats far out in the ocean, even though ships in American waters were immune from attack because Hitler did not want to provoke Roosevelt. After the United States became a belligerent, on December 7, 1941, German U-boats were let loose in American waters. At the same time, American ships were withdrawn

The Atlantic Bridge

from the Newfoundland bases to supplement the Atlantic and Pacific fleets, leaving behind only a few Coast Guard cutters. The eleven Canadian destroyers and forty-three corvettes remaining in Newfoundland were faced with almost impossible demands on their services.

Early in 1942 the centre of gravity shifted to the American seaboard, where coastal shipping was still sailing independently. American doctrine held that convoys without protection were far more dangerous than no convoys at all – a plausible view. Why place a lot of defenceless ships together and provide submarines with a huge target? Furthermore, the U.S. Navy, with its Pacific responsibilities, was desperately short of escorts.

Unfortunately this strategy took little account of the British experience, which had shown that the rate of sinkings among ships in unprotected convoys was incomparably smaller than among individual merchant vessels. The result was that in the first half of 1942 the American coastline took on the nature of a shooting gallery. U-boat commanders called this period the '*Goldene Zeitalte*,' which has been loosely translated as the 'Happy Time.' Night after night submarines rose to the surface, almost at leisure, and picked off ships, many of them silhouetted against the undimmed lights of the shoreline, with torpedoes or gunfire. From January to July 1942, nearly four hundred ships were sunk between the latitude of Cape Cod and the equator, west of the 40th meridian, for the loss of only seven U-boats.[7]

There was soon some relief from this deplorable loss rate, however. Shipping losses that summer brought about a critical shortage of fuel oil in Canada. To meet this crisis the RCN set up a convoy cycle between Halifax and the Caribbean, using Canadian corvettes as escorts, that resulted in a remarkable record: during those otherwise dismal months, not one tanker was lost and the oil crisis was averted.

The benefits of convoys – even with inadequate sea and air escorts – were finally acknowledged by American authorities, and normal traffic resumed under a convoy organization. In March 1942 the first such convoy sailed from Halifax to Boston; in July convoys began to sail further down the coast, and such was the shortage of escorts that Canada's small and already overburdened fleet was called upon to protect southbound shipping. Thus in August HMCS *Oakville* found herself in the Caribbean, where she sank one U-boat.

The Canadian coastline was not immune from the enemy onslaught. By the end of July more than forty ships, including six in convoy, had been sunk in the waters off Canada and Newfoundland, while only three U-boats had been destroyed. Between May and September 3, U-boats sank nineteen merchantmen and two escort vessels in the St Lawrence. With its heavy shipping the river was, of course, thronged with targets, but other conditions also accounted for the heavy losses. Warm and cold currents, combined with the constantly changing salinity at the river's mouth, built up layers through

38 Survivors from the torpedoed merchant ship SS *Eurymedon* coming on board HMCS *Ottawa*, September 1940.

The Atlantic Bridge

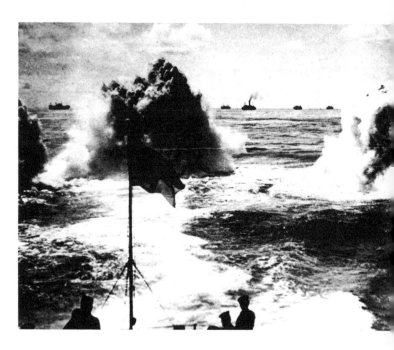

39 Depth charges being dropped over the stern of HMCS *Saguenay* before her final accident.

which sonar could not penetrate, and there was always the unending scarcity of escort vessels.

A continuous U-boat offensive resulting in many sinkings within sight of land would no doubt have brought down the wrath of the voters on the government, so, in September 1942, the gulf and river were closed to overseas shipping. The amount of cargo shipped out of Canada fell by more than 25 per cent, which amounted to a victory for the U-boats won at virtually no cost to Germany.

The RCN, with 188 warships and sixteen thousand men serving at sea, could now provide nearly half the surface escorts needed for convoys from North America to Britain. (Because of the increased availability of tankers that could fuel escorts at sea, Londonderry in Northern Ireland – rather than Iceland – became the eastern terminal for Canadian warships in February 1942.) The RCAF, with eight maritime patrol squadrons and seventy-eight general reconnaissance aircraft on the Atlantic seaboard, was carrying out increased air surveillance of the northwest Atlantic. But, as yet, air support for convoys was still incomplete. That section of the mid-Atlantic called by the Germans 'the Black Pit,' where no available shore-based aircraft could fly because of their limited endurance, harboured packs of U-boats that gathered on the surface to co-ordinate their attacks.

The only aircraft that could cover the region were VLR (Very Long Range) Liberators, which were Consolidated B-24 bombers with modifications that increased their endurance to sixteen hours. The first squadron of these, based in Britain, was not available until December 1942 and, even then, weather conditions often kept them

The Atlantic Bridge

from flying, so that at the crucial moment a number of British and Canadian convoys were deprived of air cover.

During the winter of 1942-43 the performance of both the Canadian navy and the air force was clearly less effective than that of British forces in the same period. Only eight of seventy-nine submarine sinkings on the North Atlantic convoy routes could be attributed to Canadian forces, three by ships and four by aircraft. In January 1943, the British director of anti-submarine warfare observed that "eighty per cent of all ships torpedoed in the last two months were hit while being escorted by Canadian groups."[8]

There were good explanations for this dismal situation, but they did not make the criticism any more palatable. As we have noted, the RCN had grown from about three thousand men in 1939 to about forty thousand by the end of 1943, and such rapid expansion had meant that training had become increasingly difficult and the maintenance of morale among a large number of inexperienced men an ever-present problem. Inevitably the large intake of recruits had led to a decline in selection standards and the quality of instruction suffered when operational demands reduced the available training time.

Another difficulty was poor equipment. Well after the time that the Battle of the Atlantic reached its height, Canadian ships were still without the latest technical improvements fitted in British escorts. Canadian corvettes did not have the extended foc'sles and modern bridges that afforded men a little more protection against the elements and thus allowed them to function most effectively when they contacted the enemy. Nor did they have the newest radar equipment, so that only rarely could they detect submarines on the surface. Asdics were primitive in comparison with the new models in British ships.

The only weapon they could use against submerged U-boats was the depth charge. Filled with high explosive, this 400-pound cylindrical bomb – looking more like an oil drum than a deadly missile – was dropped over the stern or thrown over the side; as it sank, a hydrostatic valve triggered the firing mechanism at a pre-set depth. If close enough to the submarine, two or more depth charges could crush a pressure hull; but to attack, the warship had to pass right over the submerged U-boat and in the process was likely to lose contact with it. British vessels had been fitted with the more advanced hedgehog, which launched twenty-four 50-pound bombs or grenades ahead of the ship. They exploded only on actual contact, thus avoiding the constant noise and disturbance of the water from the explosion of depth charges that had missed. Because of this, and because it was not necessary, with an ahead-throwing weapon, to pass right over the target, the ship had a much better chance of remaining in contact.

Canadian corvettes lacked gyro compasses and relied instead on the magnetic compass, whose needle wanders even in the calmest sea. Steering a precise course to attack a submarine was thus next to impossible. One captain recalled:

40 HMCS *Saguenay* in Newfoundland on November 18, 1942, after her collision. Badly damaged for the second time, she served as a training vessel at Annapolis, N.S., for the rest of the war.

To attack a submarine I had to station myself in the Asdic house, watch the compass, and direct the steering of the ship from this position, since there was no compass outside on the bridge. This was a bad arrangement and was subsequently altered.

To begin with it was a bit of a squash inside the Asdic house, and there always seemed to be wires leading from the compass in every direction, some attached to headphones; there was a drop-leaf table on one side and a folding stool which seemed to open up when trodden on; and there was my collapsible bunk which I had had fitted against the other side of the little compartment. Once wedged in, alongside the compass, it was a job to get yourself out. And to be able to make an exit was important. It was almost better to crane your neck in from outside through an open window. But that would have given you a distorted view of the compass card, and you would have needed the sight of a seagull to read the degrees.[9]

Many Canadian ships were also without high-frequency direction finders (HF/DF, or 'HuffDuff') which provided a rough bearing on the wireless communications of U-boat wolf-packs. Without HuffDuff, escorts had no way of locating submarines preparing to attack the convoy. These deficiencies amounted to an equipment crisis of major proportions, and even after the Admiralty authorized innovations, there were long delays in processing them through Naval Service Headquarters in Ottawa. (These appear to have been caused by the shortage of personnel, the inadequacy of staff training, and the total absence of liaison with the Admiralty on technical matters.) The

The Atlantic Bridge

41 Survivors from torpedoed merchant ships arrive at St John's, Nfld, in the British rescue trawler HMS *Northern Gift*, April 25, 1943.

result was that alterations and additions in the RCN were a year or more behind those made for the Royal Navy.

The RCN was not blind to the situation. Staff and training organizations in Ottawa, Newfoundland, and Londonderry had been trying since early 1942 to improve fighting efficiency in Canadian ships. Their efforts had been frustrated in part by the constant distractions afforded by the need for more escorts, so that Canadian ships had less time than British in harbour and had to cut short more of their training periods. The strain of being at sea continuously for more than a year affected men's efficiency and sapped their morale. "The worst time was dusk, when the dull day was fading and another ominous night was bearing down," recalled one captain. "I hated the sight of the yellowish-grey light, the dun seascape, the cold, curling waves as the evening dissolved into blackness."[10]

The shortage of equipment, the inadequacy of training, and the consequent shortcomings in performance, resulted in the replacement of Canadian escort groups in the Mid-Ocean Escort Force by British groups. The Canadians, to the chagrin of the Naval Board in Ottawa, were given escort tasks in the eastern Atlantic, where they could be

The Atlantic Bridge

provided with intensive air cover and more easily receive comprehensive training, until, in mid-1943, their increasing competence made it practicable for them to return to the northwest Atlantic. Yet amid the gloom were occasional bright spots of recognized achievements and individual successes. The constant demand on escorts made it difficult to keep Canadian ships together in permanent groups. When they could be put into a group, their efficiency improved with teamwork and the morale of their personnel rose accordingly. HMCS *Skeena* and *Saguenay* were charter members of the 'Barber Pole' Group – so named after the red-and-white markings on the funnels of the vessels – which was distinguished by its successful protection of convoys. Lieutenant-Commander K.L. Dyer, while captain of *Skeena*, invented a technique for breaking up U-boat night attacks with the simultaneous firing of 'starshell' by all escorts at the crucial moment when the enemy had gathered on the surface for the kill. The starshell released flares that descended by parachute, lighting up the surrounding sea and forcing the U-boats to submerge.

Because of such accomplishments, some Canadian naval officers in key positions were confident of the potential within the RCN and waged an ultimately successful campaign to have Canada's efforts in the Battle of the Atlantic recognized by the creation of an autonomous Canadian command in the northwest Atlantic. If this seems anomalous, or at least premature, when the efficiency of Canadian forces was in the main so questionable, it was no more anomalous than having the Canadian ships and aircraft based on Newfoundland under the control of an American officer. In 1941 the Canadians in Newfoundland had initiated the Americans into the complexities of convoy organization and anti-submarine warfare. Co-operation had been excellent and the American staff had been willing pupils. Their commander had exercised his authority with tact and offered useful assistance out of his own limited resources.

By late 1942, however, American forces had dwindled away to a mere 2 per cent of the naval escorts on the Mid-Ocean Escort route, compared with 48 per cent now provided by the RCN. Canadian aircraft squadrons in the region outnumbered American squadrons by eight to three. Thus Task Force 24, under American command, had more Canadian than American content and, whatever the shortcomings in the fleet, there were no complaints about the efficiency of the command and staff organizations at St John's and Halifax. The creation by the RCN of a Foreign Intelligence Section in 1939, under Commander Eric Brand, RN, and the subsequent formation of the Operational Intelligence Centre (OIC), modelled on the Admiralty organization of that name, allowed Canada to put the Allied intelligence advantage to good use.

Located in Ottawa, the OIC co-ordinated intelligence activities in the RCN. Among its sections OIC 5, the submarine tracking room – in co-operation with the Admiralty and the U.S. Navy in Washington –

interpreted HuffDuff data and enemy radio signals enciphered by Enigma machines and decrypted by the British Government Code and Cypher School at Bletchley Park. This 'Very Special Intelligence,' developed under the code-name 'Ultra,' enabled authorities in London and Ottawa to divert most convoys away from the patrol lines formed by German wolf-packs, at least until, in February 1942, the Germans established a new code for communications with U-boats outside European coastal waters.

It was the addition of a fourth rotor to the Enigma machines which baffled the codebreakers. No longer were precise submarine positions available, and convoy routing had to depend principally on the very approximate position estimates that HuffDuff could reveal, aided by decrypts of German coastal traffic (still using the old cypher) for an estimate of numbers sailing from enemy ports. That situation lasted for about ten months.

When Enigma decrypts from Britain dried up, the Canadian OIC found itself on much more equal terms with its British counterpart because the Canadian HF/DF network was just about as effective as those used by the RN and USN; and, in December 1942, the RCN won a bureaucratic battle to gain responsibility for the dissemination of all intelligence relating to convoys under Canadian control. Even after the Enigma 'blackout' ceased – the Royal Navy having captured a machine of the new, four-rotor type that December – the Ottawa OIC retained its status in the naval intelligence world. This created some bad feeling in Washington, but in the words of Patrick Beesley, "the acceptance of the British concept of how to handle maritime operational intelligence, adopted willingly by the Canadians and, initially, with some reluctance by the Americans, did, at the very least, save many Allied lives and much shipping."[11]

Operational intelligence, then, became for the RCN a means of exploiting to advantage a situation of strategic importance, even though rapid expansion had inhibited tactical performance in the fleet. Geography placed all great circle routes from North America to Europe close to Canada and Newfoundland, and the fortunes of war weakened both the British and American presence in those waters at a crucial period. By mastering the requirements of operational intelligence in that dominant theatre – as it was after May 1941 – the RCN was able to give Canada a role of more importance than the country's naval capacity would otherwise seem to have warranted.

The way was now open, as a result of the convoy conference held in Washington in March 1943, for Rear Admiral L.W. Murray, with his headquarters at Halifax, to become commander-in-chief of the Canadian northwest Atlantic on 30 April 1943, the first and only theatre commander in the history of the Royal Canadian Navy. It was still not a complete vote of confidence: Fleet Admiral Ernest J. King, commander-in-chief of the U.S. fleet, suggested the American commander of Task Force 24 remain in place until Murray had learned the ropes.

42 A Lockheed Hudson of No. 11 Squadron patrolling off Halifax in 1940.

Murray, who had a very good opinion of himself, was incensed, and rejected the offer with as much diplomacy as he could muster. That done, it could be said that his appointment proved the Allies recognized not only Canada's right, but also its ability, to control the sea and air forces operating in the region closest to its territory.

Within days of Murray's appointment, the battle for ONS 5, fought for the most part off the Newfoundland coast, began the series of heavy U-boat losses that led, at the end of May 1943, to the withdrawal by Doenitz of his wolf-packs from the northern routes. Over the remainder of that summer, Canadian sea and air forces under Murray's command gathered their strength for the next German move.

An important and not sufficiently recognized contribution to the Battle of the Atlantic was the ferrying of aircraft across the ocean. In 1940 Britain's minister of aircraft production, the Canadian-born Lord Beaverbrook, had persuaded Churchill to support his scheme for an Atlantic Ferry Organization (ATFERO) over the protests of the Air Ministry (which advocated transporting all aircraft by sea). Civilian pilots and crews were to fly badly needed bombers and flying boats made in the U.S.A. and Canada from ATFERO's base, in Montreal, to Britain by way of Gander, Newfoundland.

In August 1940 Sir Edward Beatty, president of the CPR, took the responsibility of setting up the scheme with a staff of men experienced in transport and aviation. Besides prominent Canadian executives in business and industry who offered their services as 'dollar-a-year' men on the administrative side, the initial crews included D.C.T. Bennett (later famous for his exploits in the Pathfinder Group of the RAF's

The Atlantic Bridge

Bomber Command), four other British and American pilots who were all first-class navigators, and a number of Canadian radio operators. P.D. McTaggart-Cowan of the Canadian Department of Transport became ATFERO's chief meteorological officer, perhaps the most important person in an organization that depended so much on the weather.

Flying the Atlantic in 1940 was a new and dangerous business. Only in 1939 had the British Overseas Airways Corporation begun limited flying-boat services across the Atlantic. Nothing was known about the behaviour of upper air currents over the ocean: before McTaggart-Cowan there was no meteorological forecasting service. In wartime there could be no assistance from ships stationed along the route to stay in communication or help guide aircraft.

Equally there was a dearth of pilots with sufficient ability in navigation to know their exact position after flying for many hours beyond sight of land. There were not enough to be found in the British Overseas Airways Corporation or from American sources to maintain a continuous ferry service on a large scale. Fortunately the few who were available proved so effective, and the civilian pilots who joined them, including many Canadians, proved so adaptable that the actual navigation and flying problems were resolved.

43 A Canadian Liberator shepherding an Atlantic convoy in 1944. It was the very long-range maritime patrol aircraft that closed the gap in the mid-Atlantic, making U-boat attacks on convoys in what was known as 'the Black Pit' hazardous in the extreme.

The Atlantic Bridge

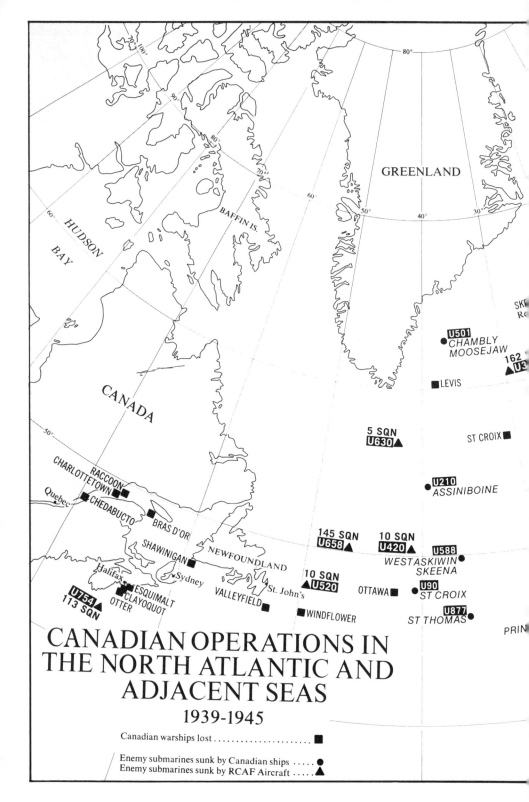

CANADIAN OPERATIONS IN THE NORTH ATLANTIC AND ADJACENT SEAS
1939-1945

Canadian warships lost . . . . ■

Enemy submarines sunk by Canadian ships . . . . . ●
Enemy submarines sunk by RCAF Aircraft . . . . . ▲

The Atlantic Bridge

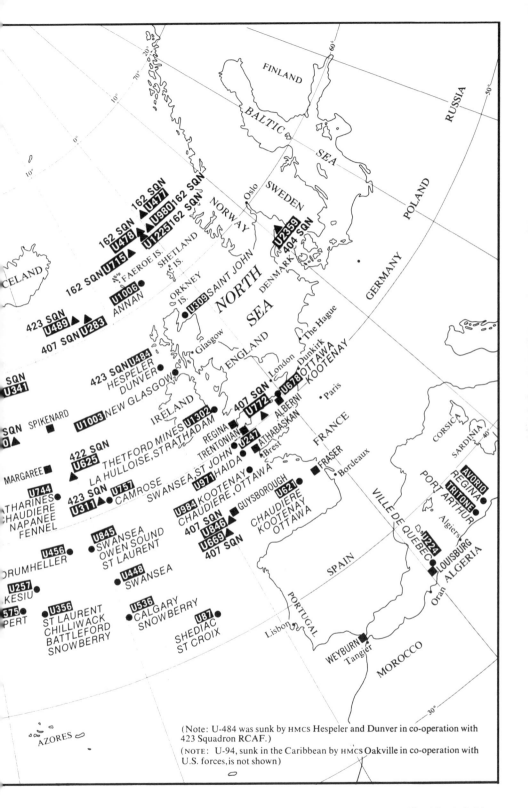

FINLAND

RUSSIA

BALTIC
SEA

POLAND

NORWAY

SWEDEN

Oslo

U2359
404 SQN

GERMANY

DENMARK

162 SQN
162 SQN
U477
U980 162 SQN
162 SQN U478
U1225
162 SQN U715

FAEROE IS.
SHETLAND
IS.

SAINT JOHN

NORTH

SEA

The Hague

U1006
ANNAN

ORKNEY
IS.

U809 SAINT JOHN

OTTAWA
KOOTENAY

ICELAND

423 SQN
U489
407 SQN U283

•Glasgow

ENGLAND

London • Dunkirk
U678
407 SQN
U772

ALBERNI

Paris

SQN
U341

423 SQN U484
HESPELER
DUNVER

U1003 NEW GLASGOW

IRELAND

U1302

ATHABASKAN

Brest

CORSICA
SARDINIA

SQN
0

SPIKENARD

U1003 NEW GLASGOW

422 SQN
U625

THETFORD MINES
LA HULLOISE, STRATHADAM

REGINA
TRENTONIAN
SWANSEA, ST JOHN

U247

HAIDA

FRANCE

Bordeaux

FRASER

U744

MARGAREE ■

THARINES
CHAUDIERE
NAPANEE
FENNEL

423 SQN U757
U311 CAMROSE

U971

KOOTENAY
CHAUDIERE, OTTAWA

U621

GUYSBOROUGH

VILLE DE QUEBEC

PORT ARTHUR

AVORIO
REGINA
TRITONE

Algiers

U984
407 SQN
U846
U669
407 SQN

CHAUDIERE
KOOTENAY
OTTAWA

U1224
LOUISBURG
ALGERIA

Oran

U845
SWANSEA
OWEN SOUND
ST LAURENT

U456

DRUMHELLER

U448
SWANSEA

SPAIN

U257
KESIU

575
PERT

U356
ST LAURENT
CHILLIWACK
BATTLEFORD
SNOWBERRY

U536
CALGARY
SNOWBERRY

U87
SHEDIAC
ST CROIX

PORTUGAL

Lisbon

WEYBURN
Tangier

MOROCCO

AZORES

(Note: U-484 was sunk by HMCS Hespeler and Dunver in co-operation with
423 Squadron RCAF.)

(NOTE: U-94, sunk in the Caribbean by HMCS Oakville in co-operation with
U.S. forces, is not shown)

The Atlantic Bridge

44 Beaufighters attacking enemy shipping in the North Sea, 1944.

There were other difficulties – deliveries from the factories to Montreal were slow, and the organization of flights was not at first very efficient – but by May 1941 the system was working reasonably well. By August, ATFERO had delivered 315 aircraft to Britain, leaving a backlog of 133 at Dorval and Gander still awaiting pilots to fly them across the ocean. The once revolutionary idea of risking military aircraft in direct transoceanic flights to their far-off destinations had taken firm hold. This being the case, and a massive flow of such aircraft being expected, British and American air force authorities no longer thought such an informal arrangement as ATFERO would be adequate to handle the large number of aircraft now expected to pass through the system.

In August 1941 the RAF established Ferry Command under Air Marshal Sir F.W. Bowhill, thus replacing the civil organization with a service one. Civilians and servicemen alike worked for the new command in both operational and military capacities, while new air and meteorological stations sprang up on both sides of the Atlantic to provide facilities for handling increased deliveries and the weather forecasting that consequently became necessary.

The Atlantic Bridge

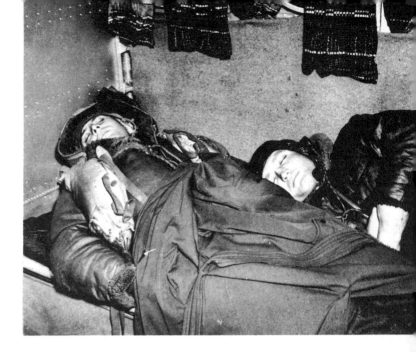

45 Two of the aircrew of a Sunderland flying boat in No. 422 Squadron snatch a few moments' sleep, 1944.

As crucial sea battles were being fought beneath them, aircraft flew from Newfoundland to Northern Ireland or Scotland in a steady stream; and by a southern route from New York to Africa, overland to the Mediterranean theatre, and even to India. Lockheed Hudsons, the first large group of aircraft ordered from the United States, were used by Coastal Command. (It may be asked why, if they could fly the Atlantic, they could not provide coverage over the Black Pit in 1942 and 1943. The answer is that, although their overload fuel tanks gave them the range to fly the 1,500-mile distance from Gander to Northern Ireland, they had an effective patrolling range with all their fighting equipment of only about 450 miles.) Consolidated Catalina flying boats, a longer-range aircraft (about 600 miles), were also delivered to Coastal Command. Subsequently, there were four-engined bombers, Liberators, and Flying Fortresses, including, late in 1942, the VLR Liberators which would play an important part in the defeat of the German attack on shipping. By June 1943, Ferry Command had delivered 2,241 aircraft, besides many important persons, mail, and much-needed equipment. In terms of tonnage and men, however, the achievement was small compared with that of the convoys.

The importance of shipping to the defeat of the Axis powers had never been more evident. At the great strategic conference at Casablanca in January and the so-called Trident Conference at Washington in May, the first object the Allies agreed to strive for in the coming year was control of the Atlantic. Upon this depended the success of the other three aims: the strategic air offensive against Germany; a full-scale invasion of Europe from Britain; and a campaign in the Mediterranean theatre to eliminate Italy from the war.

The Atlantic Bridge

The military supplies needed to take these initiatives demanded a surplus over the minimum shipping requirements for survival, not only in Britain but also in parts of the Mediterranean theatre. For three years British and American specialists in shipping control had struggled to meet increasing worldwide commitments when submarine losses constantly reduced the number of ships available to them. Increasing productivity in American shipyards and the defeat of the submarine in the Atlantic was now bringing a dramatic change in the situation. The Atlantic bridge was finally on a firm foundation. For Canada this marked the end of a severe apprenticeship and the beginning of a much-improved effectiveness in the war at sea.

The Canadian achievements of the next two years resulted from the ability to take advantage, for the first time, of the latest developments in anti-submarine warfare. In 1942, operations research scientists had demonstrated the simple mathematical truth that if you doubled the number of merchant ships, you did not have to double the number of warships needed to defend the convoy. Larger convoys became more common and in the spring of 1943 there were some escorts to spare. These formed roving 'Support Groups' that – instead of being tied to one convoy – could sail rapidly to any spot where submarines were attacking. Support Groups were particularly lethal when they included the aircraft carriers converted from merchant ships in North American shipyards and known as 'Woolworth' or Escort Carriers. Air reconnaissance for convoys was also made possible by the British invention of small flight decks on merchant ships, known as MAC (Merchant Aircraft Carriers) ships, or catapults on CAM (Catapult Aircraft Merchantmen) ships from which aircraft flew off as needed. Other inventions, including improved airborne (Air to Surface Vessel, or ASV) radar and 'Leigh Lights' (high-powered floodlights) fitted to maritime patrol aircraft, exposed surfaced U-boats to devastating night attacks.

By September 1943 there were over 21,000 Canadians at sea, most of them in the RCN's 229 major fighting ships and largely concentrated in the Western or Mid-Ocean Escort Forces. In Eastern Air Command there were 165 aircraft in eleven maritime patrol squadrons, seven of them based on the Canadian mainland or Prince Edward Island, four based on Newfoundland. In the United Kingdom's Coastal Command, of forty anti-submarine squadrons, three were Canadian, while two of the seven squadrons used for air strikes against enemy shipping off the north coast of Scotland, in the North Sea, the English Channel, and the Bay of Biscay were also Canadian. In addition, many individual Canadians flew in British squadrons.

Several 'River'-class destroyers had been acquired from the Royal Navy and a few of the new British-designed frigates, developed as a result of experience in the war, were beginning to join the fleet. Escort

46 The naval dockyard, Halifax, April 27, 1944. A MAC ship is at anchor behind the vertical crane boom, three frigates are alongside, and two frigates are manoeuvring with tugs. Also to be seen are minesweepers and a boom gate vessel.

and Support Groups usually included one or two destroyers, and thirteen Canadian destroyers were still used in this role. As for aircraft types, one Canadian squadron was now flying VLR Liberators from Newfoundland, two had Cansos (the Canadian amphibian version of the Consolidated Catalina flying boat), and the other squadrons of Eastern Air Command were flying twin-engined Hudsons or Venturas. The RCAF squadrons with Coastal Command flew Sunderland flying boats and twin-engined Wellington bombers for anti-submarine work; and Bristol Beaufighters, Wellingtons, or Hampden bombers were being used for anti-shipping strikes.

The navy was catching up slowly with British equipment as ships went into refit. Eastern Air Command squadrons were behind, in that none of their aircraft yet had the Leigh Light and the latest radar equipment was not always available, but in other respects they were up-to-date.

Both organization and training had improved immensely. Because Nova Scotia and Newfoundland weather was usually too dirty for efficient training, the Canadians, with extensive British support, set up a base in Bermuda. But the most famous and possibly the

91

The Atlantic Bridge

most effective training for ships' companies was provided in the ordinarily sleepy little harbour of Tobermory, Scotland. There a retired rear-admiral of the Royal Navy, in his wartime rank of commodore, established a reputation for rapid results by means of merciless driving, surprise, and a perverse sense of humour. Gilbert Stephenson, 'the Terror of Tobermory,' was one of the unforgettable experiences of all those Canadians who had to work up their ships on the eastern side of the ocean.

RCAF personnel in training did not receive the same sort of shock treatment – the needs of fighting an aircraft with a crew of only six or eight men were different from those of a warship. Flying skills, navigating, gunnery, and bombing were the vital requirements, carefully nurtured by hours of flying training in Operational Training Units and then in the squadrons themselves.

On September 16, 1943, the 9th Support Group (EG-9) was en route to the Bay of Biscay. One of the first groups with Canadian ships, it included the destroyer *St. Croix* and the corvettes *Chambly, Sackville,* and *Morden,* all with good combat records. As was often the case, the senior officer was in a British ship, the frigate *Itchen.* A pack of nineteen U-boats was at this same time moving into a line across the path of three convoys either at sea or about to sail.

Alerted by Enigma decrypts to a renewed attempt at wolf-pack operations on the northern Atlantic routes, British authorities diverted EG-9 to the defence of two westbound convoys leaving Liverpool. These convoys, ONS-18 and ON-202, joined forces, and by September 20, found themselves under the protection of seven British, seven Canadian, and three Free French escorts. Air cover was plentiful. VLR Liberators from Britain and, as the ships moved further west, from Newfoundland, carried out aggressive sweeps over and around the convoy. A MAC ship ensured the availability of Swordfish aeroplanes for local reconnaissance.

The Germans were hoping for a breakthrough with their new acoustic torpedo, which homed on the noise of ships' engines and was designed to neutralize the escorts before submarines tried to attack the convoy. By the time EG-9 arrived, two of the original escorts had already been damaged in engagements with submarines and forced to return to harbour. On the other hand, a Canadian Liberator, carrying out a sweep on its return to base from Britain, had attacked and destroyed U-341 on September 19. Then a British Liberator sank U-338 with a new type of British acoustic torpedo on September 20; and the destroyer HMS *Keppel* sank U-229 two days later. Two more U-boats were seriously damaged. In exchange, six merchant ships and three escorts – HMCS *St. Croix,* the British corvette *Polyanthus,* and HMS *Itchen* – were sunk.

This battle was the occasion of one of the most remarkable survival experiences of the war. When the *St. Croix* was torpedoed on September 20, Able Seaman Fisher, a stoker, obeyed orders to aban-

47 U-744 surfaces near HMCS *Chaudière* after a hunt of 29½ hours, March 6, 1944.

don ship and took charge of the ship's whaler. Amid the confusion and shock of sudden disaster – among several explosions, he heard the torpedoing of *Polyanthus* – he and his companions hauled men out of the water until there were twenty-four of them in the 27-foot open boat. Constantly taking seas over the side and leaking from several holes, the vessel drifted all night. Then the survivors were rescued by *Itchen*. The next day, September 22, *Itchen* attacked a submarine:

> There were a lot of bubbles and oil and we were sure we had got a sub and we were happy. We all went below and tried to sleep. About a quarter to nine, 22nd September, action stations went again. We went to the upper deck where it was quite cold and very dark. Around nine our searchlight went on and there was a sub in the beam.... Then the forward gun went off but the shell landed short and the bridge gunners started to fire. There was an explosion. We had been torpedoed. I was blown about thirty feet and landed against a gun deck. I got up, the ship was listing and I could hear water rushing in. I couldn't see a thing.... Just before I jumped over the side I called my chum Mackenzie, but there was no answer. So I dove over the side. As I hit the water there was a terrible explosion. I was sucked under and nearly lost consciousness. My insides seemed to be squeezed out of me. I was choking as I struggled back to the surface again, got a breath of air, and a wave took me under.... I came up ... and

93   *The Atlantic Bridge*

swam about thirty or forty feet and looked back at the propellers of the *Itchen* which were just disappearing. She had gone down in about forty seconds.

A board floated by, and Fisher hung on to it with another man. "Then ... I started to run into quite a few bodies," he recalled, "and the convoy started to pass us. The wash from the ships would wash us back and forth, we would go under and choke and there was a lot of oil and small boards that would slap us in the face. Then the star shells stopped going up and it got very dark."[12] The other man let go and disappeared after about an hour, but, miraculously, Fisher was plucked out of the sea by Polish hands from a merchantman in the convoy some time in the following hour. All his shipmates died, as did all but two of the combined ships' companies of *Polyanthus* and *Itchen*.

Terrible sacrifices: yet in the harsh currency of war they were far from worthless. After analysing the experiences of this convoy it was easy to devise a means of diverting acoustic torpedoes by towing a noise-maker astern of each warship, and the merchant shipping lost in September was replaced without difficulty. Convoy SC-143 – thirty-nine merchantmen and one MAC ship – sailed from Halifax on September 28 to run the gauntlet of eighteen U-boats. Although one of the escorts, the Polish destroyer *Orkan*, was torpedoed on October 8, British Liberators destroyed U-419 and U-643 astern of the convoy and a Canadian Sunderland flying boat of No. 432 Squadron sank U-610 more than thirty miles away. After the air escort departed that night, a submarine managed to hit one merchant ship, which sank – the sole reward for the Germans.

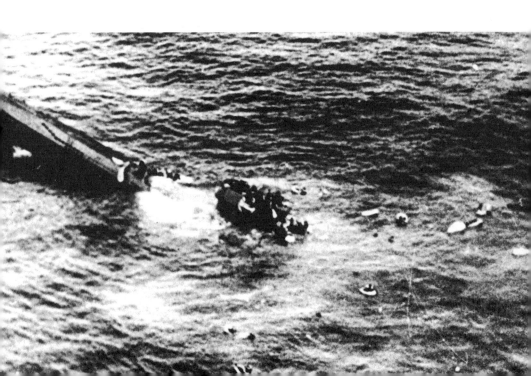

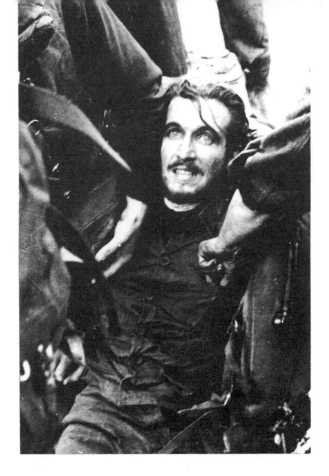

50 Searching a survivor of U-448 on board HMCS *Swansea,* April 14, 1944.

Operations in the mid-Atlantic were failing to produce results from a German perspective. In three months only 9 of 2,468 merchantmen had been sunk, in exchange for 25 U-boats – 5 destroyed by warships, 6 by American carrier-borne aircraft, 13 by shore-based aircraft (including 2 by RCAF machines), and one by warships and shore-based aircraft combined. This spelled the end of wolf-pack tactics on northern routes. Submarine warfare in the western Atlantic, in the face of such poor results, changed from aggressive group tactics to a policy of individual operations, lying in wait for targets that might pass through a submarine's patrol area. And because the German High Command had a desperate need for weather reports from the region – they were a major factor in forecasting European weather patterns – U-boats were about to become increasingly important sources of weather information.

Several manned German weather stations had been established on the east coast of Greenland since 1941, but they were vulnerable to discovery and destruction, and such, indeed, had been their fate. One solution was to establish unmanned, automatic weather stations. On October 22, 1943, U-537, a newly commissioned Type IXC boat,

The Atlantic Bridge

on its first patrol made a daring foray into St. Martin's Bay, on the coast of Labrador just south of the Davis Strait, and its crew erected one there. It was both a remarkable feat of navigation and the only known landing of German armed forces on North American soil during the war. It was blessed with extraordinary luck, because the boat had to remain surfaced, with its hatches open, for more than three days while all the equipment was carried ashore. Just a week before, an RCAF Canso from Goose Bay had flown a patrol along this part of the coast, while the annual harp seal hunt by the Inuit of the region was then being conducted within a few miles of the site. Subsequently hunters ransacked the site, but it was not until 1980, when a German researcher was compiling a history of the German weather service during the war, that its existence came to light.

Designed to transmit temperature, barometric pressure, wind force and direction, for two minutes every hour, it began sending out signals immediately. To what extent they were heard and used in Germany has not been established, but in 1944 Doenitz ordered another submarine to set up a second station in Labrador. That one was not so lucky, and was sunk by Coastal Command aircraft off the coast of Norway. Weather reports thereafter became the responsibility of designated U-boats stationed in the North Atlantic, their numbers beefed up when impending ground operations in Europe made weather forecasting particularly important.

The *Luftwaffe* had not co-operated very well with U-boats over the years, largely because of inter-service rivalry. All the same, developments by the Germans in combined sea and air attack against naval forces in European waters amounted to a serious potential danger in late 1943. Their newest weapons were glider bombs. With a speed of 300-400 knots, and carrying 1,100 pounds of explosive, they could be directed towards their targets by radio control. Their first use, in the Bay of Biscay in August 1943, had resulted in the destruction of the sloop HMS *Egret* and in serious damage to HMCS *Athabaskan*. Now glider bombs were about to be used against convoys.

The first potential victim of the new German offensive was a convoy of 66 ships and 7 escorts sailing from Gibraltar on November 14. Three lines of U-boats – a total of 28 submarines – lay in wait across the convoy's path. German reconnaissance aircraft made contact on November 16, and attacks began on the 18th. Three days later the convoy emerged from its ordeal, which included a glider-bomb attack on the 21st, with one escort damaged, two British aircraft shot down by submarines under attack, one merchantman sunk, and another damaged. The escorting forces had in turn sunk three U-boats, damaged a fourth, and shot down five enemy aircraft.

The first Canadian ships to share in the triumph of this important battle were in the 5th Support Group. On November 20 the corvettes *Snowberry* and *Calgary* combined with the British frigate

Nene to sink U-536. HMCS *Prince Robert*, an armed merchant vessel converted to an anti-aircraft ship, appeared on the scene when Heinkel 177s were in the act of unleashing their glider bombs on the 21st. Her powerful armament provided a barrage in the convoy's wake.

By this time, more and more effective Canadian naval forces were gravitating to the eastern Atlantic. This was a trend that had begun to increase in momentum late in 1942 when Canadian corvettes first went to the Mediterranean. There had also been a very small Canadian component among the flotillas of landing craft for the North African invasion in November 1942. During 1943, twenty-five landing craft of the 55th and 61st Canadian LCA (Landing Craft, Assault) Flotillas and twenty-four craft of the 80th and 81st LCM (Landing Craft, Mechanized) Flotillas would carry British infantry and mechanical equipment ashore in the invasion of Sicily on July 10. (Men of the 1st Canadian Infantry Division were landed from RN landing craft.)

It was still necessary to protect ships on the North Atlantic sea lanes, but there were very few U-boats left in the western Atlantic. Meanwhile, Canadian sea and air forces working in the eastern Atlantic, in the Arctic, and in British home waters were extremely active against the enemy. The Canso flying boats of No. 162 Squadron, RCAF, transferred from its Newfoundland base to Iceland in January 1944, did especially well as the Germans tried desperately to move submarines based in Norway against the Allied invaders of France in June 1944.

On April 17, No. 162 Squadron achieved its first success, convincingly illustrated in a series of five photographs of a U-boat's ordeal and the oil patch that marked its grave. In June, the squadron's aircraft attacked six U-boats and destroyed five of them – one with the help of another squadron. In exchange, three aircraft were lost, thirteen airmen were killed, and one was taken as a prisoner-of-war. Another aircraft was damaged by enemy fire. "I am much impressed by the spirit of the [Canadian] aircrews, who appear to be quite undaunted by the odds they are facing," wrote Sir Sholto Douglas, the air officer commanding, Coastal Command.[13]

On June 24, one of the two Victoria Crosses awarded to members of the RCAF was earned by a pilot of the squadron. David Hornell, who came from Toronto (where he had worked in the laboratory of the Goodyear Company and had been a Sunday School teacher), took his Canso flying boat in against a U-boat sighted just as the aircraft was about to turn home for base. The German fire became extremely heavy and accurate at a range of about a thousand yards. While Hornell concentrated on the best positioning for his attack, the starboard engine was hit, the wing caught fire and, as the fabric burned away leaving nothing but the ribs of the wing, the aircraft began to shudder unbearably. It was necessary to shut down the starboard engine, which meant added difficulty in controlling the machine. Meanwhile, the submarine was turning to port and Hornell had to alter course violently before dropping his depth charges. The manoeuvre demanded exceptional strength and skill by both pilot and co-pilot. Hornell then achieved a perfect 'straddle.'

As he completed the attack the damaged engine fell off, compelling Hornell to ditch his aircraft in heavy seas. At the best of times the Canso was a heavy machine to handle and alighting on rough water was always a terrifying ordeal. On the first attempt the doomed Canso bounced from a wavetop 150 feet into the air. On a second attempt it hurtled another 50 feet. Finally Hornell came in on a glide that coincided, more or less, with the slope of a wave, hauling back with every ounce of strength on the control column, and coming to rest in waves about twelve feet high. His crew managed to get out in spite of some minor injuries, but one of the dinghies over-inflated and blew up, so eight men had to share one five-man dinghy.

Their plight seemed hopeless. Although they could not know it, not one of their radio signals had been received ashore, so that nobody knew where they were, let alone in what condition. By simple good luck, a flying boat from a Norwegian squadron on a routine patrol saw one of their distress rockets and was able to send for help. This aircraft was also able to confirm that the submarine had been destroyed. Before a rescue could be effected, however, twenty-one hours after ditching – the weather becoming worse all the time – two of their number died and Hornell himself lapsed into a coma from which he could not be revived.

In the summer of 1944, most Canadian naval forces were in the English Channel and the Bay of Biscay to prevent German submarines and ships from attacking cross-Channel shipping. Canadians tried to remain distinct from the British in their own escort groups and in their own motor torpedo boat and minesweeping flotillas. Some of their efforts cannot be measured by results – there were times when the simple presence of naval formations may have been enough to inhibit enemy activity – but RCN escort groups sank three submarines in July and August. It is noteworthy that on each occasion HMCS *Ottawa*, commanded by Commander J.S.D. Prentice, was in at the kill.

The Canadian Tribal-class destroyers *Haida, Huron,* and *Athabaskan* were making their reputations in coastal warfare. In the early morning hours of April 29, 1944, *Haida* and *Athabaskan* engaged two smaller Elbing-class destroyers off the French coast. In a furious battle *Haida* drove one of the Elbings ashore and destroyed it with gunfire, but *Athabaskan* was sunk by a German torpedo with the loss of 144 men. *Haida* then conducted a daring rescue operation within range of the enemy's shore batteries and retrieved thirty-eight survivors, but she had to leave the rest behind when daylight came.

The Atlantic Bridge

She also left behind her motor cutter with several volunteers to pick up more survivors, who rescued six of the ninety-one men in the water, eluded capture by enemy minesweepers and, after an adventurous journey across the Channel, returned to safety. A relatively small incident – repeated, matched, and surpassed elsewhere, no doubt – but for a young navy it was the kind of thing on which the pride of service is built.

The two Canadian MTB flotillas also took an active part in coastal warfare during 1944. Manned by personnel who had for the most part served an apprenticeship with British coastal forces, they began Channel operations in May. From the D-Day landings until late summer the 29th Flotilla covered the beaches near Le Havre, while the 65th engaged in search and pursuit in the western Channel. They were responsible for the destruction of four enemy ships in convoy and the damaging of several others, besides sinking and damaging a few enemy torpedo and gun boats. Two Canadian MTBs fell victim to mines. On February 14, 1945, the 29th Flotilla was destroyed when high-octane fuel in Ostend Harbour suddenly caught fire and spread, burning five of the flotilla's eight boats and killing twenty-six men.

In August 1944 the RCN embarked upon naval air operations when HMS *Nabob* – although a British escort carrier, she was commanded and, for the most part, manned by Canadian personnel – joined the Home Fleet for air strikes against German targets in Norway. After only three weeks she was the victim of a U-boat attack. Not only did brilliant damage control save the ship from destruction, but aircraft from her British Fleet Air Arm squadrons, flying off a crazily angled flight deck, drove off a second submarine attack. *Nabob*, however, never again went to sea as a warship. (Initially sold as scrap after the war, she was resold to German and then Chinese owners, who renamed her the SS *Glory* in 1968.) HMS *Puncher*, the second British escort carrier commanded and manned principally by Canadians, was used to transport aircraft across the Atlantic before she began air operations in February 1945.

The U-boats had to abandon all their Biscay bases by September 1944, but they moved to Norway and north German bases and continued to threaten lines of communication. A revolutionary new development, the 'Schnorkel' mast, allowed air to be drawn into a submarine while submerged and exhaust fumes to be expelled, thanks to a valve arrangement that, when waves broke over the mast, also prevented water from pouring into the vessel. Thus it became possible for U-boats to run their diesel engines while submerged, and consequently to charge batteries and proceed under water at speeds previously only attainable by surfaced submarines. As 1944 drew to a close, new and very large Type XXI U-boats with Schnorkels were coming into service for distant operations. Other Type XXIII boats, similarly fitted but smaller, were also approaching completion. Had it not been for the disruption of factories, shipyards, and canals caused by strategic bombing, these new vessels would have been ready in larger numbers early in 1945, providing a serious new threat because they were so difficult to find at sea. Only after they had attacked could convoy escorts realize their presence: it was a throwback to the dark days of 1940.

In the western Atlantic, U-boats had finally abandoned wolf-pack operations after the defeats of late 1943. Instead, they conducted lonely, individual patrols, a policy that led to a long-drawn-out war of nerves marked by occasionally devastating confrontations and endless days (and nights) of ships and aircraft chasing elusive clues to the whereabouts of their prey. Schnorkel boats did not need to surface, were few in number, and so did not offer many opportunities for a sighting. They still had to use their radios, however, and therefore regularly betrayed their exact positions to Allied intelligence. Routing authorities consequently knew where not to send convoys, and established 'datums' – last known positions – on which air/sea searches could be based. Shipping losses remained negligible, U-boats remained, for the most part, on the defensive, and their successes fell off significantly.

The RCN and RCAF, aided by the OIC in Ottawa, ensured the safe and timely arrival of hundreds of convoys on the northern routes. At the same time U-boats operated with relative impunity in Canadian waters, benefitting from the strong currents, temperature gradients and tidal effects that played havoc with sonar. They did so, under the occasional intrepid commander like Kurt Dobratz of U-1232, with enough success to earn the extravagant praise of Doenitz himself, in Enigma messages duly decrypted at Bletchley Park. The last eighteen months of the anti-submarine war foreshadowed conditions that would govern developments in this field through the post-war decades. It was the dawn of a new era.

Convoys still sailed across the Atlantic in 1945 and Canadian forces continued to provide a very large proportion of the escorts. Besides ten squadrons of Eastern Air Command, there were eight escort groups of minesweepers and corvettes and three support groups of destroyers and frigates based on Halifax.

As we have already noted, other small ships, based on Halifax, St John's, Newfoundland, Saint John, Sydney, and Gaspé, looked after coastal convoys and patrolled coastal waters. In the last year of the war they were roughly handled by U-boats returning to the western Atlantic. HMCS *Valleyfield* had been torpedoed off Newfoundland on May 6, 1944. The corvette *Shawinigan* was lost in the Cabot Strait on November 24, 1944, and the Bangor-class minesweepers *Clayoquot* and *Esquimalt* on the Halifax approaches on December 23, 1944 and April 16, 1945, respectively.

The continuing danger of submarine attack ensured a continuing demand for Canadian anti-submarine sea and air forces in European

The Atlantic Bridge

waters. In trying to visualize Canadian efforts here, one must resort to statistics. At least 25 per cent of the 426 escort vessels in British home waters in 1945 were Canadian. W.S. Roskill, the British official historian, observes that the RCN "thus came to carry as large a share of the struggle for control of Britain's coastal waters as it had borne in the Atlantic convoy battles of earlier phases."[14] Results show that the effort in the eastern Atlantic late in the war was, in fact, much more significant than earlier convoy battles – and, indeed, in the light of more recent research, more significant than indicated in the first edition of this book. Of the 33 U-boat kills credited to the RCN between 1939 and 1945, 25 occurred east of the 35th meridian of longitude, and 18 of those took place after November 20, 1943.

The air effort showed similar tendencies. In May 1945 there were 784 aircraft in Coastal Command, 511 of them used in anti-submarine warfare and the remainder for attacks on enemy shipping. They flew from bases as far north as Iceland and as far south as Gibraltar. A measure of the Canadian contribution to Coastal Command must include all Canadians who took part in its activities. Canadian squadrons formed just under 10 per cent of the total force and, in addition, many RCAF aircrew were to be found in British squadrons. Of 178 submarines destroyed by aircraft of Coastal Command during the whole course of the war, 15 were credited, in whole or in part, to Canadian squadrons.

In anti-shipping operations, Canadian squadrons participated in the destruction or damage of 85 vessels, or 17 per cent of the total for Coastal Command. Most of the successes took place towards the end of the war: all the submarines sunk or damaged in the eastern Atlantic by Canadian aircraft met their fate after May 1943, and 67 of the 85

51 Survivors of HMCS *Esquimalt,* which was torpedoed off Halifax in April 1945.

The Atlantic Bridge

U-190, at Bay Bulls,
Nfld, on May 14, 1945,
after surrendering to
HMCS *Victoriaville* and
Thorlock on May 11.

surface vessels sunk and damaged were a result of operations in 1944
and 1945. Like the RCN, therefore, the RCAF was proving itself a highly effective force now that it was on the enemy's doorstep.

After May 8, 1945, victory in Europe gradually reduced the hectic
pace. The navy immediately declared more than half its ships 'surplus
to requirements' and all except two squadrons of Eastern Air
Command could now be disbanded. On May 10, 1945, a Liberator
from No. 10 Squadron sighted U-889 on the surface, 250 miles southeast of Cape Race. Two Bangor-class minesweepers hove in sight and
began to escort the submarine to harbour. The frigates *Buckingham*
and *Inch Arran* took over the task and, on the afternoon of May 13,
received the U-boat commander's official surrender just off Shelburne,
N.S. Two days earlier U-190 had surrendered at sea to the frigate
Victoriaville and the corvette *Thorlock*.

On the other side of the ocean, on May 19, a support group
including one British and four Canadian frigates escorted fifteen surrendered U-boats into Loch Eriboll, in northern Scotland. The long
black hulls aroused feelings of revulsion in the men who had been
fighting them for so long, but they must also have felt a sense of relief.
Even though the war against Japan still had to be won, the return to
Europe was finally complete, unhampered by that tenacious German
menace to the sea lanes.

Canadian seamen and airmen had played a memorable part in
the sea war against Germany. Bridging the Atlantic would have been
a longer and, perhaps – given the strategic importance of
Newfoundland and the Mid-Ocean Escort Force – an impossible task
without them. Their efforts are remembered in Canada every May, on
Battle of the Atlantic Sunday. But the truth is, Canadians did not
achieve their potential until after that battle had been won in 1943.
It was not until the last year of the war against Germany that
Canadian airmen and seamen – following British techniques and
trained to a very large extent by the Royal Navy and Royal Air Force

The Atlantic Bridge

– proved themselves in versatile combinations of long-range patrol aircraft, anti-submarine escort groups, MTB and destroyer flotillas skilled in coastal warfare, and carrier task forces operating in the crowded waters of the northwest European littoral.

CHAPTER 5

The Army Overseas, 1940-1943

The 1st Division, still largely untrained and unequipped, sailed for England in December 1939, since training could be better carried out in the milder English winter climate. It soon settled in at Aldershot, the Victorian garrison town near Salisbury Plain, and training began during the second week of January. The chief of the Imperial General Staff, General Sir Edmund Ironside, informed McNaughton that his division would not be required in France "until early May."

As it turned out, the British had entered upon their coldest winter since 1894. While to the Canadians it was mild enough in terms of temperature, they were used to a drier cold and to insulated houses, storm doors and windows, and central heating. Moreover, the barrack blocks in which they found themselves housed were bleak and frigid structures of Boer War vintage, with one tiny open fireplace – for which there was never enough coal! – to heat each spartan dormitory room. There was no provision for hot water or showers and even the cold water supply was limited.

There was also a shortage of equipment for training, and imagination was a poor substitute. As they practised the esoteric art of gunlaying without either guns or targets, Canadian gunners found themselves "in odd postures making strange movements in response to barked out orders, the centre of attraction being a particular individual who would squat on an airy seat, twiddle his fingers and stare fixedly at nothing."[1]

Another problem arose over the fact that the British were still relying on much of the tactical doctrine developed during the First World War. Military theorists like Liddell Hart and J.F.C. Fuller had long been advocating more modern techniques of warfare based on mobility, flexibility, speed, and co-operation of all arms. They were largely ignored by the so-called Imperial General Staff, though their ideas had been enthusiastically adopted by the Germans.

Canadian doctrine and training faithfully followed British practice. For the Hastings and Prince Edward Regiment, "the 1918 Pamphlet of Field Engineering was the Bible.... Miles of trenches grew and spread across Salisbury Plain and the pathetic futility of it went quite unnoticed. No voice cried out against that monumental folly."[2]

On April 9, however, the 'phoney war' came to a sudden and violent end when the Germans launched their invasion of Norway and Denmark. Caught badly off balance, the British and their French allies responded in a confused and ill-considered fashion, hoping to stop the enemy somewhere in central or northern Norway, and they hastily cobbled together an expeditionary force to do so. The Canadians were caught up in the prevailing tumult, McNaughton agreeing that his troops might be used in an amphibious attack on Trondheim, a key port in central Norway. Control of Trondheim would block the German drive to the north and secure the light railway that brought Swedish iron ore – which could be worked into particularly high-grade steel – to tidewater at Narvik.

McNaughton, who never lacked drive and enthusiasm in those early days, accepted the British plan without referring it to Ottawa for Cabinet approval. Lester B. Pearson, then a foreign-service officer on the staff of the Canadian high commissioner in London (and eventually to become a Canadian prime minister), felt that "if the whole thing turns out badly ... then I would not wish to be in McNaughton's shoes if he agrees to the use of Canadians in this way without prior authorization from Ottawa."[3] And, indeed, although nothing came of it at the time, McNaughton's initiative was not appreciated by the pettifogging lawyer, J.L. Ralston, minister of finance and (very briefly) acting prime minister, who would become minister of national defence on the death of Norman Rogers in early June.

Nevertheless, by April 19 a contingent 1,300 strong, composed of the most advanced units in training, was waiting to embark at Dunfermline, Scotland, expecting to be the first Canadian ground forces to see action in the Second World War.

Perhaps luckily for everyone concerned, their hopes were soon frustrated. The Trondheim plan was abandoned and the Canadians found themselves back on Salisbury Plain while British and French forces bumbled ineffectually about the Norwegian coastline for another five weeks. The last British troops left Narvik on June 8, but by that time a far greater disaster had overtaken the Allies and the chaotic Norwegian operations had faded from the headlines.

On May 10, 1940, the Germans launched their attack in the west. Armoured *Panzer* divisions, supported by dive-bombers, swept across the Netherlands, Belgium, and northeastern France, ripping great holes in the British and French defences. The main thrust came through the tangled hills and forests of the Ardennes, which Allied strategists had dismissed as quite unsuitable for a major armoured attack. The Germans then swung north to cut off the British Expeditionary Force and the northern group of French armies from the main French forces in the south.

Again a scheme to employ the Canadians was quickly devised. They would be landed at Calais to secure a port through which the BEF could be evacuated to England if necessary. McNaughton, who was to command British troops in the Calais area as well as his own men, was given orders to keep open the coast road to Dunkirk, but only hours after an advance party consisting of McNaughton himself, four staff officers, and ten 'Mounties' of No. 1 Canadian Provost Corps arrived at Calais, the road was cut by German spearheads.

53 At the end of a brief leave, Canadians feed the early-morning pigeons in a deserted Trafalgar Square, London.

At almost the same moment, Canadian units began to arrive at Dover and by 11:00 a.m. on May 24 the first of them were embarked and ready to sail. They waited the rest of that day while the British Cabinet and the War Office debated what should be done. Their eventual conclusion was that there was now no purpose in sending the Canadians across the Channel and that night they were ordered back to Aldershot. "A very flat feeling for all of us who had been highly keyed up," recorded the 1st Brigade's diarist.[4]

As for the isolated BEF, a combination of luck and dogged determination in the face of adversity enabled the greater part of it to escape by way of Dunkirk. Between May 26 and June 4 the Royal Navy, and what the Admiralty euphemistically described as "other little ships," lifted more than a quarter of a million men (including 70,000 Frenchmen) from the harbour quays and another hundred thousand off the open beaches to the east of the town, and took them all back to England. Britons rejoiced at the 'miracle of Dunkirk,' but Winston Churchill, their new prime minister, grimly reminded them

The Army Overseas, 1940-1943

54 Major B.M. Hoffmeister (who as a major-general was to command a Canadian armoured division before the war ended) leading B Company of the Seaforth Highlanders of Canada down an English road in the summer of 1940.

that "We must be careful not to assign to this deliverance the attributes of a victory. Wars are not won by evacuations."

With the British gone and the French thoroughly demoralized, the German *Blitzkrieg* fanned out to the south and west, bypassing Paris. The Italians, anxious for a share of the spoils, declared war on Britain and France and invaded France from the south on June 10. It still seemed possible, however, that a western redoubt might be established in Brittany and, early in June, the two divisions in England still fit to move and fight – one British and one Canadian – were dispatched to Brest. The 52nd (Lowland) Division, already under orders to move, started to cross on June 7 and the next day the Canadians began to follow them.

"The general idea ... was that these troops would not be available for operations until the division had concentrated," McNaughton recalled later,[5] but the now customary incompetence of British planning and staff work ensured that the first Canadians to land were sent forward piecemeal towards Le Mans, sometimes with neither officer

The Army Overseas, 1940-1943

nor senior NCO in charge. Wine was plentiful and the Canadians were popular; not all of them arrived at their destinations in a soldierly manner and there were "some reports of drunkenness and reckless driving." Perhaps fortunately, the nearest Germans were still more than forty miles away.

On June 14, the day Paris fell, the War Office came to terms with reality and ordered the evacuation of this second Expeditionary Force. The Canadians withdrew, leaving behind most of the 1st Brigade's transport and heavy equipment but bringing off their own artillery and a number of invaluable Bofors anti-aircraft guns belonging to British units that had abandoned them in Brest. The French were now out of the war, except for that gallant minority that chose to follow Charles de Gaulle into exile and form the genesis of Free France.

Back in England and concentrated once again, the Canadians found themselves the only division in the country equipped to fight as a formation and still mobile enough to move quickly to any threatened point. They promptly became the mobile reserve – "McNaughton's travelling circus," they called themselves – held ready to counter-attack any landing on the English coast as the islanders, now isolated by the fall of France, buckled down to fight a serious war. While strong points and anti-tank defences were hurriedly constructed along 'stop-lines' throughout the south and east of England, while young boys and old men flocked to join the Home Guard and the RAF and the navy guarded the Channel, the army's training was stepped up to an unprecedented intensity and degree of toughness.

Only two months earlier, in April, Ironside had confided to his diary his wish that "our [British] commanders had the terrific energy of McNaughton in the Canadians."[6] Now Ironside was replaced by Sir John Dill, who obviously felt the same way. McNaughton was given a key appointment: command of the newly formed British VII Corps, which included his own division – now placed under Major-General G.R. Pearkes – the British 1st Armoured Division, and two brigades of New Zealanders. VII Corps formed GHQ Reserve, Channel coast.

The concepts of the First World War were entirely abandoned. The countryside erupted in a rash of tank-traps, roadblocks, machine-gun nests, strong points, and barbed-wire obstacles. The whole shape of infantry training changed with a new emphasis on air defence, dispersal, and the use of one-man slit-trenches instead of elaborate trench systems. Nothing typified this realistic approach to war more than the forest of steel posts that sprouted on British army parade grounds, intended to destroy any troop-carrying enemy gliders that might attempt to land there. Drill did not stop but was carried on between and around the posts. At the same time, equipment began to arrive in increasing quantities from British, Canadian, and American factories. The worst English winter in half a century was followed by

55 Canadian soldiers cross an obstacle while training at a battle-school in England. They were kept moving by instruction staff – one can be seen in the second line not carrying a rifle.

one of the finest summers, and Canadian morale rose even as rations were reduced.

Meanwhile, having reorganized his forces after the defeat of France, Hitler was planning the invasion of Britain. The first step was to establish air superiority over the Channel and southern England, but the *Luftwaffe* faltered and the second step – putting troops ashore – could not be taken.

As the year wore on, a steady flow of additional units from Canada to the United Kingdom made practicable the formation of a second Canadian division and the creation of a Canadian corps, which on Christmas Day 1940 inherited the VIIth's commander and its GHQ Reserve role. Before long the Canadians were training for an eventual return to the European mainland – though no one yet knew how they would be transported there or established once they arrived. "A dagger pointed at the heart of Berlin," McNaughton called them, in a melodramatic phrase that was quickly picked up by the media.

For Canadians, at home and abroad, his words echoed through the next two years – proudly at first, then with an ironic note, and finally with a kind of forlorn and increasingly vocal resentment as Britons, Australians, New Zealanders, Indians, South Africans, and, eventually, even Americans went into battle on different fronts while most battle-trained Canadians still languished on garrison duties in England. A tank brigade (complete with Canadian-built tanks) reinforced the infantry divisions already in Britain during June 1941, followed by the 3rd Division and then the 5th Armoured, while the 4th Division was temporarily retained for home defence in Canada.

The routine of training, at individual, unit, and formation levels in turn, was broken briefly only after Hitler had attacked the Soviet Union on June 22, 1941. A balanced force of brigade strength went off in late July to raid the Norwegian-owned Spitsbergen archipelago. From these remote islands in the Arctic Ocean, which lay close to the now-vital convoy routes to Murmansk in northern Russia, radio stations had unwittingly been aiding the anti-shipping operations of the *Luftwaffe* with their weather transmissions. After a landing that was unopposed and bloodless, the Canadians evacuated the total population of the islands and destroyed all stores and facilities. In September they were back in southern England.

On the other side of the globe from Spitsbergen lay Hong Kong. The British chiefs of staff had long recognized that their Chinese outpost was indefensible in the event of war with Japan. In the summer of 1941 the colony was garrisoned by four battalions of British infantry, hostages to fortune who were there primarily for reasons of prestige, morale, and the maintenance of civil order. However, when Major-General A.E. Grasett, the Canadian-born British officer who had just relinquished the Hong Kong command, returned to Britain via Canada in August 1941, he discussed the colony's situation with his old RMC classmate, Major-General H.D.G. Crerar, who was then the chief of the General Staff. In England, he went on to convince the War Office of the desirability of increasing the Hong Kong garrison, a reinforcement that the British soon argued "would have a very great moral effect in the whole of the Far East and ... show Chiang Kai-shek we really intend to fight." Perhaps Grasett also mentioned his chat with Crerar on the subject, for the War Office quickly asked Ottawa to "give consideration to providing for this purpose one or two Canadian battalions from Canada."

There were two good reasons why this should not be done, the first being the vulnerability of Hong Kong and the second that there were no adequately trained and uncommitted troops in Canada at the time. However, the Canadian prime minister's comprehension of strategy and logistics was not very profound and in this essentially military situation his customary political insight deserted him. For J.L. Ralston, the First World War veteran who was now the minister of national defence, and for General Crerar, it is less easy to find

56   After landing at
Victoria, the capital and
port of Hong Kong, on
November 16, 1941, men
of the Royal Rifles of
Canada and the
Winnipeg Grenadiers
march through the streets
watched by a thin crowd
of curious Chinese. A
month later Japanese
assault troops were ashore
on the island.

excuses. On their advice the Canadian government agreed to send two battalions to Hong Kong.

The best-trained units in Canada were those of the 4th Division, now preparing to join McNaughton's forces in the United Kingdom. At the other end of the scale were nine battalions which, "due either to recent employment requiring a period of refresher training, or to insufficient training, are not recommended for operational consideration at present." Two of the latter, the Royal Rifles of Canada (of whom, perhaps a quarter were French-speaking) and the Winnipeg Grenadiers, had already served overseas in Newfoundland and Jamaica respectively. General Crerar, however, apparently chose not to distinguish adequately between garrison duties in islands remote from the prospect of battle and the hard realities of combat. He simply noted that they "are both units of proven efficiency" and assigned them to Hong Kong.

When they sailed, on October 17, 1941, neither unit had had any consistent training at the battalion level, nor had all their men completed their Tests of Elementary Training for all weapons. Both units had needed large drafts to bring them up to strength and now found themselves, in the words of their brigade commander, with "a number of men who did not know, and were not known by, their officers."[7]

However, their battle worthiness was an academic question under the circumstances they were soon to encounter. Not even *Panzer Grenadiers*, or Guardsmen, or Marines in such meagre numbers, could have withstood for long the blow that was about to fall on Hong Kong. The Canadians landed on November 16 and the Japanese launched their attack three weeks later. In ten days they were across the straits that separated the New Territories from Hong Kong proper and began to push their way across the island.

By December 23, the battle-weary garrison was split in two and pinned into peninsulas on the south and west of the island. There was no air cover or support and the defenders had no more than a dozen anti-aircraft guns. "Very heavy shelling, mortaring and dive bombing all morning and extremely difficult to maintain communication," signalled the senior British naval officer on the island. "Further fighting will be uncontrolled.... No water in hand and all men physically exhausted after days of continuous fighting."[8]

Canadian morale remained high. After seven days of brutal and almost uninterrupted fighting the Royals' War Diary could still optimistically (and quite incorrectly) confide that "Lack of ammunition [is] all that saves the Nips from being shelled off the island." The struggle got closer and closer, until ammunition was hardly the most important factor. On Christmas Eve a subaltern of the Winnipeg Grenadiers found himself the first (perhaps the only) Canadian to engage in hand-to-hand combat with the enemy in the Second World War.

make hands with us !!

This is the only and best way remained for you!

就是你們要圖幸福之

民的方法 !!

HONG KONG 香港

57 A Japanese propaganda leaflet dropped on Hong Kong during the battle for the Crown colony. Despite its crudity, it provides a substantially accurate impression of the situation that actually existed.

58 When the Royal Rifles were re-formed after the fall of Hong Kong, a poster previously used by the regiment was reworked.

I was able to knock his rifle and bayonet out of the hands of one of the Japs, and with my new weapon managed to run through another of the enemy. Unfortunately I had difficulty withdrawing the blade and while endeavouring to do so I was lucky enough to catch the flash of a sword being raised to strike.

Quite subconsciously I jumped for my assailant, grasping the blade with my right hand, and circling his neck with my left arm, forcing his head against my chest.... While struggling in this fashion we both lost our footing and rolled down a small slope for about ten feet.... I managed to regain approximately the same standing advantage I had enjoyed earlier, except that by now we had both lost our grip on the sword. Since my opponent's face was tucked against my chest I endeavoured to turn his head in such a way as to enable me to deliver what I hoped would be a knockout with my fist. Unfortunately, I failed to notice that I had forced his steel helmet down over most of his face and the net result of a terrific uppercut was a sprained thumb for

The Army Overseas, 1940-1943

me.... I had completely forgotten that I carried a pistol up to this moment and in something of a frenzy I endeavoured to reach it.... Complications arose here, for I found after inserting my right forefinger through the trigger guard [that] the cut I had received on this finger when I had first grasped the [sword] blade had deprived it of the necessary strength to squeeze the trigger. Still further difficulties arose when I attempted to withdraw the finger and found that the flesh, acting much the same as the barb on a fish-hook, rendered it difficult to remove that finger from the trigger guard. However, I did manage and pressing the pistol to the base of my opponent's neck, finally ended the struggle.[9]

Very early the next morning, as a company of the Royal Rifles organized themselves for a last stand at Stanley Barracks, a telephone call from the senior British officer in the vicinity ordered the re-siting of their reserve platoon, which was occupying the Officers' Mess. "I have a definite promise from the Brigadier that no troops will be allowed in the Officers' Mess," he announced, according to the regimental records. Only hours later came the inevitable order to surrender and the guns fell silent.

The Canadians had lost nearly three hundred killed and five hundred wounded in the course of the fighting, out of the nearly two thousand who had sailed from Vancouver. Company Sergeant-Major John Osborn of the Winnipeg Grenadiers won, posthumously, Canada's first Victoria Cross of the war. "An inspiring example to all throughout the defence," ran the citation in the *London Gazette*, four years later, "... in his death he displayed the highest quality of heroism and self sacrifice."

Those who survived were marched into Japanese prison camps. There, under atrocious conditions, another 260 died during their years of captivity. In Canada, a Royal Commission appointed to investigate the circumstances under which the Canadian force had been dispatched eventually decided that the expedition had not been either "ill-conceived or badly managed," a delicately phrased verdict that seems to have evaded the real questions of competence and judgement at the highest level.

In England, fatigues and 'duties' (which took up at least half of every regimental soldier's time) followed monotonously on one another and drills followed drills. Unsuccessful exercises brought numerous repetitions in their train, while successful ones brought only more advanced exercises. Thus First Canadian Army, formed in April 1942, practised its assigned 'break-out' role for the still-distant, but now inevitable, bridgehead that would eventually be established somewhere on the coast of western Europe. Some day, somewhere, somehow, Allied troops would have to create a 'Second Front,' if only to make sure that

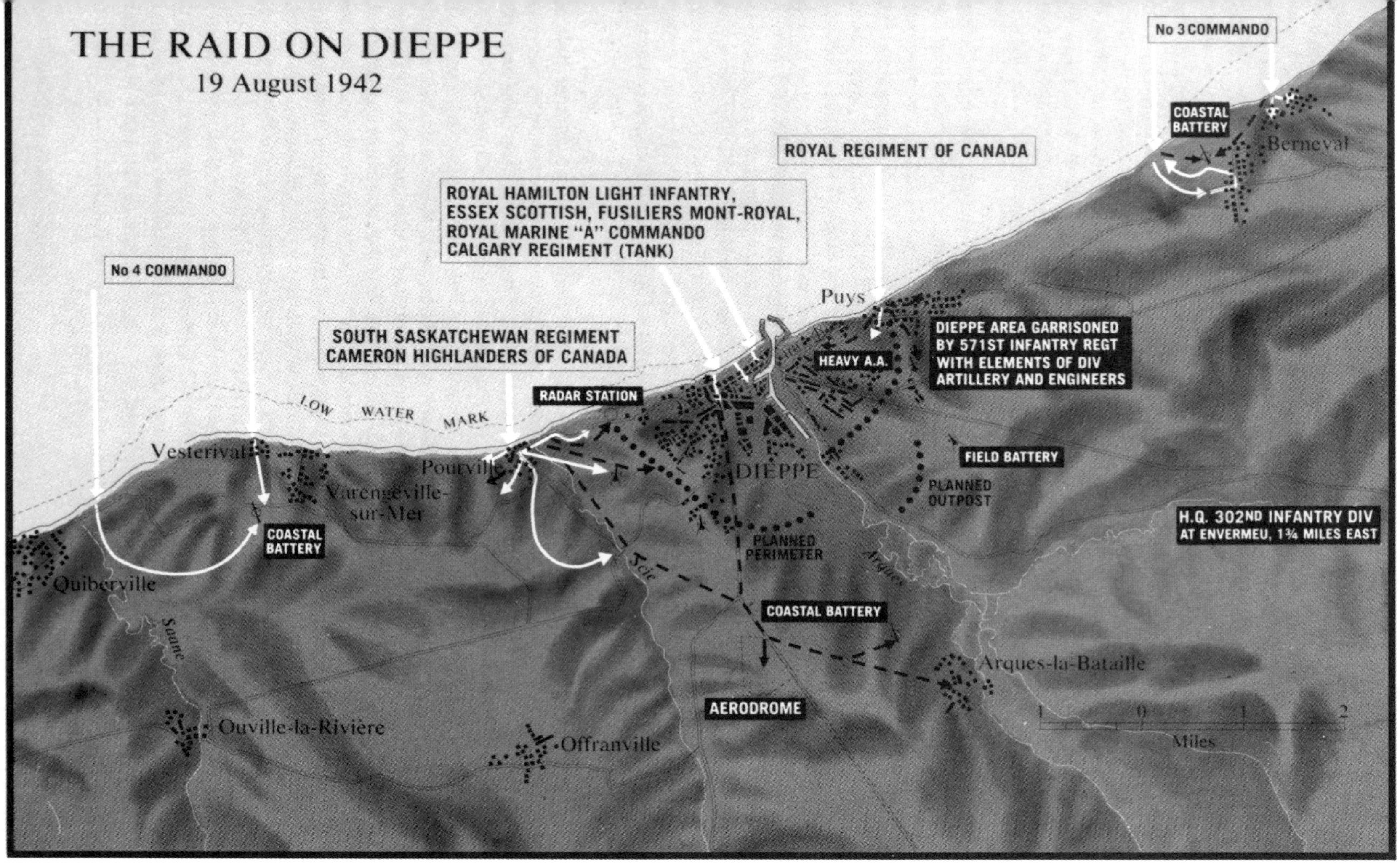

THE RAID ON DIEPPE
19 August 1942

No 3 COMMANDO

COASTAL BATTERY

Berneval

H.Q. 302ND INFANTRY DIV AT ENVERMEU, 1¾ MILES EAST

Arques-la-Bataille

2

1

0

Miles

ROYAL REGIMENT OF CANADA

DIEPPE AREA GARRISONED BY 571ST INFANTRY REGT WITH ELEMENTS OF DIV ARTILLERY AND ENGINEERS

FIELD BATTERY

PLANNED OUTPOST

HEAVY A.A.

Puys

Arques

COASTAL BATTERY

PLANNED PERIMETER

DIEPPE

AERODROME

Scie

Offranville

ROYAL HAMILTON LIGHT INFANTRY, ESSEX SCOTTISH, FUSILIERS MONT-ROYAL, ROYAL MARINE "A" COMMANDO CALGARY REGIMENT (TANK)

RADAR STATION

SOUTH SASKATCHEWAN REGIMENT CAMERON HIGHLANDERS OF CANADA

Pourville

LOW WATER MARK

Varengeville-sur-Mer

COASTAL BATTERY

Ouville-la-Rivière

No 4 COMMANDO

Vasterival

Saane

Quiberville

the Russians would not totally dominate Europe in the post-war era. Before that day arrived, however, the Canadians were to be involved in one more combat situation even briefer and more costly in human terms than the Hong Kong débâcle.

The Russians were continually demanding that their allies open a Second Front and relieve the German pressure on them. The Americans, for their part, were anxious to strike directly at the enemy. Churchill would have liked to oblige them, but was convinced that such a project was still beyond the capability of Anglo-American forces. However, since British staff planners still believed that the immediate capture of a moderately large port more or less in working order would be essential to the Second Front when it was initiated, it might be – and was – argued that a 'reconnaissance in force' should be made to discover whether or not that was possible.

Even so, "there is a mystery about the decision to execute the raid on Dieppe, for it can easily be shown that the British Government, and the Chiefs of Staff in particular, had been convinced for more than a year that this sort of operation made little sense," Professor Brian Villa has written in a study which has compelled the rewriting of several paragraphs of this book. "It was extremely hazardous and was unlikely, even if it were to succeed to be worth the cost."[10]

An outline plan was prepared and, on April 30, Lieutenant-General Sir Bernard Montgomery, the British officer under whom the Canadians were now serving, broached to McNaughton the idea of employing Canadians, telling him he believed that those of the 2nd Division "were those best suited." After learning more about the plan, McNaughton agreed that two brigades of the 2nd Division, under Major-General J.H. Roberts, should form the bulk of the force. By May 20, the troops were on the Isle of Wight to begin intensive training in amphibious operations that culminated in two full-scale 'dress rehearsals' on a stretch of the Devonshire coast resembling the Dieppe area. Neither went well, although the second was an improvement on the first.

Throughout the planning process there were difficulties with the Royal Navy and the Royal Air Force over the vital question of adequate fire support. The Admiralty was unwilling to risk major vessels in the mine-strewn waters of the English Channel and Bomber Command thought it a misuse of its resources to plaster the port with bombs. In the end, the attackers were left with the 4-inch guns of seven Hunt-class destroyers and a few squadrons of light and medium bombers from Army Co-operation Command to provide that vital element of a frontal attack.

Only when they embarked on the ships that were to carry them across the Channel, on July 2 and 3, were the Canadians told what their objective was. But unsettled weather now interfered with the mounting of Operation *Rutter*, and the ships never left harbour. On July 8, after the troops had been held on board in their cramped quar-

59 Landing craft carrying Les Fusiliers Mont-Royal race for the beaches of Dieppe when the reserve wave of infantry was ordered in.

ters for five or six days, the project was reluctantly abandoned and the men marched ashore. Over the next three weeks, however, the proposal for another *Rutter* – this time code-named *Jubilee*, but still with Dieppe as the objective – was gradually revived. Amazingly, this was done without any formal authorization from Prime Minister Churchill (who was also minister of defence) or his chiefs of staff, although they must have known unofficially – or at least suspected – what was going on.

There was a clear possibility that the enemy knew about *Rutter* by now, and that Dieppe had been the target. Indeed, Villa has argued, in an epilogue to the second (1993) edition of his work, that they may have been deliberately told about *Jubilee* – and not expected to believe it – as part of a very complicated deception plan that extended far beyond the subject of this book. That is as may be. At the same time, however, it could be – and was – argued that the Germans would never expect Dieppe to be the objective again, so soon after the aborted *Rutter*, and, in fact, Professor John Campbell's research has confirmed, beyond any reasonable doubt, that in early August 1942 they attached no more significance to Dieppe than they did to other likely objectives.[11] However, there was every reason for them to believe that a major raid – perhaps even an attempt at a Second Front – would come somewhere along the coast before the summer was out. On that basis they were maintaining all their coastal defences at a high level of readiness.

The main attack was to be launched against the town itself, along a three-quarter-mile arc between the harbour mole and a point just west of the Casino, a large white building standing in solitary splendour on the promenade, behind a low sea wall. In front of the wall a shingle beach sloped down quite steeply to sand or water, depending on the state of the tide. As six squadrons of fighter-bombers hit the buildings closest to the beach, the eastern half – code-named 'Red Beach' – was to be assaulted by the Essex Scottish; the western half –

'White Beach' – by the Royal Hamilton Light Infantry. Behind them would land the Churchill tanks of the Calgary Regiment – a baptism of battle for this new tank type – while a floating reserve of Les Fusiliers Mont-Royal and a Royal Marine Commando would be committed as required. A mile away to the east, at the hamlet of Puys, the Royal Regiment of Canada and three companies of the Black Watch of Canada were to land on 'Blue Beach' and hook inland, towards the town; on the other flank the South Saskatchewan Regiment would land on 'Green Beach' at Pourville and swing east into Dieppe, while the Cameron Highlanders of Canada were to drive south nearly four miles, to Arques-la-Bataille where the local German headquarters was believed to be located.

As the assault force closed in on the French coast in the early hours of August 19, 1942, the easternmost part of it, carrying No. 3 Commando, which was assigned to neutralize a coast defence battery of heavy guns, encountered a small enemy convoy *en route* from Boulogne to Dieppe. In the brief but bloody fire-fight that followed, one German ship became a total loss, three British escort vessels were "seriously damaged," and the landing craft widely scattered, with some of them hard-hit. The sounds of battle alerted the garrison at Petit Berneval, where part of the commando was to land (so that only the boatload that landed to the west was able to make any headway,

60 This German photograph of the Dieppe beach – from the West Headland, where the Germans had machine-guns entrenched – was taken within a day or two of the raid. The Casino and the buildings behind it (extreme right) were subsequently demolished by the Germans to improve their fields of fire in the event of another attack.

61 During a rehearsal for Dieppe, a Landing Craft (Assault) carries Canadian infantry towards an English beach.

although they succeeded in suppressing the enemy battery for nearly two hours before re-embarking), and at Puys, but no special precautions seem to have been taken in the central or western sectors.

In the event, however, no special precautions were needed. The customary German state of dawn readiness was to prove quite enough to handle the raiders when, supported directly only by light naval gunfire and six squadrons of fighter-bombers, the first of almost 5,000 Canadian soldiers began to land on the beaches in front of, and on each side of, Dieppe. By an hour after noon nearly 900 of them were dead or dying and over 1,000 were wounded. About 1,900 were prisoners of war and only 2,200 (many of whom had not landed) were on their way back to England.

Only at Pourville were the Canadians lucky enough to achieve some degree of surprise. At Puys the Royal Regiment and the Black Watch were virtually annihilated by some eighty German soldiers admirably placed on the cliffs at each side of the short beach. A score of men, led by the battalion's commanding officer, climbed the steep slope that blended into the western cliff, only to go to ground in a convenient copse and stay there until the battle ended. Of those that landed, two hundred were killed and another twenty later died of wounds. All the rest were taken prisoner.

The Army Overseas, 1940-1943

62 An infantry landing craft after the battle at Dieppe, with most of its overhead cover ripped off and the interior littered with bodies and equipment – destroyed, most likely, by a mortar bomb exploding inside and setting off more explosives carried on board.

In Dieppe itself, where the landings were timed to take place half an hour later than on the flanks, machine-gunners in the upper windows of buildings beyond the promenade and in concealed vantage points on the cliffs on each side of the town, and mortarmen further inland, waited for the raiders to land. The fighter-bombers arrived early, three minutes before the landing craft touched down, so that by the time the Canadians began to storm ashore the Germans had recovered from the momentary bombing and strafing of the aircraft.

The overwhelming impression as the first troops landed was one of horrendous noise, which stunned the mind and made it difficult to formulate or comprehend the simplest sentence. High explosive bursting on shingle, the rattle of machine-gun fire, the dull roar of distant naval guns and sharp report of high-velocity field pieces, the howling of aircraft engines, the screams of wounded men – these sounds in deafening combination numbed the minds of soldiers who had never before been under fire. "People had shot over us and around us," recalled the battle adjutant of the Royal Regiment, landing at Puys, "but nobody had ever shot at us – and there's a big difference, a very big difference ... as I left the assault craft I saw perhaps a hundred dead men."[12] His reaction was common to those landing on every beach.

The Army Overseas, 1940-1943

63 The RHLI's padre, the Rev. John Foote, won his Victoria Cross dragging and carrying wounded men across this Dieppe beach to Tank Landing Craft No. 5, where the battalion's wounded medical officer, Captain D.W. Clare, had established a makeshift regimental aid post. Note how the tank has bogged down in the shingle.

In the centre "it was unbelievable that anyone survived," according to a platoon commander of the RHLI. His landing craft was still nosing into the beach when

> we were hit; the Bangalore torpedoes exploded among the toggle ropes and grappling irons. I only remember the sound because I was blinded. The boat filled with water and I was soon up to my neck. I couldn't hear at all after that for a long while but later there were faraway noises as if I were listening to something over a very poor connection on a long distance 'phone call.'[13]

Blinded for life, he and one private were the only survivors of his platoon.

Alongside the Hamilton men the Essex Scottish were faring even worse. Thirty-two officers and 521 other ranks had embarked for Dieppe, but only 2 officers and 49 other ranks (27 of them wounded) sailed home again. On all the beaches except the one at Pourville, where the initial opposition was less ferocious, masses of men, stupified by the intensity and brutality of battle, huddled behind derelict tanks and landing craft or under the sea walls. Enfiladed by machine-guns and scythed by mortar shrapnel and splintered flints, the result

The Army Overseas, 1940-1943

of mortar bombs bursting on the shingle, they were slaughtered where they lay.

Very early on, a warrant officer of the Essex Scottish led a dozen men in pushing a Bangalore torpedo – lengths of pipe filled with explosive that could blow a gap in wire entanglements when the contents were detonated – through the barbed wire on the top of the sea wall on 'Red' beach. When the torpedo exploded, the group made a mad dash across the promenade. They entered a number of buildings and cleared them of the enemy, working their way through the town, but there were too few of them to make a major impact, or to hold their positions once the Germans began to concentrate against them. They fought their way back to the beach. "I lay it 90 per cent to good luck, and the fact that we were in the very centre [of the beaches]," reported Stapleton in a post-war interrogation. "You would think that everybody on the hills [sic] could very easily have concentrated on us; but they were all so busy with what was going on in front of them that they weren't [looking about] probably the way they should have been."[14]

Some of the 'Rileys' got into the lower floor of the Casino, where they fought the Germans from room to room for several hours. While that struggle went on, another little group burst into the town, penetrated as far as the church at St Rémy, and established themselves in a theatre that they held until 10:00 a.m. Then they struggled back to the Casino, part of which continued to be occupied by Canadians until the evacuation from the beaches was under way.

Only about half of the Calgary tanks were able to get ashore, and those were not able to make much headway. Half of them were stopped on the beach, either by shingle banks or the sea wall. Nevertheless, the tank hulls were proof against any weight of fire that the local defences could bring to bear and no crewmen were killed or wounded inside their machines. Some tanks continued to fight even though immobilized; some surmounted the sea wall and roared up and down the esplanade, only to find the narrow roads leading into town blocked by massive concrete obstacles. The unprotected sappers who were supposed to blow them away were all being 'blown away' themselves. (Royal Canadian Engineer casualties were proportionately the heaviest of all during the raid.) The tank gunners did what they could to suppress German fire. One tank flushed some German infantry from trenches on the esplanade and "made a dash for them ... Both gunners opened up and we got plenty of them. Even had the pleasure of running down one who tried to dodge us."[15] But it, too, was immobilized before very long.

Aboard his headquarters ship, the destroyer HMS *Calpe*, General Roberts had little idea of what was happening. Many of the radio operators on the beaches were being picked off by German snipers. Others had their radios destroyed by shrapnel, and even when communication with *Calpe* was possible, the confused, smoke-shrouded

The Army Overseas, 1940-1943

fighting was difficult to comprehend from disjointed wireless conversations. A garbled message suggested that the Essex Scottish were making headway on 'Red' beach and Roberts ordered the Fusiliers Mont-Royal to reinforce them. In fact the remnants of the Essex were still pinned against the sea wall.

It made little difference. Most of the French-Canadians were landed by some mistake on 'White' beach, behind the 'Rileys.' One of their warrant officers afterwards remembered

> the wounded and dead who lay scattered on the beach. Some of the wounded were trying to swim out to the boat [and] many were bleeding heavily, reddening the water around them. [Once ashore,] mortar bombs are bursting on the shingle and making little clouds which seem to punctuate the deafening din ... close to me badly mutilated bodies lie here and there. The wounded scream ... the blood flows from their wounds in a viscous, blackish tide.... For myself, I am absolutely astounded to have reached the shelter of a building. I was certain that my last hour had arrived.[16]

A dozen men of the Mont-Royals, led by a sergeant, got into the maze of ancient streets behind the promenade and fought their way through them to the inner harbour. Then, with their grenades and ammunition all used up, they were forced to surrender. Their captors stripped the Canadians of their weapons and outer clothes, left them in the hands of a single armed guard, and went back to the battle.

Sergeant Dubuc induced the guard to come within arm's reach by begging for water, and then grappled with him while another Canadian beat his head in with a piece of iron pipe. Free again, the Canadians dashed off, each man for himself. The spectacle of unidentifiable men in their underwear sprinting through the middle of a battle apparently unnerved every German they passed, because they got back to the beach unharmed.

One man who seemed impervious to his own danger and to the sights and sounds of conflict that engulfed him was the RHLI's chaplain, John Foote. He picked up the wounded, man after man, and carried them to the Regimental Aid Post established in the lee of a grounded, burning tank landing craft. Not a bullet or a splinter touched him. During the evacuation he helped carry more wounded to the boats but, in the end, chose not to leave himself, explaining that the men who were being left behind needed him more than those returning to England. He won the only Victoria Cross ever awarded to a Canadian chaplain.

At Pourville, on the right flank, where the South Saskatchewans and the Cameron Highlanders had landed between 4:52 and 6:00 a.m., the initial opposition was light. Really heavy fire developed only as the South Saskatchewans crossed the River Scie, Lieutenant-Colonel

The Army Overseas, 1940-1943

Cecil Merritt leading them with a reckless bravery that earned him a VC, and hooked left towards Dieppe proper. They were stopped well short of the town. Indeed, they could not even take the radar station that was dug into the headland above Dieppe. However, the Camerons, landing behind them, pushed two thousand yards inland, towards Arques le Bataille, before the evacuation order was issued.

As the two battalions withdrew, "the wide concrete promenade was strewn with bodies," wrote Wallace Reyburn, a war correspondent. When his turn came to leave,

> the beach was dotted with prone figures on the sand and men running out to the boats.... From each end there was the raking fire of machine guns.... Mortar shells exploded on the beach and sent cascades of sand and pebbles far and wide. Snipers picked off men as they ran. Focke-Wulfes came roaring down low and spat their machine guns and cannon fire at us. I watched a Junkers 88 that had managed to slip through our fighters, come trundling (it seemed so slow and laborious compared to the speed of the Focke-Wulfes) along about a hundred feet above the beach and drop its bombs as it got over the boats.[17]

The struggle for air superiority did not begin with the first landings. Two RAF fighter squadrons cruised over Dieppe for half an hour until the *Luftwaffe* appeared. Then, as the numbers of enemy aircraft increased, forty-eight squadrons of fighters, including six RCAF ones, fought in relays to maintain a local air superiority that would protect the troops below from enemy air attack and permit the fighter-bombers providing direct support for the ground forces to work without *Luftwaffe* interference. At times during that disastrous morning the haze over Dieppe was full of wheeling and diving aircraft as German and Allied pilots chased each other around the sky.

Two more Canadian squadrons formed half the wing assigned to tactical reconnaissance duties. Their work required that they fly low, in pairs – easy targets for prowling German fighters or for anti-aircraft fire. Their Mustangs ranged fruitlessly over the surrounding countryside, searching for approaching reinforcements (which the Germans did not need) and suffering a higher casualty rate than any other air units engaged in the battle.

Altogether, the Canadian squadrons lost 14 aircraft and 9 pilots (with another 10 machines damaged and 3 pilots wounded) among the total RAF/RCAF losses of 99 machines and 81 pilots and aircrew. Ninety-one German aircraft were alleged to have been 'destroyed' at the time, with 38 'probables' and another 140 damaged, so that it could be argued that the air battle over Dieppe was a resounding success; but we now know that enemy losses totalled only 48, with 24 damaged – not nearly such a satisfactory result. However, the Allies were far more able to bear such losses as occurred and their record

64 *Luftwaffe* soldiers, probably from an anti-aircraft unit, examine the personal papers of a Canadian wounded at Dieppe.

The Army Overseas, 1940-1943

does look better than that of the Germans when the ratio of losses to sorties flown is examined. They lost only one fighter for every 27.2 sorties flown but the enemy lost one per 7.6 sorties.

German losses amounted to a third of their fighter strength in the west, while the Allied loss totalled less than a tenth of theirs. On the other hand, since the fight took place over German-held territory or close to the coast, the *Luftwaffe* certainly recovered more of their airmen.

Dieppe was not the unmitigated disaster that Hong Kong had been, despite the fearsome losses. The lessons that were learned might just as well have been learned in realistic exercises, but they were lessons for all that. Objectives must be more realistic, tactics more sophisticated, and training more rigorous. Communications must be more comprehensive, equipment more appropriate, and, most of all, fire support by sea and air must be overwhelming. Moreover, some method must be found to put vast numbers of men and matériel ashore on open beaches – in fact, research had already started on 'portable harbours' – for the prospects of taking an established port by storm were obviously dim. The 'boffins' – research scientists and engineers – went to work on AVREs (Armoured Vehicles, Royal Engineers), amphibious (DD) tanks, 'Mulberry' pre-fabricated harbours, and 'PLUTO' (Pipelines Under The Ocean) that could pump fuel directly across the Channel. Casualties were replaced from the reinforcement depots and the men who had been lucky enough to get away from the beaches went back to the apparently endless cycle of training, fatigues, 'duties,' and exercises, benefiting from the trial by fire at Dieppe – and remembering, perhaps, that it is the last battle that decides every war.

In Canada the first reaction to the news of Dieppe was one of pride and admiration for the heroic conduct of the troops, as it was described by war correspondents such as Ross Munro, Wallace Reyburn, and the American Quentin Reynolds. Families were left to mourn their dead, or worry over sons and brothers in German prison camps, as the full casualty figures were released gradually, over the better part of a week. Subsequently public opinion began to veer towards criticism of the Establishment – politicians, senior civil servants, and general officers – for sending Canadian soldiers on such an ill-starred endeavour.

The first faint criticisms came from Toronto's *Globe and Mail* (August 23), which questioned whether the methods used at Dieppe were really the best ones. The *Montreal Gazette* headed its first editorial on the raid "The Dagger is Whetted," but, by September 17, that journal was asking if the dagger had been blunted at its first thrust. *Saturday Night* (September 9 and October 23) carried articles suggesting that the Dieppe concept and the planning of it were almost exclusively the work of Canadian officers and that the failure of the raid demonstrated the bankruptcy of Canadian generalship.

65 Prisoners are marshalled in the streets of Dieppe after the battle. The Canadian in his underpants may have abandoned his battledress trousers in a last-minute and unsuccessful attempt to reach the departing ships.

Only the second allegation was true, but Canadian generals – McNaughton and Crerar – had approved of British planning after Mountbatten, the chief of combined operations, had skilfully removed from the chain of command such critical figures as Sir Bernard Paget, the overall commander of Britain's Home Forces, Montgomery, and the original, clear-thinking, naval force commander, Admiral T. Baillie-Grohman, replacing them respectively with the two Canadians and his personal toady, Captain John Hughes-Hallett, who took Baillie-Grohman's place.

It might have been argued that the army should never have accepted an invitation to send its untested troops into such a potential killing ground on the basis of a thoroughly inadequate plan. But how could any Canadian general have refused to commit his men to battle when such an opportunity arose after two years of preparation, especially when so much of the country's leadership, media, and public had been pressing to see Canadians in action? Nevertheless, McNaughton and Crerar did have a responsibility to ensure that their men were committed under circumstances that presented a reasonable prospect of success. There was little such prospect for *Jubilee*.

The Army Overseas, 1940-1943

Despite the criticism, the government refused to provide formal scapegoats. (Although General Roberts was relieved of his appointment shortly afterwards and never held another operational command.) The strictures gradually died away, leaving in their wake (in the words of the official historian) "something to undermine the hitherto unassailable position of General McNaughton with the public."

CHAPTER 6

Sicily and Southern Italy

By Christmas 1942, elements of the RCN and RCAF had accumulated a considerable amount of battle experience in their respective spheres and a growing number of Canadian sailors and airmen could claim fighting records equal to those of the men of Allied sister services. But Canadian soldiers were still relatively raw material: to be no more than "a dagger pointed at the heart of Berlin" was an unsatisfying role when other armies were actually lunging at the Germans day by day.

The British – after defeats in France, Greece, Crete, Malaya, and Burma – had swept across North Africa to link up with American forces in Tunisia; the United States had been in the war for only a year, but already its Fifth Army had had several months of combat experience in the Mediterranean theatre; the Russians, having stemmed the German juggernaut at Stalingrad, were beginning to drive it back through eastern Europe in the course of the most massive battles the world has ever known. Canadian soldiers, however, lacked either a record, or the immediate prospect, of sustained action. Parades, training, and fatigues filled their days. Only a combination of common sense and tightening discipline kept their morale at a satisfactory level.

At home, discontent was much more apparent and vociferous. Perhaps the emotional need to hear of Canadian troops in action reflected problems of national identity and the still uncertain direction of Canadian society – problems that the uniformed soldier overseas did not have. As the Dieppe catastrophe faded from the headlines, demands for a more active role for our ground forces became insistent. During November 1942, in the space of five days, the *Winnipeg Free Press* editorialized that Canada should "send a full division to some theatre of war" at once; the *Vancouver Sun* reported a decorated veteran of the Great War harrumphing to his old comrades of the Canadian Corps Association that "soldiers sitting idle in England ... [were] ... the greatest disgrace of the war"; the Montreal *Gazette* exacerbated the situation with a caustic story headlined "Mental Illness in Overseas Army Laid to Inactivity and Anxiety" (such cases were very few); and nearly every daily newspaper and radio station in the country quoted former prime minister R.B. Bennett's needling comment that he knew of "no good reason why the Canadian Army should have to spend its fourth Christmas in Britain without firing a shot" – the last phrase of which must have grated on the survivors of Dieppe.

Even the minister of national defence, J.L. Ralston (who had crossed swords with McNaughton more than once when the latter was chief of the General Staff), was now in favour of getting the army into action as soon as possible. Lieutenant-General Ken Stuart, the current CGS, was also seeking a more active role for the army. Moreover, despite General McNaughton's clear preference for holding the Canadians together in one unified (and Canadian) command, his protégé and the next most senior officer overseas, Lieutenant-General Harry Crerar, was busily undermining his superior's position. The chief of the Imperial General Staff, General Sir Alan Brooke, wrote in his diary for February 10, 1943, "Harry Crerar to dinner, and a long harangue from him as to the necessity of getting some Canadians fighting soon for imperial and political reasons."[1]

Hume Wrong, the assistant under-secretary at External (now Foreign) Affairs, expressed similar opinions in a memorandum to Mackenzie King. Pressed on all sides, in the middle of March the prime minister reluctantly set about defusing this potentially explosive issue by rejecting McNaughton's view and notifying Whitehall that Ottawa would now favour the employment of some Canadians in extended operations. It was still understood, however, that troops sent to combat theatres (the Mediterranean was, in effect, the only possible one) would be returned to First Canadian Army before the opening of a Second Front.

On April 23 the British formally responded to King's signal by asking permission to employ a Canadian infantry division and a tank brigade "to undertake certain operations based on Tunisia," and the Cabinet quickly approved the request. General Dwight D. Eisenhower, the American who had been appointed Supreme Allied Commander in the Mediterranean theatre, intended to secure the Mediterranean shipping routes and capture Sicily as a base for possible further operations against southern Europe. (At that time, such operations were far from certain.) Now he would do so using British, American, and Canadian forces. The troops assigned to join the famous Eighth Army, under General Sir Bernard Montgomery, were those that had been overseas longest – the 1st Canadian Infantry Division and the 1st Canadian Army Tank Brigade.

These two formations moved north to Scotland for special training in amphibious and mountain operations. Meanwhile, it was decided that Major-General H.L.N. Salmon, the 1st Division's commander, should go at once to Egypt, where the Eighth Army's share of the Sicilian landings was being planned. His aircraft left on April 29 but crashed into a Devonshire hillside shortly after take-off with the loss of all on board. Into his place as commander of the Mediterranean contingent stepped Canada's youngest general, Guy Granville Simonds. Promoted to command the 2nd Division only a few days earlier, at the age of 39, the arrogant, hard-driving Simonds had begun the war as a captain on the staff of the Royal Military College at Kingston. His subsequent meteoric rise had culminated in his appointment to a divisional command after a spell in Tunisia as a senior staff officer with a British corps, in order to gain some insight into the battle experience that the Canadians were conspicuously lacking.

Simonds therefore already knew the Eighth Army, its generals, and something of its methods. Within twenty-four hours of his arrival in Cairo he had been briefed by Lieutenant-General Sir Oliver Leese, the commander of XXX (British) Corps in which the Canadians would serve; made a Canadian plan; and cabled it back to Britain so that his staff could start organizing the combat loading of the assault ships for Operation *Husky*, the code-name for the Sicilian landings.

The Canadians sailed from the Clyde in several convoys towards the end of June, still uncertain of their destination, although the replacement of their Canadian-designed and -built Ram tanks with American Shermans (standard in the Mediterranean theatre) probably gave them some idea. They were told their objectives on Dominion Day, 1943, and for the next ten days they drilled, exercised, studied the assault plans, and played endless games of bingo (legally) and poker (not so legally). On July 4 and 5 the convoys passed Gibraltar and entered the dangerously enclosed waters of the Mediterranean. While they steamed towards Sicily, Allied air cover – including the RCAF's No. 417 Squadron, which had been serving with the Desert Air Force since April – kept them free from the attentions of the *Luftwaffe*. Enemy submarines did succeed in sinking three vessels, however, all of them off the North African coast between Oran and Algiers. Of the nine hundred Canadians on board, sixty were lost.

The initial landings on Sicily were made by British and American airborne troops in the pre-dawn darkness of July 10. Unexpected winds left many of those who jumped from aircraft scattered over a wide area. Others, who were aboard gliders being towed by Dakota aircraft, were drowned after poor navigation led to their gliders' being cast loose far out to sea. These misfortunes might have had serious repercussions for the seaborne assault forces if opposition to the landings had been strong. But the bulk of the quarter-million men in Sicily were second-line Italian garrison troops. The Germans were holding their two divisions on the island – the 15th *Panzer Grenadiers* and the Hermann Goering *Panzers* – in reserve for a counterattack, as they waited for a point of Allied main effort to become apparent.

There was no single point of main effort, however. Just after dawn the Canadians, forming the left flank of five British landings that spread over forty miles of shoreline, landed near Pachino, close to the southern tip of the island, while the American Seventh Army, under General George Patton, established three more beach-heads spread over another forty miles of coast as far again to the west. The opposition was negligible everywhere on the Anglo-Canadian beaches, and although some of Simonds' troops were up to two-and-a-half

66 In the grey Sicilian dawn the first Canadian infantrymen to land in Europe since Dieppe plunge through the shallow water of a Cape Passero beach on July 10, 1943.

hours late in getting ashore, by 6:45 a.m. he was able to report that "all Canadian objectives had been taken."

Twenty minutes earlier, General Eisenhower had broadcast from Algiers an announcement of the initial assault that made no mention of Canadian participation. The omission, which was instantly picked up in Ottawa, was corrected within ten minutes by another announcement from the Pentagon in Washington, but it provided a disturbing background to the more significant issue of Allied relationships that was to be raised within the next few days.

On the Canadian beach everything was tranquil. A private in the Seaforth Highlanders of Canada – a Canadian-born Tennessean who had gone north to enlist in 1939 – has described the scene:

> We were ordered now to advance. The cane-brakes ended and farm fields began. We walked through the fields of ripe tomatoes, stopping momentarily to pick a few.... Two houses loomed ahead. Near the large white house on the right was a heavy middle-aged man, dressed in dark pants, white shirt, and black vest. He merely looked at us with a little interest before he resumed his work of repairing a window.... We passed on through another cane-brake and into another field.[2]

Two days later the Canadians were more than thirty miles inland, despite a shortage of wheeled transport that had been aboard the lost ships and an enervating combination of heat, humidity, malarial mosquitoes, and fine white dust. Soon they were moving up into the

Sicily and Southern Italy

ITALY
3 September 1943 –
25 February 1945

GULF OF GENOA

EMILIA

Genoa

Bologna

Reno

Senio

Ravenna

GOTHIC LINE

Pistoia

Pisa

Arno

Florence

Rimini

Tomba di Pesaro

Pésaro

TUSCANY

Foglia

Metauro

FIRST CANADIAN CORPS

Arezzo

Siena

L. Trasimene

Ancona

ELBA

CORSICA

Perugia

MARCHES

UMBRIA

ADRIATIC SEA

Viterbo

Tiber

LATIUM

ROME

ABRUZZI

WINTER LINE

Ortona

Villa Rogatti

SARDINIA

Anzio

SIXTH U.S. CORPS
JAN 1944

FIRST CANADIAN CORPS

Liri

Ceprano

Cassino

&

Sangro

MOLISE

Biferno

Termoli

Campobasso

Vinchiaturo

ADOLF HITLER LINE

GUSTAV LINE

Volturno

Naples

CAMPANIA

Foggia

APULIA

Melfi

SEVENTY-EIGHTH BRIT DIV & FOURTH ARM'D BDE
22 - 23 SEP 1943

Bari

TYRRHENIAN SEA

Salerno

Gulf of Salerno

FIFTH U.S. ARMY
SEP 1943

LUCANIA

Potenza

Taranto

FIRST BRITISH AIRBORNE DIV
9 SEP 1943

GULF OF TARANTO

SICILY
10 July – 6 August 1943

Trapani

Palermo

Sciacca

Agira

Leonforte

Regalbuto

Mt Etna

Valguarnera

Adrano

Piazza Amerina

Catania

Licata

Grammichele

Augusta

SEVENTH U.S. ARMY
10 JULY 1943

Ragusa

Syracuse

Modica

Rosolini

Ispica

Pachino

EIGHTH BRITISH ARMY
10 JULY 1943

Messina

Strait of Messina

Reggio

CALABRIA

Catanzaro

EIGHTH BRITISH ARMY
3 SEP 1943

Messina

Reggio

FIRST CANADIAN DIVISION

0 10 20 30 40 50
Miles

0 20 40 60 80 100
Miles

Sicily and Southern Italy

67 During the first day of the Sicilian landings, shipping steadily piled up off the beaches and a stream of transport and mechanized equipment poured inland along bull-dozed tracks. In the fore-ground one of the first Italians to surrender stands unguarded and ignored.

mountainous centre of the island, but it was not until the fifth day, just outside the village of Grammichele, that they first came under German fire. Men of the 1st Infantry Brigade and tanks of the Three Rivers Regiment took the village by noon at a cost of twenty-five casualties. The next day, July 16, fighting over higher, rockier ground unsuitable for tanks, the infantry lost another twenty-seven men clearing Piazza Armerina.

The Germans, recognizing the inability of their two divisions to throw ten times their number of Allied soldiers back into the sea, had now resolved to withdraw into the mountain bastion around Mount Etna. *Feldmarschall* Albert Kesselring's tactics were to establish numerically weak rearguards in naturally strong positions, to have

Sicily and Southern Italy

68 Sherman tanks of the 12th (Three Rivers) Armoured Regiment drive through the shattered streets of Regalbuto. The capture of this key point, defended by men of the crack Hermann Goering Division, gave the Canadians their hardest fight of the Sicilian campaign.

them resist fiercely for a stipulated time and then disengage quickly and fall back through the next selected strong point. The battlefield, like most modern battlefields, seemed deserted – sunburnt hillsides lashed by sudden bursts of machine-gun fire and the sporadic 'krrumph' of exploding mortar shells. In a matter of days the men of the 1st Division learned more about the practice of their trade than they had in the previous three and a half years.

Another cause of Allied dissension now cropped up. McNaughton had arrived in Algiers on the first day of the landings, bent on visiting his soldiers in the field as soon as possible. But on July 17, when the Canadians were moving on from Piazza Armerina, he learned from Montgomery that, "owing to shortage of transport no visitors will be allowed on the island during active ... operations." When McNaughton, who was no ordinary visitor, argued his case with General Sir Harold Alexander, the deputy supreme Allied commander, that suave soldier backed Montgomery. The Canadian, a crusty character at the best of times, went fuming back to London to express irascibly to the chief of the Imperial General Staff his com-

Sicily and Southern Italy

mitment to the principle that "representatives of Canada could visit Canadian troops at their discretion."[3]

Montgomery subsequently claimed that he was concerned with keeping from General Simonds the additional strain of entertaining his superior officer while fighting his first battle as a formation commander – "For God's sake, keep him away," he reports Simonds as saying[4] – but, at the time, the brusque manner of his refusal certainly exacerbated a difficult situation. This little contretemps, involving McNaughton with all three top British commanders, was to play its part in events later in the year.

While the American forces, under the swashbuckling Patton, were sweeping around the western coast of the island, the British component of Montgomery's desert-wise Eighth Army was not performing as well as expected in the close country of the narrow Catanian plain, under the southeastern flank of Etna. Only the Canadians, high in the central mountains on the Eighth Army's left flank, were still pushing forward. Kesselring, intend on maintaining his perimeter and thereby control of his withdrawal, began to strengthen his mountain line. The best part of two more German divisions had now reached him from the mainland and, in the battles of Agira and Regalbuto, the 1st Canadian Division, reinforced by a British brigade, had to meet and overcome the stiffest opposition of their campaign.

The Canadians were beset by problems of command and control. Some of their inexperienced regimental officers responded uncertainly to the concentrated pressure of battle, maps were read wrongly, and their radios too often failed them at vital moments. On the positive side, however, they had courage, tenacity, and the hard-driving energy of their commander to carry them through, plus an enormous weight of fire power: the complete divisional artillery, ninety bombers, and more than a hundred fighter-bombers were allocated to support one battalion attack by the Royal Canadian Regiment.

Agira was taken on the 28th, after five days' hard fighting and at a cost of 438 casualties. With its fall, and as Patton made rapid progress along the northern coast of the island, the Germans began to scurry back towards the Straits of Messina. Their departure was hastened by the dramatic news that Mussolini had been deposed in a coup d'état. *Mareschal* Pietro Badoglio, the leader of the ministry that replaced him, announced that the war would go on, but Hitler was under no illusions regarding the peaceful intentions of the new régime.

On July 30, before Badoglio could open negotiations with the Allies, masses of German troops were sent south through the Alpine passes to ensure that Italy remained a German satellite. The formal Italian surrender did not come until September 8, when the Italians were granted a status of 'co-belligerency' – something less than full membership in the Grand Alliance – but the change came too late for the Allies to derive any real military advantage from it. By then northern and central Italy were firmly in German hands.

For the Canadians, the Sicilian campaign ended on the banks of the Upper Simeto River, west of Adrano, when they were withdrawn from combat on August 7 to rest and prepare for the assault on the Italian mainland that was now being planned. In his *Memoirs*, Montgomery commented that "the Canadians were magnificent in the Sicilian campaign," and his praise was well warranted. They had fought their way across 150 miles of mountains, outflanking the Germans who had tied down the British divisions on the coastal plain, and progressed from the status of military apprentices to journeymen soldiers at least, at a total cost, in the 1st Division, of 562 killed, 1,664 wounded, and 84 taken prisoner by the enemy.

On August 10 the Germans began to evacuate the sixty thousand men they still had on the island across the Straits of Messina. Messina itself fell on August 17, the Americans entering the town from the northwest a matter of hours before the British arrived from the south.

The capture of Sicily reinforced and made irrevocable Allied control of the Mediterranean and secured the shortest route (via the Suez Canal) to the Far East, but the decision to continue the fight on to the Italian mainland was strategically questionable. The British, anxious to delay the Second Front in France for another year at least, were eager to continue the campaign up the Italian 'boot,' but militarily the 'soft underbelly of Europe' was a myth. Churchill's vivid metaphor was intended to win converts to a political strategy aimed at reaffirming British influence in southern Europe.

The nature of the ground – a central mountain spine with a succession of steep and rugged ridges dropping towards the sea on both sides of the peninsula – would favour the defence. It would also ensure that the Allies' overwhelming technological and numerical superiority was largely negated. Even along the narrow coastal plains the 'closeness' of the country – village and terraced vineyard, river and ravine – meant that armoured forces could rarely be deployed *en masse;* nor could their inherent mobility be properly exploited.

Anglo-American armies were to force their way northwards for the next eighteen months, breaking through the Gustav/Hitler, Caesar, Trasimene, and Gothic Lines with an enormous toll of Allied resources in both men (including a substantial number of Canadians) and matériel.

The successes of the 1st Division in Sicily had been properly celebrated at home and the Cabinet apparently felt that much of the glory was reflecting on the government. Now, instead of reuniting the Mediterranean component with the core of the overseas army, still in England, it was decided to add a second division, together with a corps headquarters, to the Canadian forces in Italy: put simplistically, more troops in action without an exorbitant butcher's bill would

69 A badly wounded German officer is given immediate treatment by two Canadian medical officers while an orderly waits to drive him to the nearest field hospital.

bring more favourable publicity for the government and more opportunities for distinction to senior officers.

McNaughton objected, further irritating those who were critical of his desire for a unified army. His views now carried little weight, however, in the face of his political masters' determination. Preparations were begun to increase the Mediterranean contingent to corps strength.

The Eighth Army's attack on Reggio di Calabria at the very tip of the Italian 'toe' on September 3, 1943, was preceded by an immense artillery bombardment from the Sicilian shore, although the enemy had already withdrawn out of range. Kesselring had no intention of offering serious resistance within the limits of effective Allied fighter cover, which reached north as far as Naples. Marching ashore at Reggio with the British 5th Division, the Canadians met the only actual opposition shortly after they left the beaches. "There is a zoo in town and our shelling broke open some cages," Montgomery wrote to Alan Brooke. "A puma and a monkey escaped and attacked some men of the HQ, 3rd Canadian Brigade, and heavy firing was opened by the Canadians. It is a curious war...."[5]

Sicily and Southern Italy

While the Fifth U.S. Army stormed ashore at Salerno on the lower 'shin' of the boot, the Canadians drove along the 'sole,' heading towards the great naval base at Taranto. High in the 'instep' they swung inland, north towards Melfi, which was reached on September 26, leaving Taranto to be occupied by British airborne troops. With the 1st Division were the tanks of the Calgary Regiment; of the other units of the 1st Army Tank Brigade, the Ontarios were with the British 5th Division on the western coast and the Three Rivers Regiment, which had borne the brunt of the Sicilian fighting, remained in Sicily until September 24.

The ease of the initial advance during the Canadians' first three weeks on the mainland of Europe was reflected in their light casualties – 32 killed, 146 wounded, and 3 taken prisoner. North of Melfi, however, German resistance began to stiffen and the rate of advance slowed noticeably.

During October the Canadians found themselves pushing into the central mountain range as the Allies drove north from Naples and Foggia, the American Fifth Army on the left of the Appenines and the British Eighth on the right.

The October mornings were heralded by thick, heavy mist that quickly soaked clothes and equipment and, as often as not, each day brought a steady drizzle of cold rain. War artist Charles Comfort wrote of his visit to a regiment of field artillery at about this time: "Officers and men, wearing all the clothing they possessed, mud to the knees, huddled about small charcoal fires, made in biscuit tins or oil cans. In our improvised lean-to, we felt that the limit for resistance had been reached."[6] For the combat infantrymen, skirmishing still further forward and about to find themselves up against the Gustav Line – the forward edge of the Germans' first major defensive position – things were a good deal worse.

A thousand miles to the northwest, in London, General McNaughton found himself being pressured out of the command of the army he had built so carefully. At 56, he had been doing two men's jobs for nearly four years, as a formation commander and as senior Canadian officer overseas, and undoubtedly he was tired. He had still never led men in battle on a formation level – his First World War reputation had been built on impeccable staff work and an innovative technical approach to gunnery – and it was claimed by higher British commanders that his battle-command capability was doubtful. He seemed to them to lack both operational understanding (a judgement based solely on training exercises) and the capacity to deal ruthlessly with his subordinates – an essential qualification when so many lives would be at stake.

Could the irascible McNaughton have ever served under the domineering Montgomery, especially after the Sicilian episode? Probably not. But perhaps a more significant factor in his removal

Sicily and Southern Italy

70 Men of the Carleton and York Regiment hunt snipers in the narrow, stepped streets of Campochiaro in October 1943. The body lying across the street, between the first two soldiers, is that of an Italian civilian, caught in the crossfire.

from the scene was his concern with maintaining Canadian autonomy in the maelstrom of military intrigue that swirled about the British and Canadian Cabinets and their chiefs of staff, once the United States was in the war and eventual victory was assured. As we have noted, he was also at loggerheads with his own superior, the minister of national defence, who "clearly favours early action for all or most of our men," as Mackenzie King confided to his diary.[7] Ralston, a confirmed anglophile, did not object to splitting Canadian forces and putting parts of them under British control.

Personally, the prime minister agreed with McNaughton on the subject of a united Canadian army, but although he might have been willing to cross swords with Ralston he was clearly not prepared to question the British assessment of McNaughton's fitness to command. At the end of December 1943 McNaughton went, as gracefully as circumstances permitted, into semi-retirement. (It was announced that he was taking sick leave.) In Ottawa Lieutenant-General Ken Stuart, Ralston's right-hand man, relinquished his appointment as chief of the General Staff in Ottawa in order to go to London as chief of staff at Canadian Military Headquarters there. As the *Manchester Guardian* astutely observed at the time, "General Stuart comes to England as

Sicily and Southern Italy

71 General Montgomery, General Crerar, and Colonel Ralston, outside Montgomery's tactical headquarters at San Pietro in November 1943, immediately after the arrival of I Canadian Corps HQ in Italy.

Colonel Ralston's senior service lieutenant and thus will bring Canadian troops overseas under the direct control of the Minister."

The Gustav Line was the southern edge of a defence in depth intended to hold the Allies at least for the rest of the winter. Stretching across the narrowest part of the Italian peninsula, its eastern half was based on the virtually impregnable peaks of the Abruzzi in the central mountain spine and on a succession of swift-flowing, volatile rivers that dropped out of the hills to cut across a narrow coastal plain to the Adriatic Sea.

Once again the 1st Division, now commanded by Major-General Chris Vokes (Simonds had been posted to command the newly arrived 5th Armoured Division so that he could get experience in commanding armour), found itself in mountains, threatening an attack across the upper Sangro – the first of the river barriers – while V (British) Corps – which included the three Canadian tank regiments, now remustered as the 1st Canadian Armoured Brigade – in Montgomery's words "hit the Germans a colossal crack" further downstream. At the end of the month the whole of the ridge commanding the lower Sangro had been taken and the Canadians were ordered down into the plain, slated to spearhead the drive for Ortona with their own armoured brigade in support.

Sicily and Southern Italy

72 Men of the Edmonton Regiment move down a street in Ortona to take their turn at 'mouse-holing' and sniper hunting.

Along the coast the weather was milder but wetter, and the heavy clay soil was quickly churned into a thick, voracious slurry by the passage of hundreds of vehicles. Towns and villages – key points in the flow of battle – were reduced to heaps of rubble by the bombing, shelling, and mortaring of both sides. The mine-sown fields and vineyards between them were cut by deep gullies that created natural traps for attacking armour and convenient entrenchments for defending infantry.

Air support was inevitably sporadic and uncertain in the cloudy, rainy weather, although Kesselring thought that "the Allies had an air superiority which was only tolerable because their air operations were so systematic and, in our view, not pushed home." Meanwhile, the Canadians slogged forward against a resolute and well-conducted German defence from the Moro to the Riccio Rivers, covering only a distance of less than five miles in more than a month. The chaplain of one of the armoured regiments remembered later how "we used to watch the infantry going up into the line. Single file they trudged along, guns carried anyhow, ammo slung round them, trousers bagged

73 A street in Ortona as the battle ebbed away. A Canadian Bren carrier and two motorcycles are damaged while a truck and jeep burn as a result of German mortaring.

and down at heels. No war loan posters at home would show them that way. The P.B.I. [Poor Bloody Infantry] going into the line."[8]

The Canadians lost 2,400 killed, wounded, or taken prisoner, and over 1,600 sick. In the third week of December cases of battle fatigue (included in the sickness statistics) rose to 20 per cent of all casualties, and every rifle company in the division had lost at least 50 per cent of its original strength. As they fought their way into Ortona, Captain Paul Triquet of the 'Van Doos' won French Canada's first Victoria Cross of the war at Casa Berardi on December 14 – the first of three to be awarded to Canadians in Italy.

In Ortona the principal problem from a tactical perspective was co-ordinating the efforts of infantry, armour, and engineers.

> The infantry would be brought up to form a bridgehead over a rubble pile. It would be necessary for them to clear mines under the cover of smoke, or else to extend the bridgehead further to allow the sappers [engineers] to work. Under such circumstances, the leading infantry got to a point where it [sic] needed tanks in support, to shoot up the

Sicily and Southern Italy

74 Christmas in a part of Ortona taken by the Allies (not quite as close to the front line as the scene described by Matthew Halton). The brigade headquarters staff enjoy their Christmas dinner in the Church of Santa Maria while the signals officer plays carols on the organ. The men are looking happy partly because it is Christmas and partly because they are not in one of the rifle companies actually in the line.

upper floors of buildings. If the infantry lost contact with the sappers, the tanks did not get up in time.[9]

The alternative was to advance through the buildings that lined the streets and, against most stubborn German resistance, the Canadians perfected a technique of street fighting that would become standard for the rest of the war. Since anyone on foot was a sure target in the rubble-strewn streets, which were mostly impassable to armour, groups of three or four men – a half-section at the most – moved through the shell- and bomb-blasted houses on each side, 'mouse-holing' with high explosives the stone walls of each top floor and then clearing them of German paratroopers from the top down with grenades and sub-machine guns. Only those who were quick, careful, and lucky survived to tackle the next street. Booby traps were common and sometimes the enemy mined a house before leaving through his own 'mouse-hole.'

No one seemed quite clear why Ortona was so important. On December 22 an Associated Press correspondent noted that "for some unknown reason the Germans are staging a miniature Stalingrad in hapless Ortona." Knowing nothing of that report, Kesselring blamed

75 When Ortona became a battlefield in December 1943, this Italian family moved out into the countryside and dug caves in a sandy hillside. They were still living there in mid-February 1944 when this picture was taken by a *Toronto Star* correspondent.

it on the British: "We do not want to defend Ortona decisively, but the English have made it as important as Rome ... you can do nothing when things develop in this manner; it is only too bad that ... the world Press makes so much of it."[10]

The fighting increased in intensity. It was "a carnival of fury," said CBC correspondent Matthew Halton, who was there on Christmas Day. "Christmas dinner in the shelled, broken church in Ortona. Candles and white tablecloths ... not four hundred yards from the enemy, carol singers, the platoons coming in in relays to eat a Christmas dinner – men who hadn't had their clothes off in thirty days coming in and eating their dinners, and carol singers singing 'Silent Night.'"[11]

Ortona finally fell on December 27. But, musing over a brilliantly successful raid that his Van Doos carried out just a few weeks later, in which "daring and momentum carried the day" rather than obstinate perseverance, Lieutenant-Colonel J.V. Allard wondered "whether our superiors had been right in doggedly attacking Ortona head on, with the ensuing heavy losses. Would it not have been better to bypass Ortona completely?"[12]

147   *Sicily and Southern Italy*

76 Men of the Saskatoon Light Infantry mortar German positions as a prelude to a night attack in the Ortona salient.

The 5th Armoured Division had arrived in Italy on November 8, 1943. Two divisions in the field now justified the creation of a corps headquarters, over ten thousand strong, including four regiments of heavy artillery and all the usual support units, among which were two general hospitals of six hundred and twelve hundred beds respectively. On December 23, command of the new corps was given to Lieutenant-General Harry Crerar, who was now clearly being groomed to take McNaughton's place at the head of First Canadian Army. When the 5th Division began to filter into the front around Orsogna in early February 1944, an entire Canadian corps was in action for the first time since the First World War, under circumstances not too unlike those their fathers had known in Flanders.

The weather had shown no signs of improvement and the cold winter rain was saturating everything and everybody.

In mid-January 1944, Simonds pushed his new command into a poorly planned and worse executed attack across the Riccio, just beyond Ortona, sending a succession of inexperienced 11th Brigade units to assault positions on the Arielli ridge held by almost equal numbers of battle-hardened German paratroopers. Despite massive fire support, the inevitable happened and the Canadians were driven

Sicily and Southern Italy

back in confusion, with heavy losses, with their morale predictably shot to pieces.

A month later, the offensive finally petered out as Allied planners began to turn their attention to the western flank of the Appenines and the possibility of capturing Rome. General Montgomery had already left for the United Kingdom to play his part in Operation *Overlord* – the invasion of northwest Europe – and over the rest of the winter three veteran British divisions had followed him. The failure of the Canadian government to ensure that their two divisions also went back when both Crerar and Simonds left to join the *Overlord* team, made it seem quite unlikely that the Canadians would ever fight as a unified force, as McNaughton had planned.

Montgomery was succeeded by General Sir Oliver Leese, in whose XXX Corps the Canadian 1st Division had fought during the Sicilian campaign. Major-General E.L.M. Burns, who had commanded the 5th Armoured Division since General Simonds' departure for northwest Europe (but entirely lacked the charisma required to restore morale so gravely damaged by Simonds' blunder), was promoted to command the newly formed I Canadian Corps in March. A dour, introverted intellectual, Burns was nicknamed 'Smiling Sunray' by his troops in ironic recognition that he hardly ever did smile. ('Sunray' was the radio code-name for any commander at any level.)

In the spring of 1944 the Germans had stopped the Allied armies in their tracks on the Gustav Line, a series of well-sited defensive positions that stretched across the whole width of the peninsula. The best prospect of breaking this deadlock seemed to be at the western end of the Line, where the valley of the southward-flowing Liri River pierced those defences before joining the Rapido River to become the Garigliano. If only the enduring bastion of Monte Cassino, which dominated the mouth of the valley, could be subdued, the Allies would be well positioned for a drive on Rome.

Moreover, on January 22 an amphibious landing had been made by two corps – one American (which included the unique 1st Special Service Force, a commando-type unit of one Canadian and two American battalions under an American commander) and one British – at Anzio, about thirty-five miles south of Rome. Kesselring had succeeded in keeping them pinned in a relatively small bridgehead, however, where a well-judged counterattack might conceivably throw them all back into the sea at any moment. In order to relieve Anzio while concentrating as much pressure as possible on the Germans' weakest point and, at the same time, forcing them "to commit the maximum number of divisions in Italy at the time that *Overlord* is launched" (in the words of General Alexander's chief of staff), it was decided to move part of the Eighth Army across the mountains and commit it to a major attack up the Liri valley. In April the Canadians began their move, leaving behind them in Ortona the graves of 1,372

77   Under enemy observation and fire, an artillery FOO (Forward Observation Officer) with the PPCLI sprints across fifty yards of open ground that was once the vineyard and olive grove of an Italian farm. The two wine bottles in the lower left corner had been carefully 'booby trapped' by the Germans.

of their comrades – nearly a quarter of the total number of Canadians who would be killed in the Mediterranean campaign.

On May 11, British, French, and American troops attacked the western flank of the Gustav Line. The Canadian Corps was held in reserve at this stage, but the independent 1st Canadian Armoured Brigade played an important role in providing close support fire for the initial crossings of the Garigliano by the 8th Indian and 4th British Divisions.

In a night attack the British and Indians established precarious footholds on the northern bank, but the crossing-points were dominated by German guns, and getting reinforcements across to expand the bridgeheads would be difficult. One prefabricated bridge was erected by dawn, but to put up another in daylight seemed impossible. Then two tanks of the Calgary Regiment appeared, bearing between them a complete hundred-foot span of bridging that had been put together well behind the front. Alongside both tanks – the first of which was turretless – walked the designer of this curious device, Captain Tony Kingsmill of the Royal Canadian Electrical and Mechanical Engineers, coolly controlling their speed and direction by field telephone even though he was wounded before very long. Driving up to the river bank under heavy fire, the first tank went straight into the water, its crew escaping just as it became submerged to the top of its hull. The rear tank kept going and the bridge slid over the top of the first tank to the far side of the river.

Sicily and Southern Italy

"YOU SCRAM! THERE AINT ROOM FOR THREE HERE."

The pusher tank then disconnected and presto! – a new method of bridging small rivers had been proven in the field. It was no fault of Kingsmill that his bridge was temporarily put out of action by German shellfire after only four of the Calgary's tanks had crossed. He was rewarded with a Military Cross – dramatic evidence that bravery in battle was not restricted to members of the so-called 'combat arms.'

Eventually, lodgements were secured. In the second phase of the assault, on 12 May, the Canadian 1st Division was thrust into the mouth of the Liri valley to 'open up' the hole appearing in the Gustav Line. It was spring and the countryside was at last beginning to resemble that sunny Italy beloved of peacetime travel agents. Armour and air support was plentiful. In two days the Canadians stabbed forward five miles and were pressing against a new set of German defences. On their right the British 78th Division kept abreast of them, while on the left a Free French corps and the II (U.S.) Corps of the Fifth Army were also across the Garigliano and driving north towards Anzio and Rome. Cassino finally fell to the Eighth Army's Polish Corps on 17 May. (Its thousand-year-old abbey was pulverized by Allied bombing, but has since been rebuilt, largely with American money.)

The next obstacle was the Hitler Line, another prepared defensive position. Immensely strong but quite shallow, it split off from the Gustav Line in the central mountain massif and, where it crossed the Liri valley, lay about eight miles further north. Overcoming it demanded a carefully co-ordinated set-piece assault, and this time General Leese assigned the key role to the Canadians. General Vokes, whose 1st Division was to lead the way, selected an axis of advance on the east bank of the Liri where the ground seemed most suitable for the tanks of the 5th Armoured Division, which would follow through to exploit any success. The 5th was commanded by Major-General Bert Hoffmeister, a pre-war captain in the Seaforth Highlanders of Canada, who had already distinguished himself leading an infantry brigade and who was to be one of the two militia officers to command a division in the field during the war. (The other, Major-General Bruce Matthews, only held his command for the last six months of the war.)

Beginning on May 19, each night, after dark, infantry and engineer patrols cautiously probed the forward edge of the German defences, lifting mines and reconnoitring tank routes. On May 22, the chaplain of the Seaforth Highlanders noted in his diary that "my boys move in tonight.... New boys with fear and nerves and anxiety hidden under quick smiles and quick seriousness. Old campaigners with a far away look. It is the hardest thing to watch without breaking into tears."[13]

He might indeed have cried had he known what was to follow. The next morning Vokes' men charged forward under a barrage of fire from more than eight hundred guns and every available plane of the Allied tactical air forces. Nevertheless, by nightfall the Seaforths had lost more than a quarter of the battalion killed, wounded, or prisoner, the heaviest losses they suffered in one day throughout the war. The 2nd Brigade's losses totalled 543, the division's nearly 900. Once again flaws in control and communications at various levels, coupled with the initial failure of the British 78th Division to take their objective on the Canadians' right flank, served only to emphasize the effect of a masterly German defensive plan.

The supporting armour was devastated by a combination of well-sited minefields, enemy artillery concentrations, and the fire of 'Panzerturme' – tank turrets mounted on concrete underground bunkers, whose 75-mm guns dominated nearly every line of advance with their interlocking fire. The Ontario Regiment, for example, lost twelve tanks to the Panzerturme and one to mines, while all its other machines took one or more direct hits from high explosive shells. The infantry were left to plunge forward without immediate fire support, funnelled into 'killing grounds' – a hail of mortar bursts of machine-

79 The only men in this company of the PPCLI to get a noonday meal were those who were resting at company headquarters – four hundred yards from the enemy, north of Ortona – after a patrol the previous night. Men in the line ate only twice a day unless they were lucky enough to have a candy bar.

gun and rifle fire. The Seaforth Highlander whose description of the Sicily landing has already been quoted was wounded in this attack only seconds after the events he describes:

> My mind had but one thought; get through the barrage, get through the barrage.... No one except the wounded or the dead stopped.... Over to the left a German jumped up and seemed to be raising his hands when he was killed by one of our fellows. Directly ahead and about fifty yards away a Jerry stood up and held his machine gun in his arms. A long burst tore into eight platoon to my right. I fired two rounds from the hip at the same time that others must have fired. The Jerry folded up and fell. I stepped on his bloody head as I passed over the position a few seconds later.[14]

The Hitler Line was broken on May 23, 1943. "I send my greetings and congratulations to your magnificent fighting men," signalled General Alphonse Juin, the commander of the Free French corps, who had watched the Canadian attack from the high ground on the other side of the Liri. "You have done great things in this valley."

The 5th Armoured began to move forward, to exploit the break. As the Germans were forced back on May 23 and the breach deepened and widened, General Leese inserted his XIII Corps into it on the Canadians' right. That was a mistake. The valley was becoming

Sicily and Southern Italy

80 A photograph of Adolf Hitler and two pictures of himself taken in happier days lie beside the body of this *Luftwaffe* sergeant of the Hermann Goering Division.

too narrow to carry two corps abreast, each under its own entirely separate headquarters, and if more troops were necessary, they should all have been put under one command. However, both the Canadians' 5th and British 6th Armoured Divisions began to pour through the hole punched by the Canadian infantry.

Hoffmeister's men set off in fine style. On May 24 the Lord Strathcona's Horse were leading in their Sherman tanks. A tank commander has recalled the advance:

> "Push on now" came the Colonel's voice over the wireless and sixty tanks began to roll forward, spreading out into formatio.... [A] feeling of exhilaration began to take hold. Others had been hit but I was indestructible. Then it happened. One moment, the world around me was full of vivid colour ... and then suddenly, in the fraction of an instant, everything had turned to inky blackness.... At that same instant, from what seemed a long way off, there came a mighty metallic clang as though some great anvil had been struck by a giant sledgehammer.
>
> I think I knew right away what the trouble was. This was not the blackness of unconsciousness or the blackness of death. I was alive, that was certain, but I was blind.... I

154   *Sicily and Southern Italy*

slumped forward in the turret, hands rubbing at eyes, trying to brush away the veil, trying to see something, anything, that would tell me it wasn't true.[15]

Regrettably, it was all too true. In a Caserta hospital a doctor told him, "I'm sorry, but we have had to remove both eyes. You see, there was no hope of saving them." By then his division had forced a crossing of the Melfa, a tributary of the Liri, where Major J.K. Mahoney of the Westminster Regiment won a Victoria Cross. But when the British armoured division was blocked by a German rearguard and forced over to the left, the Canadians were ordered to sidestep to the left also, thus dangerously compressing their front.

Jammed against the Liri, with the British squeezing in from the right and the 1st Division following up immediately behind, the 5th (and corps headquarters) got into something of a tangle. Relatively inexperienced commanders and staffs were put under tremendous pressure. The advance lost momentum and the control problem was further complicated by a botched bridging job that held up Hoffmeister's armour for twenty-four hours as it shifted to a new axis of advance. On May 28 the Canadians finally crossed the Liri. However, on June 3 General Leese ordered them 'pinched out' of the front so that Juin's Free French, moving up on the left with extraordinary rapidity, might slide on to the Canadian axis and press the pursuit towards Rome – an objective finally attained by Americans whose vain and publicity-conscious commander, General Mark Clark, disobeyed orders in his anxiety to be first into the Eternal City.

The operations of the Canadian Corps in the race for Rome demonstrated their lack of experience in fluid battle conditions. At Ortona they had proved themselves in static warfare as bitter and vicious as that at Stalingrad a year earlier, even though it had been on a much smaller scale. The Hitler Line, too, had been a set-piece affair. Mobile fighting, however, involved much more complex military problems. On May 23 General Burns had been in command of the corps for only ninety days; Hoffmeister had never handled a division of any kind in battle, never mind an armoured one; and Vokes probably lacked the capacity for that kind of command. Their staffs were also short of practical experience in handling mobile operations at their respective levels. These weaknesses – based on inexperience and greatly exacerbated by General Leese's blunder in pushing forward two corps abreast – made the Canadians the last choice to pursue the Germans further.

The Americans on the left of the French linked up with their troops in the Anzio bridgehead on May 25 and Rome fell to them on June 4. Its capture was quickly overshadowed by the launching of Operation *Overlord* just two days later.

CHAPTER 7

Operation *Overlord*

Planning for the invasion of northwest Europe may be said to have begun in October 1940, when the Joint Planning Sub-Committee of the British chiefs of staff first considered the problems involved in returning to the continental mainland from which the BEF had so recently and rudely been ejected. When the United States entered the war, in December 1941, the principle of an invasion through France had been confirmed. Indeed, the Americans thought it might be mounted in late 1942, but a British refusal to consider it at that time (unless the Russian front looked like totally collapsing) compelled them to think again.

The Americans next argued for an attack in 1943, but the British remained chary of mounting a premature assault and, as we have seen, were more interested in reaffirming their influence in the Mediterranean theatre. Bowing to British experience, their new allies reluctantly accepted the postponement of a cross-Channel assault in favour of the attack on Sicily and, subsequently, Italy.

In March 1943, however, an Anglo-American planning staff began to consider in detail the strategy and logistics of invading France. The requirement for air cover from fighters limited the possible area of assault to the French and Dutch coasts between Cherbourg and Flushing. The Dieppe experience had taught that the attack should probably not be launched through a port – but not every beach would be suitable. Such technical considerations as tides, beach slopes, roads, and regional topography soon narrowed the possibilities to two main areas: the Pas de Calais or the Baie de la Seine.

In many ways the Pas de Calais was the most suitable, but for those very reasons it was also where German defences were strongest. The Baie de la Seine, on the other hand, was much more lightly defended and the port of Cherbourg lay nearby, to the west, where a short thrust across the base of the Cotentin peninsula would isolate it from further reinforcement. At the eastern end of the Bay, albeit on the other side of the Seine estuary, lay Le Havre – the second largest port (after Marseilles) of pre-war France.

On August 15, 1943, in the course of the second day of the Anglo-American summit conference at Quebec, code-named *Quadrant*, the basic plan for Operation *Overlord* was accepted by the Combined Chiefs of Staff. It outlined an assault via the Baie de la Seine to take place in late May or early June 1944. Ten months of detailed planning and meticulous rehearsal followed. On Christmas Eve 1943, General Eisenhower, who had been commanding Allied forces in the Mediterranean theatre, was appointed supreme commander, Allied Expeditionary Force, with Air Chief Marshal Sir Arthur Tedder as his deputy. Admiral Sir Charles Little would command the Allied naval forces and Air Marshal Sir Trafford Leigh-Mallory, the combined air forces.

The hard-driving, mercurial American general, George Patton, had fallen into disfavour by physically assaulting a battle-fatigued soldier in a Sicilian field hospital, apparently disqualifying himself from higher command. The only other obvious choice for overall ground force commander was Montgomery, but because of his egotistical, abrasive, schoolmasterish temperament, almost guaranteed to upset the Americans in the long run, no overall commander-in-chief was appointed for the ground forces. General Omar Bradley would command the American 12th Army Group, while the far more experienced Montgomery would have only the British 21st Army Group, composed of Second British and First Canadian Armies. However, Montgomery, who had been the key figure in planning *Husky*, would be responsible for the initial assault and for the tactical co-ordination of all ground forces during the early stages of the battle, until the number of men ashore justified setting up the two army group headquarters.

The landing phase of *Overlord*, called Operation *Neptune*, was postponed for twenty-four hours by forecasts of poor weather. But in the early hours of June 6, 1944, five thousand ships of every conceivable function, shape, and size were moving steadily into the Baie de la Seine. Far out on each flank, nine Canadian destroyers of the River class, eleven frigates, and nineteen corvettes, together with six RCAF coastal reconnaissance and maritime strike squadrons, shared the task of protecting the vast armada from German interference. In mid-channel, Tribal-class destroyers of the naval covering force, including HMCS *Haida* and *Huron*, kept their stations along each side of the invasion 'corridor' ready to repel attacks by anything that might evade the outer defences. A U-boat commander was to write in his memoirs of "a steel screen of ships and guns ... a dark umbrella of aircraft. Sixteen of the latest Snort [Schnorkel] boats sailed out to meet the allied armada. One got through."[1]

Fleet-class destroyers assigned to beach bombardment duties led the long lines of landing ships and assault transports, among them the Canadian ships *Prince Henry* and *Prince David* and five flotillas of Canadian landing craft, totalling more than forty vessels. In the van of this vast armada steamed the minesweepers, including the 31st Canadian Minesweeping Flotilla, and scattered among the other flotillas were six more Canadian sweepers. Working to precise limits under the most exacting conditions, every sweeper faced not only the danger of being mined itself but also the threat of shore-based gunfire, air attack, or the onslaught of German E-boats – extremely fast, heavily armed motor launches.

81 With the shoreline and immediate vicinity secured, the Landing Craft (Infantry) on D-Day were able to run right up the beaches, and men and matériel were soon coming ashore in ever-increasing numbers.

One in three of the ships in the minesweeping force sailed as a reserve against expected casualties. As things turned out, the reserve was not needed. "In the early evening we were still 40 miles off the French coast," a Canadian sailor wrote in his diary.

> We hadn't met any opposition at all so far. We couldn't understand it.... The sky was still overcast, but an hour or two after nightfall we could just make out the deeper darkness of the French coast, now only 14 miles away off our starboard bow.... Then, in the flat perspectiveless light before dawn, we could see the ships that had followed us in. They'd found the channel all right.... There were ships everywhere, big troop transports, cruisers, destroyers, and landing craft of every description. Soon we could see that the landings had indeed begun. The shore was lined with beached craft, and beyond them the land lay under a pall of smoke. Cruisers were pouring out salvo after salvo in support of the troops, but I couldn't see any answering fire at all.[2]

Special assault vessels, each bearing eleven hundred 3-inch rockets and thus firing a salvo equivalent to the gunfire of a hundred cruisers, drenched the shore with high explosive. Self-propelled artillery being carried in landing craft blazed away at the coast ahead. Supported by this overwhelming weight of firepower and led by flail tanks and the AVREs of the Royal Engineers, the first troops stormed ashore. "We are getting close now and the bombardment stops," wrote a subaltern of the Regina Rifles.

> So far not a shot has been fired from the defenders on the beach. Will it be a pushover? We soon have the answer in the form of machine gun fire and shells from pill boxes which

Operation Overlord

**VICTORY
IN EUROPE**
6 June 1944 – 8 May 1945

**CANADIAN
ASSAULTS
"D" DAY**

are apparently still open for business despite the terrific pounding they have taken.[3]

The Americans landed on two beaches, 'Omaha' and 'Utah' at the western end of the bay. The 3rd Canadian Division, under Major-General R.F.L. Keller, was assigned to 'Juno,' with the British 3rd and 50th Divisions to its left and right respectively, on 'Sword' and 'Gold.'

159   *Operation* Overlord

The most difficult assignment proved to be that on Omaha, those on Utah and Sword the easiest – although none were very easy. On Juno, the padre of the North Shore Regiment recalled how

> the beach was sprayed from all angles by the enemy machine guns and now their mortars and heavy guns began hitting us. Crawling along in the sand, I just reached a group of three badly wounded men when a shell landed among us killing the others outright. As we crawled we could hear the bullets and shrapnel cutting into the sand around us.... A ramp had been placed against the [sea] wall by now. Over it we went ... two stretcher bearers ahead of us stepped on a mine ... half-dazed, we jumped down again behind the wall.[4]

A sergeant in a British engineer company busily neutralizing mines watched two Canadians bash in the skull of a German.

> We were up in the dunes at the top of the beach, just on the other side of the Seulles river ... and as we got to the top of a rise I saw my first German. He was alive but not for very long. These two Canadians who were with me were running up the beach behind me with their rifles. Just as they went up behind me through this opening in the sea wall, the Jerry came up out of the emplacement with a Schmeisser [sub-machine gun]. I thought – Christ! They haven't seen. I had-n't got a Sten gun, it had gone in the drink. But they just didn't stop running, they just cracked their rifle butts down on the German and that was that.[5]

Near the Anglo-Canadian boundary between the two 3rd Divisions, some elements of the 21st *Panzer* Division came into action against the British during the afternoon. Their counterattack was broken up by a combination of anti-tank artillery and naval gun-fire. On the whole, though, the German reaction was untypically slow. Their commanders were at first uncertain whether this was a subsidiary attack to one that might come further east at any time, or whether it was the long-forecast opening of the Second Front. This uncertainty the Allies had fostered with complex deception schemes.

At the end of the day the Allies had succeeded in establishing themselves on all five beaches, but they had not reached any of their assigned objectives several miles inland. Nor had they achieved the intended build-up of men and matériel. Plans had called for 107,000 men to be put ashore with 7,000 vehicles and 14,500 tons of supplies, but only 80 per cent of the men, 50 per cent of the machines, and 30 per cent of the supplies had been landed. Nevertheless, the Germans were unable to exploit the situation, since their static coastal divisions had sustained heavy losses in both men and equipment, and Allied tactical air power was preventing the enemy from quickly filling the

82 Men of the Royal Winnipeg Rifles plunge ashore from a Landing Craft (Assault) on D-Day. Within minutes they – together with a squadron of the 6th (1st Hussars) Armoured Regiment – were attacking a strong point that had not been put out of action by the preliminary bombardments. In the words of the official historian, "When the strong point was clear, 'B' Company had been reduced to the company commander and 26 men."

vacuum immediately behind his front caused by placing his reserve divisions too far back.

The Canadian spearheads dug in at nightfall three or four miles inland, ready to call down upon any counterattack an overwhelming weight of naval gunfire. Six battleships, two 15-inch gun monitors, twenty-three cruisers, and seventy-seven destroyers assigned specifically to fire-support duties were lying off the beaches all night. On the surface, and in the ceaseless propaganda being pumped out by Allied media, all was going well. Yet, paradoxically, they were probably going wrong just as much as they were going right. Montgomery's maps might show a steadily expanding bridgehead, but all the Allied thought and effort had been directed to establishing themselves ashore – little attention had been paid to what should be done next in tactical and operational terms.

For example, no one on the American front seems to have considered in advance the problems inherent in advancing through the *bocage* – the raised hedgerows of western Normandy, their roots interlocked in three-foot-high earthen banks, that inhibited tank movement and gave such enormous advantages to defending infantry. On the Anglo-Canadian side, some of the "Battle Notes" distributed in the days immediately before embarkation seem, by their emphasis on minefields, patrolling, and 'digging-in,' and their failure to affirm the need to 'press on regardless' once the enemy was off-balance, to have been prepared with some kind of trench warfare in mind. Consequently, battles of attrition is what they got until Operation *Cobra* – the American breakout of July 24-31 – began.

On June 7 the Canadian 7th Infantry Brigade, on the right, reached its D-Day objectives before noon, the first Allied formation to do so. The 9th Brigade, however, leapfrogging through the 8th, on

Operation Overlord

83 German prisoners,
taken during the early
stages of the landing, carrying a wounded
Canadian down to the
beach. The Canadian
clutches German boots
and a helmet picked up as
souvenirs. A Canadian
corporal follows the
stretcher; the sergeant and
private on the left are
British.

the left, and pressing towards Carpiquet airfield, met with a sudden reverse. Elements of the 12th SS *Panzer* Division came into action, driving them back several miles to a point only slightly further inland than the one they had reached the day before. Here, around Buron and Authie, the Canadians fought and lost their first real battle in northwest Europe. They fought, in the words of the official historian, "with courage and spirit but somewhat clumsily." Communications with the navy failed and their supporting artillery regiment, slow off the mark that morning, found itself too far back to supply covering fire at the vital moment, so that "at a time when the 9th Brigade's leading troops were in sight of its final objective, the Carpiquet air-field, they had been thrown back for over two miles, and the ground thus lost was not to be recovered for a full month."[6]

They showed weaknesses that were to bedevil the Anglo-Canadian armies throughout the campaign: a ponderous approach to battle; poor co-operation between infantry, artillery, and armour; a failure of regimental or battalion commanders to keep their superiors quickly and fully informed of what was happening; and a disconcert-ingly unprofessional approach on the part of senior officers that too often expressed itself in a tendency to trust their troops' raw courage and self-confidence instead of relying on careful planning and calcu-lated judgement. These last two problems were perhaps more in evi-dence among the Canadians (and continued to be evident through-out the rest of the war) than among the British.

The first few weeks of fighting in the bridgehead were probably as bitter and malevolent as anything seen on the more notorious Eastern Front, although the summer weather of Normandy was very different from that of winter in Byelorussia or the Ukraine. A certain ruthlessness was exhibited by both sides. On D-Day a British seaman aboard a landing craft unloading at Courseulles had watched Canadian soldiers march six Germans behind a sand dune some dis-tance away. Bent on getting a souvenir from the prisoners, he ran up the beach only to find the six "all crumpled up.... Every one had had his throat cut."[7]

84 Canadian casualties
wait to be taken off the
D-Day beaches surround-
ed by British engineers
and medics digging pro-
tective trenches to place
them in, and with an
abandoned German can-
non looming ominously
above them.

There was dirty work like this on both sides in the heat of battle. The losers, of course, were more apt to suffer for it. Kurt Meyer, the commanding officer of 25 SS *Panzergrenadier* Regiment (a part of the 12th SS *(Hitler Jugend)* Division that he later commanded), which joined the battle on June 7, was eventually convicted of countenanc-ing the killing of Canadian prisoners at the Abbaye d'Ardennes by men of his regiment in a court martial held in December 1945. He was sentenced to death, but despite a public outcry the sentence was commuted to life imprisonment. Meyer was subsequently released from Dorchester Penitentiary in September 1954. Wilhelm Mohnke, commander of 26 SS *Panzergrenadier* Regiment, whose troops also murdered Canadian prisoners, was taken prisoner by the Russians at the end of the war and held by them until the 1950s, by which time

85 Servicing a Spitfire at a forward airstrip in Normandy. This lightweight aircraft, with its comparatively wide and stable undercarriage, could land and take off from grass runways if necessary.

the Canadian government had apparently lost interest in pursuing the matter. (The suggestion has been made that this was at the instigation of the United States government, which had received useful information from Mohnke on his return from Russia.) In 1989, a Canadian Commission on War Crimes sparked renewed concern but a lack of living witnesses – Mohnke himself was still alive – precluded any further prosecution.

The German formations were soon greatly outnumbered by the Allies, but a high percentage of enemy officers and NCOs had seen much hard fighting in the east and their battle wisdom and leadership did much to compensate for their comparative lack of men and matériel. Moreover, although their turrets had to be cranked around by hand, the enemy's Panther and Tiger tanks were superior in armour and armament to most of the Allies' Shermans and Cromwells – although the 'Firefly' Sherman, with its 17-pounder gun and power-operated turret, was, by and large, a match for any German tank.

The scale was turned by Allied airpower, and most particularly by tactical airpower. "On the morning of June 10," wrote Gehr von Schweppenberg, the commander of the *Panzer* army in Normandy, "I saw a Panzer Regiment in action against the Canadians. It was hellish but in this case the hell came from the sky."[8] Three hours later, wounded, he was being helped from the ruins of his headquarters after an attack on it by British and Dutch light bombers and fighter-bombers of the 2nd Tactical Air Force.

The foundation of Allied air superiority had been laid long before D-Day. For the past two years, 'circuses' and 'ramrods' – the fighter pilots' terms for massed fighter sweeps over France and the Low Countries – had been paring away German fighter strength in the west, while the bomber offensive over Germany pinned the largest part of the enemy's day and night fighter arms to the defence of the Fatherland itself. By D-Day the *Luftwaffe* in France had been reduced

Operation Overlord

to only 319 aircraft in a state of operational readiness, less than 100 of the total being fighters. Against them were ranged some 6,000 to 7,000 Allied aircraft, including more than 3,000 fighters and fighter-bombers.

Three RCAF fighter wings of Spitfire IXs – each three squadrons strong and led by Canadian Wing Commanders Lloyd Chadburn and George Keefer, together with the British ace (and one of the top-scoring Commonwealth pilots of the war) 'Johnnie' Johnson – formed the core of the Canadian contingent. They were backed by a fighter-reconnaissance wing of Spitfires commanded by Group Captain E.H.G. Moncreiff (J.M. Godfrey became his 'Wingco (Flying)' on July 2) and by a wing of Typhoon fighter-bombers led by Wing Commander R.T.P. Davidson, RAF.

It was primarily the fighter-bombers – 'Jabos' (short for *Jagdbombern*), the Germans called them – that supplied "the hell from the sky" that so impressed von Schweppenberg. The *Luftwaffe* made only a nominal and cursory appearance over the beaches on D-Day; it turned up in somewhat greater numbers on June 7, when Keefer's wing was credited with twelve destroyed, one probably destroyed, and four damaged; and again on June 15, when No. 127 Wing – whose first leader, Lloyd Chadburn, had been killed in a mid-air collision two days earlier, to be succeeded by Bob Buckham – claimed another nine destroyed and two damaged.

German planning had called for 600 fighters to be brought forward from Germany in the event of an invasion, and these formations began to move on June 7 and 8. However, the weight of Allied bomber and fighter-bomber attacks on their assigned tactical airfields destroyed so many of the incoming machines before they could be made fit to fight, and caused such havoc in the enemy's logistics system that, after June 12, no more than 250 German fighters were ever available for operations. The total was often much less.

In this absence of serious opposition the Tactical Air Force was able to play a major role in the land battle, slashing at the German supply lines as well as strafing and bombing in close support of the ground troops. Fighter-bomber attacks on road and rail bridges, locomotives, and trucks were very effective in slowing the rate at which the enemy's reinforcements reached Normandy. The 2nd SS *Panzerdivision*, for example, which was stationed in the vicinity of Toulouse, on France's west coast, was ordered forward in the early hours of June 6, but the last of its fighting units did not reach the battlefront until June 23, having taken seventeen nights to travel 450 miles that could have been covered in less than a quarter of the time under normal conditions.

During the first four days of *Overlord*, Allied fighters and fighter-bombers flew out of English bases, so that the duration of their missions over France and the weight of weaponry they could carry had to be balanced, one against the other. Extra tanks of gasoline or additional bombs were alternatives that limited either flight time or the potential damage that each aircraft could inflict on the enemy. But on June 10 the first airstrip in the bridgehead was ready, and that morning Johnson's wing of RCAF Spitfires became the first Allied aircraft to land there.

As more airstrips were carved out of the countryside, where aircraft could refuel and rearm, air support for the ground forces became both continuous and intense. Any reported movement of German tanks, any massing of his armour, brought an immediate and violent response from the fighter-bombers, so that the techniques of blitzkrieg and mobile warfare were useless to the Germans. Powerful Panther and Tiger tanks, the vaunted cutting-edge of the *Wehrmacht*, were compelled to adopt a largely static role as nothing more than armoured strong points during daylight. "Branches and twigs were carefully cut out of a hedge and the tanks decorated with them until they seemed to have been spirited away," wrote the historian of the élite *Panzer Lehr* division. "Next, the tank tracks in a field of oats had to be obliterated, or they would be a clear signpost for any fighter-bomber. Laboriously each blade was bent back again and made to stand upright."[9]

86   The wreck of a German destroyer that had been driven ashore on the Île de Bas by HMCS *Haida* and *Huron* on June 9, 1944. Its destruction was completed by rocket-firing Beaufighters of No. 404 Squadron RCAF.

The German attempts at sea to interfere with the development of *Overlord* were no more effective than their efforts in the air. On the evening of D-Day an anti-shipping strike wing of Coastal Command – consisting of fourteen rocket-armed Beaufighters of No. 404 Squadron RCAF, and seventeen from No. 144 Squadron RAF, with Mosquitos of the RAF's No. 235 Squadron providing fighter cover – surprised three German destroyers steaming north, about thirty miles southwest of St Nazaire on the French Atlantic coast, and attacked out

87 HMCS *Haida* at speed, photographed from HMCS *Huron*.

of the setting sun. It was reported in the diary of the Canadian squadron that "when the formation left, the centre destroyer was on fire and the leading destroyer was sinking."

Very early the following morning, however, six of the Canadian Beaufighters found all three destroyers still afloat some distance to the northwest of their previous position. When they arrived on the scene, "the centre destroyer was smoking slightly" and in the subsequent attack "an explosion was observed in the 2nd or 3rd ship which lit up the ship ahead. The explosion burst to a height of 200 ft and when it subsided the ship was afire internally from stem to stern."[10] Post-war studies show that no German destroyers were actually lost, despite this dramatic report. However, the prime aim of the strikes was achieved: these three warships played no further part in the prosecution of anti-invasion operations.

Four more German destroyers slipped out of Brest on the dark squally night of June 8 and started up-Channel only to be picked up by the radar of a patrolling Allied destroyer flotilla whose eight ships included HMCS *Haida* and *Huron*. As soon as visual contact was

Operation Overlord

established, the Germans launched salvoes of torpedoes, then turned away to the west and north. 'Combing' the enemy torpedo tracks, *Haida* and *Huron*, together with HMS *Tartar* and *Ashanti*, took up the chase. In the running fight that followed, *Tartar* was hit and her signalling and radar equipment were badly damaged; *Ashanti* sank one of the German ships; and *Haida* and *Huron*, although their guns scored some hits, were frustrated when their respective adversaries escaped by cutting unwittingly across a British minefield without further damage.

While steaming back to their patrol stations, however, the Canadian ships raised another radar contact that proved to be the destroyer that had crippled *Tartar*. Again their enemy avoided them with a lucky dash across a minefield, and the Canadians "swung back northwards to skirt the barrier in an agony of suspense lest this destroyer should also elude them." Twenty minutes later they found the enemy again and resumed their pursuit. Soon all three ships were bearing down upon the rock-bound French coast at high speed. While the enemy's guns were still slightly off target, however, *Haida* and *Huron* were now hitting their quarry repeatedly, and, in the palest light of dawn, the burning enemy destroyer was forced onto the jagged rocks of the Île de Bas. Later that day, the Canadian-crewed Beaufighters of No. 404 Squadron completed its destruction.

On June 15 a heavy bombing attack on the docks of Le Havre disabled four more destroyers and ten motor torpedo boats. The only remaining German naval forces that might be brought into action were a number of light, high-speed gunboats (all of which found it virtually impossible to penetrate the Allied destroyer and MTB screens) and the submarine fleet. During the first week of the invasion, forty-three U-boats left from bases in Norway and on the Atlantic coast. Twelve had to return prematurely with mechanical defects or damage caused by Allied depth-charges, eighteen were sunk, and only thirteen succeeded in completing their patrols. During the first three months of *Overlord* the U-boats managed to sink between them just seven small warships (from destroyer escorts to minesweepers), three landing craft, and thirteen freighters, totalling some 55,000 tons – an infinitesimal fraction of the invasion fleets.

On June 24, approximately fifteen miles northwest of Ushant, U-971 was destroyed by the depth-charges and guns of *Haida*, working in conjunction with HMS *Eskimo*. After two hours of depth-charging, the submarine was forced to surface, and gunfire from *Haida* blew open the base of its conning-tower and set it on fire. Two weeks later, on the eastern side of the invasion corridor, the Canadian destroyers *Ottawa* and *Kootenay* shared in the destruction of U-678.

Two of the seven Allied warships sunk by U-boats in the course of *Overlord* were Canadian. During June each of the Canadian corvettes made at least six return trips to the Normandy beaches. Despite attacks by the occasional enemy bomber, guided glider bomb, or E-boat, they suffered no serious damage – though an American destroyer mistakenly put a shell through the engine room of the *Trentonian*. Fortunately there were no casualties.

Things were much the same in July – *Alberni* was credited with shooting down a Ju-88 bomber over the beachhead – but in August the Canadians' luck turned sour. On the 8th, *Regina* went to the aid of a freighter reported mined off Trevose Head. In fact she had been hit by a torpedo, and while *Regina* stood by the crippled ship, she, too, was hit by a torpedo and sank in a matter of minutes with the loss of 30 men and the serious injury of 10 others. Two weeks later, *Alberni* was torpedoed east of the Isle of Wight, rolling over and sinking in seconds with the loss of 60 men. The corvettes were the hardest-hit category of all the Canadian naval forces involved in *Overlord*, losing altogether 90 killed and 30 wounded, out of the total RCN casualties of 120 killed and 159 wounded.

Early in July, the desperate Germans had resorted to somewhat ineffectual methods of attacking Allied shipping. Using man carrying and manually guided torpedoes, ridden to the vicinity of a target by 'frogmen' in wet suits, they succeeded only in sinking two minesweepers and damaging the obsolete old cruiser HMS *Dragon* seriously enough to warrant scuttling her as an additional breakwater for the *Mulberry* artificial harbour off Arromanches. Remote-control motor boats, loaded with explosive to the gunwales, were also employed rather fruitlessly, and aerial minelaying in the invasion corridor gradually became more intense, but within its carefully layered air and sea defences the invasion build-up continued unabated. The result of the German efforts to interrupt it can best be summarized by pointing out that, in the first month after D-Day, only 261 vessels were destroyed or damaged by all kinds of enemy action, as against 606 lost by bad weather or human error. In the same time 875,000 men, half a million vehicles, and several hundred thousand tons of stores and equipment were landed in Normandy.

The area of the Allied toehold in France expanded much more slowly than expected. It took the Americans until June 26 to capture Cherbourg; and on the eastern flank, where Montgomery had planned to take Caen on the first day, Anglo-Canadian progress was even slower. The Canadians who had been in the environs of Carpiquet on June 6 did not succeed in occupying the village and the northern half of the airfield there until July 4, and even then the North Shore Regiment and the Régiment de la Chaudière suffered nearly two hundred casualties in clearing a hamlet that was defended by only fifty *Panzergrenadiers*. It had been intended that, by the end of June, the front line would run through Lisieux, Alençon, and Laval, west of Rennes, and then to the coast west of St Malo; but when that time came Allied forces found themselves still confined to a bridgehead less than a quarter of the planned size, that did not include either Caen or St Lô.

This compression caused very real problems as more and more equipment and facilities was crammed into a limited space. Men and matériel were trussed together in such a fashion that lateral mobility on any scale was virtually impossible, and even movement along the various axes of advance from the beaches was frustratingly slow and difficult. The rate of reinforcement had to be deliberately restricted and among those formations that were held back temporarily were the headquarters and a major part of First Canadian Army.

Even though General Crerar had arrived in France on June 18 and set up a small tactical headquarters, his 3rd Division remained, for the time being, under the operational control of Second British Army. So, too, did the headquarters of II Canadian Corps, under General Simonds, and the whole of Major-General Charles Foulkes' 2nd Division (including the veterans of Dieppe), which began to move to France on July 7 and first entered the line on the 11th.

If the Germans had been able to employ their armoured divisions *en masse* against this solid but shallow lodgement, they might well have cut their way through to the coast and then destroyed the Allied armies piecemeal. Although Montgomery enjoyed an overall superiority of five or seven to one, he could never have manoeuvred his troops or deployed reinforcements quickly and effectively in such a press. Time after time, however, German tank concentrations were broken up by the dreaded *Jabos* before they could be launched against the Allies.

Montgomery pushed forward at a snail's pace, trying to do with mass what he could not do by manoeuvre. Eventually heavy bombers based in England were brought in to supplement the immense weight of artillery, armour, and infantry in Normandy. On July 9 the British and Canadians finally took Caen, the hinge of the whole bridgehead.

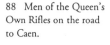

88 Men of the Queen's Own Rifles on the road to Caen.

The Americans had started to chew their way through the *bocage* in the western sector. To stop them, the enemy began reinforcing that part of his front with some of the armour that had previously been deployed against the British and Canadians in the east. Montgomery's strategy now called for holding the weight of German forces around Caen, so that the Americans, on the other flank, could break out to the south and then sweep round to take the enemy in the rear. Pressure must therefore be maintained on the Germans in the vicinity of Caen, and to that end a series of attacks were launched in mid-July that gained little ground but cost Montgomery's forces dearly. The Canadians – who had lost 1,194 men in two days while taking Caen – lost another 1,965 in four days' fighting, between July 18 and 22.

Nevertheless, this intense pressure all along the front was weakening the Germans. On July 20 *Generalfeldmarschall* Gunther von Kluge, who had just succeeded Gerd von Rundstedt as the German commander-in-chief in the west, predicted that "the moment is fast approaching when this over-taxed front line is bound to break up," and events were soon to prove him right. Five days later, co-ordinated attacks were begun all along the front by Americans, Canadians, and British, as a week-long battle of attrition began, with HQ First Canadian Army easing slowly into a command role: it took under command I British Corps on July 23 and II Canadian Corps on July 31.

By the end of the month the Americans had taken Avranches, the springboard for their intended breakout into open country, and, on August 1, their Third Army, under the dynamic Patton, began its dramatic exploitation of the hole that was opening up on the extreme left flank of the German front. Von Kluge's worst fears were about to be realized.

After driving thirty miles south from Avranches, Patton swung eastwards, enveloping the German Seventh Army and part of *Panzergruppe West* in what would subsequently become known as the Falaise pocket. The mouth of this pocket initially stretched from Verrières in the north to Argentan in the south, with the ancient Norman stronghold of Falaise roughly in the centre. The boundary between British and Americans had been set just north of Argentan, so that the Americans were forbidden to push north, and the troops best sited to close the pocket from the northern side were those of II Canadian Corps.

The whole of the Canadian combat force in northwest Europe was in Normandy by this time, Major-General George Kitching's 4th Armoured Division having begun to move to France in mid-July. A subaltern of the British Columbia Regiment, in that division's 4th Armoured Brigade, wrote on July 29:

> Here I am a veteran of two days and though I have not seen any action I have had the opportunity to see most of the battlefields that the Canadians have fought in. I have seen

89 Canadian armour moves up to the 'start line' for Operation *Totalize*. The tank in the foreground is equipped with a 'Flail' – chains fastened to a revolving drum in order to explode anti-tank mines before the tank can be disabled by them. Another flail tank can be seen immediately behind the jeep.

towns in utter ruin where not a building is standing; I have seen trenches abandoned by the enemy in their hasty withdrawal inland; trenches, dug-outs and fox holes littered with equipment ... and big stuff like knocked-out tanks with their dead crews still in them; machine guns and artillery with shells still in the breach and indicating the crew were killed before they could fire.[11]

On July 31, 1944, the 4th Division entered the line as part of Simonds' II Canadian Corps, in turn now a part of Crerar's First Canadian Army – which was, however, less than half Canadian in its total content, because, as well as I British Corps, the Polish Armoured Division had also been placed under Canadian command. On the evening of August 3, Montgomery instructed Crerar to "break through the enemy positions to the south and south-east of Caen" as soon as possible.

It could not have been an unexpected assignment because planning was already well in hand. Operation *Totalize* – the Canadians' biggest operation to date – was launched within four days. The first phase was keyed to a preliminary bombardment by a thousand heavy bombers of the RAF and a night attack by the 2nd Armoured Brigade and the 2nd Infantry Division, whose infantry were mounted on improvised armoured personnel carriers (soon to be known as 'Kangaroos' since each carried ten men in its 'pouch') – an innovation designed to add speed and weight to the assault.

Operation Overlord

Initially things went well enough. The first of two major defensive lines was overrun, even though the darkness brought some confusion and several units lost direction and strayed from their proper axes of advance. Soon after first light, the Canadians had pushed four miles down the road towards Falaise and the 4th Canadian and 1st Polish Armoured Divisions were marshalling their forces for a second phase that would carry them right through the German defences, with the 3rd Canadian Infantry Division moving up to support them.

The second phase of the attack was scheduled for the early afternoon of August 8, and was to be preceded by an hour and a half of 'carpet' bombing by the U.S. Eighth Air Force. Most of the fifteen hundred tons of bombs landed in the right places, but in the cold jargon of their official history, "in one case faulty identification of the target by the lead bombardier led him to drop near Caen.... In the second instance a badly hit lead bomber salvoed short and the rest of the formation followed in regular routine."

These bombing errors inflicted more than three hundred casualties on the Poles and Canadians, and the 3rd Division's Major-General Keller was wounded and had to be evacuated. Keller had been showing signs of stress since the earliest days of the landing, and Montgomery had been cautiously seeking a way to remove him without upsetting Canadian sensibilities: now the USAAF had, all unwittingly, smoothed his path. However, probably nothing hurts morale more than losses inflicted by one's own side, and the unexpected loss of a commander – even a desperately overstressed commander – inevitably upsets command and control arrangements. In the ensuing depression and confusion the pace of the advance was unexpectedly slow and by dusk the Canadians had pushed forward only another two miles. Momentum was entirely lost and the Germans were enabled to bolster their defences as the armoured units laagered where they were, or even withdrew to more secure defensive positions, harbouring in the manner to which they had all become accustomed during years of training in England. Two squadrons of the Canadian Grenadier Guards, for instance, fell back more than a mile to find themselves a suitable berth for the night. The next morning German resistance was predictably stiffer.

Moreover, during the day poor navigation and careless map reading had brought the virtual destruction of one Canadian battle group. Swinging left from their proper axis of advance, two squadrons of the 28th (British Columbia) Armoured Regiment – going into action for the first time – and two companies of the Algonquin Regiment ended up on a patch of high ground on the wrong side of the Falaise road and some 6,500 yards northeast of their true objective.

They then reported their believed position by radio to their brigade headquarters, but, by an error in transmission, the map reference figures were transposed from 0946 – where they should have been but were not – to 0964, a position several miles to the rear of

Operation Overlord

both their actual and believed positions. Through the night they waited patiently for reinforcements that, in the circumstances, could never come; and early the next morning they were discovered by an SS *Panzergruppe*.

Throughout that day they were subjected to an intermittent but devastating fire. Eight tanks finally escaped and a number of wounded were taken out in half-tracks; at dusk those survivors who could made their way back on foot to the Polish lines. The British Columbians had lost forty-seven tanks and over a hundred men in their first days' fighting, while the Algonquins incurred about 50 per cent casualties.

"Such losses would have been deeply regrettable even had they been the price of success," wrote C.P. Stacey in his official history of the campaign. "Unfortunately they were suffered in the course of a tactical reverse which did much to prevent us from seizing a strategical opportunity of the first magnitude." But perhaps the best epitaph on the many contradictions of *Totalize* came from the pen of a North Shore officer who was there. "Fighting heavy," he noted in his diary for August 8. "Bumped into quite a hornet's nest. Large signs up: 'It is a Court Martial Offence to Dig Potatoes in the Fields and Gardens.'"[12]

General Simonds promptly ordered another attempt to close the gap, calling it Operation *Tractable*. (It was *Tractable* to the planners and staff, but to the troops who participated it would ever afterwards be known as "the mad charge.") This was to be a daylight version of the first phase of *Totalize*, hooking slightly to the left, with smoke providing the cover that darkness had given to the latter.

Because an officer carrying a copy of the plan accidentally drove into their lines (where he was killed) the night before the attack, the Germans not only expected it but also knew precisely how it would develop and adjusted their defences accordingly. In the event, this knowledge did them little good, however, for their numbers were growing less with each Canadian attack and the sheer pace of *Tractable* proved too much for them.

On the morning of August 14, much of the 4th Armoured Division – temporarily commanded by Brigadier K.G. Blackader – packed into Kangaroos; behind them, trucks and more trucks carrying men of the 3rd Infantry Division formed up in two dense, close-packed columns. It was a perfect summer morning and the atmosphere on the start line was reminiscent of a small town carnival with men sitting atop their vehicles, whooping, hollering, and waving their helmets at friends and neighbours. Just before noon, the massive columns began to roll forward against the scattered, determined remnants of 12th SS *Panzer*, down to its last thirty tanks and forty or fifty anti-tank guns.

90 Massed tanks of the 4th Canadian Armoured Division line up for Operation *Tractable*.

From time to time the infantry had to leave their vehicles in order to clear the enemy from wooded areas or buildings, but the overall impression – especially among the tank crews – was of a headlong chaotic rush towards Falaise.

> The smokescreen supposed to blind the enemy turned out to be a thick dense mist in the path of our advance, soon supplemented by the dust clouds created by the terrific bombing; the area was 'Vision Zero!' Very little could be done to keep direction, except by aiming the tank 'at the sun.' Speed, nothing but speed, and on we went, crashing through obstacles at 20 to 25 m.p.h., very rough inside a tank going across country.... We just barged ahead, some of the tanks appeared to be going on at crazy angles, and in the confusion I did not know who was right and who was wrong, I just kept charging 'at the sun,' blasting everything large enough to hide a field gun, and taking a terrible whipping in the turret of the bucking 32-ton monster.[13]

Close behind them came the infantry in their Kangaroos and trucks (Troop Carrying Vehicles, or TCVs).

> As the speed of the movement increased, a cloud of dust rose that outdid the efforts of the artillery's smokescreen. The parade-ground formation was broken and a careening mass of vehicles herded southwards cross-country, completely dis-

Operation Overlord

regarding roads, ditches, fences, or any other obstacle except hedges. Each time the vehicles approached a hedge, they pressed together to pass through the narrow gaps made earlier by the tanks. Many a TCV driver's heart was in his mouth as he competed with half-tracks, anti-tank guns, tanks and flails to reach the opening before his neighbour.[14]

Again, many heavy bombers, this time of both the British and American air forces, were attacking German defences in the path of *Tractable*, but a number of aircraft of Bomber Command, including some from No. 6 (RCAF) Group, had failed to time their runs from the coast accurately and bombed short. "In the direction from which the column had come was a huge air fleet systematically bombing our own troops in the rear areas, causing nearly 400 casualties and the usual confusion and depression among the survivors."

General Crerar, noting that far more bombs had fallen on the enemy than on Canadians, reported that the bombing "contributed greatly to the great success" of the attack. Much of its momentum was lost, however, as the tanks reached a small stream, only some six or eight feet across but with four-foot-high wooded banks in many places that effectively stopped the rush. The tanks had to spread out in order to find places where they could cross, and the enemy had concentrated his anti-tank guns to cover those spots. Consequently, the rate of progress slowed down considerably as the afternoon wore on, although by nightfall the Canadians had broken the German line and taken nearly 1,300 prisoners in an advance of some five miles. Nevertheless, they were still some way from closing the Falaise pocket.

There was bitter fighting in Falaise itself, and the fall of the town, two days later, deprived the Germans of their best line of retreat from the pocket, but they still held one main road running east from Trun and a number of secondary routes. Along these roads the Germans were now escaping from the pocket in great numbers as the Allied tactical air forces gave their main attention to targets further east, including the crossings of the Risle and Seine rivers. On August 18 the bulk of the German forces were reported on the east bank of the Orne River, already more than halfway out of the pocket. However, under the pressure of events the Germans were compelled to readopt a pol-

91 Racing across a partly harvested grain-field, each vehicle in Operation *Tractable* raised its own small cloud of dust, which soon contributed to one vast fog of battle. In the foreground are 6-pounder anti-tank guns of the 3rd Canadian Anti-Tank Regiment; behind them are some of the new 'Kangaroos' – the first armoured personnel carriers.

92 Perhaps the most famous Canadian war picture: Major D.V. Currie at St-Lambert-sur-Dives supervising the collection of German prisoners. When this picture was taken, Currie (on the left, with a pistol in his hand) had been fighting for three days to close and hold closed the German escape route from Falaise. No other VC winner has been photographed so soon after the events that won him his cross.

icy they had abandoned in the first few days of the invasion: large-scale road movement in daylight.

The fighter-bombers fell upon them like wolves upon sheep. The 2nd (British) Tactical Air Force alone claimed 124 tanks destroyed and 96 damaged and nearly 3,000 transport vehicles destroyed or damaged. On August 19, 52 tanks were destroyed, 92 damaged, and 1,500 other vehicles destroyed or damaged. One squadron among many – the RCAF's 439 Squadron, which was flying Typhoons – recorded that "any pilot engaged in attacking the 3000 M[otorized] E[nemy] T[ransport] in the area was more in danger from air collision than from enemy resistance. The congestion necessitated the maintenance of a left hand circuit.... A grand harvest was reaped by the squadron."[15] But that night the weather worsened and low-level operations became too restricted to have a large-scale effect.

The pocket was loosely closed at Chambois on August 19. A mile to the northwest, at St-Lambert-sur-Dives, Major D.V. Currie, with a squadron of the 29th Armoured (South Alberta) Regiment and three companies of infantry, was blocking a German attempt to break out towards Camembert, on the other side of the finely wrought Canadian block. Currie and his men held back many times their own number of Germans for the best part of three days before they were relieved.

Operation Overlord

Currie's personal gallantry in this action brought him the first Canadian VC of the northwest Europe campaign. Despite his efforts, however, a desperate German assault briefly re-opened a corridor to the east on the 20th, and some 40 per cent of the encircled enemy scrambled out of the pocket. The scene they left behind was one to awe the most combat-hardened veterans. "The road, as were all the roads in the area, was lined and in places blocked by destroyed German vehicles of every description. Horses and men lay rotting in every ditch and hedge and the air was rank with the odour of putrefaction."[16] But even though their material losses were enormous and their organization shattered, the Germans had got the bulk of their fighting forces out before the pocket was firmly sealed.

Since June they had lost some 400,000 men, 1,300 tanks, 500 assault guns, 1,500 field guns, and 20,000 vehicles. The Allies had lost 206,000 men altogether – 124,000 Americans, 64,000 British, and 18,500 Canadians – of whom nearly a third had been killed. The 3rd Canadian Division had suffered more casualties than any other division in 21st Army Group and the 2nd Canadian Division was next – regrettable distinctions that reflected their commanders' limitations as well as the courage and tenacity of Canadians in battle.

CHAPTER 8

The War in the Air

In spite of the moderate expansion program begun in 1936, as war clouds gathered over Europe, the Royal Canadian Air Force could accommodate very few of the hundreds of young men who saw in themselves the successors of the Canadian aces of the preceding generation. They crossed the Atlantic to join the British Royal Air Force in such numbers that by the fall of 1939 there were far more Canadians flying with the RAF than with the RCAF. The ranks of Fighter Command soon contained so many that the British, at Ottawa's request, obligingly formed an 'all-Canadian' fighter squadron from a small proportion of them.

By the end of November, No. 242 (Canadian) Squadron RAF, equipped with Hawker Hurricanes, mustered twenty-one Canadian pilots and nearly two hundred British ground staff under the command of Squadron Leader F.M. Gobeil, an RCAF officer who had been on an exchange posting with the RAF when war broke out. In April 1940, orders were issued for it to join the Air Component of the British Expeditionary Force in France, but the move had to be postponed owing to the German attack on Scandinavia. When the blitzkrieg subsequently struck France in May, the squadron was still stationed in Yorkshire.

By then, the RAF units in France were providing air cover for the British ground forces as well as vainly attempting to slow the German advance by destroying key bridges behind the *Panzer* spearheads. Their losses were heavy and in the last two weeks of May, as the better led and equipped *Luftwaffe* mauled Allied air and ground forces, a number of pilots from squadrons in England, including some from No. 242, were detached to reinforce Hurricane squadrons already in France. Some went to No. 85 Squadron, where another Canadian, Flying Officer A.B. Angus, had already been credited with five victories and awarded a Distinguished Flying Cross before being killed in action. Others were split between Nos 607 and 615 Squadrons, and it was while serving with the latter that Pilot Officer W.L. McKnight claimed No. 242's first victory on May 19; this initiated a personal score that totalled $16^1/2$ before his death in January 1941, during one of the early fighter sweeps over occupied France. In eleven days in May, Flight Lieutenant M.H. Brown, a Manitoban serving in No. 1 Squadron RAF, registered $8^1/2$ victories. Brown was credited with the fourth-highest Canadian score of the war – 18 – before he was killed over Sicily in November 1941.

As the Germans closed in on Dunkirk, the balance of No. 242 Squadron, still based in England, moved south to Biggin Hill in Kent

93 Hurricanes of No. 242 Squadron RAF, the 'all-Canadian' Squadron, turn for home at the end of a patrol over northern France.

and began flying patrols across the Channel to protect the evacuation of the BEF. On May 23, Fowler Gobeil became the first RCAF pilot (as opposed to Canadians in the RAF) ever to meet an enemy in aerial combat. A Messerschmitt (Me) 109 smartly evaded him, but two days later an Me 110 was less fortunate and Gobeil claimed the RCAF's first victory.

After the evacuation of the bulk of the British Expeditionary Force from Dunkirk, there were still the best part of three British divisions in western France, together with three RAF fighter squadrons. Two more squadrons, Nos 17 and a reunited 242, were despatched from England on June 8, to provide additional air cover. Their task, of course, was hopeless. Ten days later, they flew back to England, having lost one more pilot and claiming at least six victories. Once the fighting had begun, however, replacements were rarely Canadian. After its return to Britain, the remainder of the squadron rapidly became anglicized, and when the legendary, legless British ace, Douglas Bader, took command from Gobeil at the end of June, No. 242's last link with anything formally Canadian was cut.[1]

After the fall of France, Britain's position seemed perilous indeed. Now the Germans held air bases along the entire Continental semicircle to the south and east that stretched for 1,300 miles from Brest to Bergen. Stopping enemy bombers in the Battle of Britain, which

The War in the Air

94 Twenty years of peace had brought an unacceptable rigidity to the tactical formations and combat theory of Fighter Command. Tactics had needed to be more flexible in the light of experience against the *Luftwaffe*. Here, pilots of No. 1 Squadron RCAF discuss a new tactic in October 1940. Flying Officer W.C. Connell (left) survived two operational tours and left the air force in 1946; Flying Officer Ken Boomer (centre) became a squadron leader before being killed in action in October 1944 during his third operational tour; and Flight Lieutenant Ed 'Pappy' Reyno (right) went on to become vice chief of the Defence Staff and deputy commander-in-chief of the North American Defence Command (NORAD). General Reyno retired in 1972.

The War in the Air

lasted from July to October, was going to require every man and machine that could be found – even with the aid of radar (it was originally called Radio Direction Finding, or RDF) and the sophisticated, ground-based fighter control that the RAF had developed.

Two RCAF squadrons were already at hand, but only one of them was equipped and trained for air-to-air combat. No. 110 Squadron had arrived in England during February 1940 and begun specialized training in army co-operation duties with the intention of accompanying the 1st Canadian Division to France. Its pilots were not trained in fighter tactics and, even if they had been, its Westland Lysanders – two-seater observation machines, lightly armed, with a top speed of 220 mph – were totally unsuited to the role. No. 1 (later 401) Squadron, on the other hand, was equipped with a modern, eight-gun fighter, the Hawker Hurricane.

No. 1, still lacking operational training, had been sent overseas in June 1940 under the command of Squadron Leader E.A. McNab. On August 24, its first day of operations, it shot down two RAF Bristol Blenheims, mistaking them for enemy bombers, and severely damaged a third. That kind of accident was not an uncommon occurrence among neophyte aircrew, but McNab understandably called it "the lowest point of my life."

Two days later, however, the squadron became the first RCAF unit to meet an enemy in battle when its Hurricanes encountered a formation of Dornier 215s, shot down three of them, and damaged four more. The first fell to McNab, who was subsequently forced down unhurt by damage resulting from his victim's return fire. Flying Officer R.L. Edwards was not so lucky. He destroyed a Dornier but was hit by his opponent, driven into an uncontrollable spin, and killed in the ensuing crash. The third victory was credited to Flight Lieutenant G.R. McGregor.

One pilot for three was a barely satisfactory ratio of losses in the cold logic of the Battle of Britain, but in fact the Canadians had been lucky, for they were still novices in combat. The next time they saw action, on the last day of August, their inexperience cost them dearly. While patrolling the Dover coast at 22,000 feet they were attacked out of the sun by high-flying Messerschmitts and three of them were shot down without loss to the enemy. Thus they learned painfully and expensively the truth of the old First World War adage: 'Beware of the Hun in the sun!'

The Battle of Britain was building to its climax. On September 15 the British exultantly claimed a total of 185 German aircraft shot down, with the loss of only 27 British machines and 11 pilots. Another 11 pilots, wounded or injured in crash landings, would live to fight again. Post-war research has settled on a figure of 60 German aircraft actually brought down; but the *Luftwaffe* had lost twice as many planes and nearly five times as many pilots as the RAF.

95 The first class of observers graduated by the BCATP journeyed from their Canadian training school to bomber squadrons of the RAF in the U.K. in November 1940. One year later half the men in this picture were dead and several of the rest were prisoners of war.

In fact, over the course of the whole battle Allied losses were slightly more than half of the German total, although no one knew that at the time and it was believed that the disparity was much greater. The claims of the Canadian squadron were more conservative (and more realistic) than those of many others during that crucial month: in the eight weeks following August 26 it was credited with destroying thirty enemy aircraft, the probable destruction of eight, and the damaging of as many as thirty-five more.

The Hurricane was not really a match for the Me 109, however, and while Hurricanes accounted for the majority of enemy machines shot down, most of their successes were achieved against bombers while the technically superior Spitfires concentrated on attacking the bombers' fighter escorts. The Canadians played their part as best they could. McGregor and his fellow flight commander, B.D. Russel, in particular, had begun to build themselves solid reputations. Otherwise the record of the squadron was unremarkable until September 27.

On that day the *Luftwaffe's* last major daylight attack was launched and the Poles of No. 303 Squadron RAF and the Canadians attacked the first wave of enemy bombers together. Flight Lieutenant John Kent, a Canadian in the British service who was leading the Polish squadron, remembered how

we saw the hordes of German bombers and escorting fighters coming in.... As the RAF fighters got stuck into them, we could see them falling away, plunging down with smoke pouring from them. It almost seemed that there was an

The War in the Air

96 RCAF ground crew in England lived in Nissen huts made from corrugated iron sheets fastened to a semi-circular wooden frame and heated by a small stove (centre foreground). The airman laying his shirts to dry behind the stove wears a T-shirt that originated with the Central Navigation School at Rivers, Man.

invisible barrier over a certain point and that as soon as the bombers reached it large numbers of them suddenly began pouring smoke and going down.[2]

That day, thirteen RCAF pilots flew twenty-six sorties, during which they claimed seven enemy aircraft destroyed, one probably destroyed, and another seven damaged.

No. 1 Squadron was still to see some hard fighting before it was withdrawn to Scotland for rest and retraining late in October, but after September 27 there was a noticeable reduction in the weight of enemy air attack. The *Luftwaffe* could not beat the British fighters from the skies and gain the air superiority that would be necessary to cover the landing and re-supply of an invasion force. Nor was there much future in trying to cripple British war industry in the face of an improving air defence which, by now, could shoot down one in ten enemy aircraft that appeared over England during daylight.

By mid-November, day attacks had virtually ceased and the enemy had turned to night raiding, focussing at first on the London and Liverpool docks. Against this type of action, Fighter Command was relatively ineffective. Ground-based radar could not guide night fighters on to the enemy with the pin-point precision needed if the fighter crews were to pick up their targets visually: airborne radar was still too undeveloped for aircraft to 'home' on the enemy with any degree of consistency, even when ground radar brought British planes within two or three miles of a potential victim. However, the *Luftwaffe* was also unable to locate targets precisely at night and its policy of aimed bombing – the only practicable one for the limited force of light and medium bombers, which were all the Germans had – soon degenerated into a sporadic and necessarily indiscriminate campaign that caused very little concern when measured against the totality of British

The War in the Air

industrial or moral resources. London, Coventry, Liverpool, Manchester, Plymouth, and Glasgow were all raided heavily during the winter, but with the coming of shorter summer nights in 1941 these attacks tailed off. London, hit by some seven hundred bombers on the night of April 19-20, 1941, was not assailed seriously again until the coming of the V-1 'flying bombs' in the summer of 1944.

With the airspace over the United Kingdom secured by day, Fighter Command turned to an offensive of its own by "leaning forward into France" in early 1941 – an approach that cost it dearly throughout that year and much of 1942. In many ways, this campaign was the mirror image of the Battle of Britain. Although Fighter Command had an enormous advantage in numbers, early on it became clear that its 'sweeps,' 'circuses,' or 'ramrods' were no match for the *Jagdfliegern* when the latter could fight on their own terms. Often they declined to fight (since the aggressors proved unable to do significant damage to anything on the ground) but, when they did choose to do so, casualty ratios were consistently in the region of four to one in favour of the enemy – and this time, it was the German pilots who could parachute to safety, surviving to fight another day.[3]

Meanwhile, another enemy offensive had been growing in intensity. In March 1941 the *Luftwaffe* had moved into Sicily and North Africa to support General Erwin Rommel's *Afrikan Korps'* initial drive over the Egyptian border; in April Hitler pushed his troops into the Balkans; in May Crete fell. By June, only the island fortress of Malta, partially blocking the enemy's supply routes to North Africa with its aircraft and submarines, kept the central Mediterranean from becoming an Axis lake. In the course of the air battles that preceded and accompanied these operations, four more Canadian airmen in the RAF played notable parts.

Flying a Gloster Gladiator (the RAF's last operational biplane fighter), Flight Lieutenant Vernon Woodward – "the imperturbable Woody" – had been credited with eleven Italian aircraft destroyed in the Western Desert before moving to Greece. Switching to a Hurricane, he claimed three more Italian and six German planes there, and then – back in the desert – brought his total score up to twenty-two, a record that made him by September 1941 the second-highest scoring Canadian fighter pilot of the war.

Pilot Officer R.W. McNair, who had already claimed one Me 109 and damaged another while flying with the RCAF's No. 411 Squadron in England, arrived on Malta in March 1942. In his subsequent three-month tour, he claimed nine enemy aircraft. (Later he went on to command 126 [Canadian] Wing of the RAF's Second Tactical Air Force in 1944, and to become the sixth-highest scoring Canadian, credited with sixteen victories.) His time in Malta overlapped with that of H.W. McLeod, who arrived in May and was credited with twelve 'kills' during his tour. McLeod became the highest-scoring RCAF pilot of all, with twenty-one victories before being killed

The War in the Air

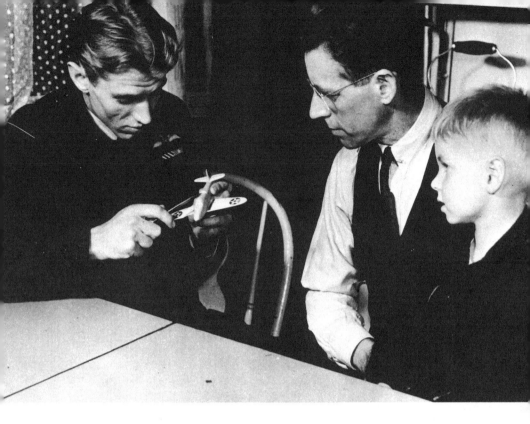

97 "All over North America kids by the tens of thousands are whittling flying models," wrote Flying Officer George Beurling, DSO, DFC, DFM, and Bar, in his autobiography, *Malta Spitfire*. While recuperating from the wound that ended his tour on Malta in October 1942, Beurling gives his youngest brother a few whittling tips.

in a dogfight over Holland on 27 September 1944, by which time he had reached the rank of squadron leader and been awarded the DSO and DFC and Bar.

However, the exploits of Woodward, McNair, and McLeod have been largely overshadowed by those of a moody, solitary, cantankerous prodigy from Verdun, Quebec, George Frederick Beurling. Learning to fly at sixteen, Beurling had tried to join the pre-war RCAF but was rejected because he lacked the necessary educational requirements. Going to England at his own expense, he was accepted by the British in September 1940, but his early career in the RAF was stormy. Long-range sweeps over France by large, tightly disciplined formations were just coming into vogue when Beurling embarked on his operational flying career, and that was a style of fighting that he either could not, or would not, adapt to. Often to the anger of his superiors, not to mention his fellow flyers, he would break away to chase the enemy on his own.

Although this approach brought him his first two victories, it did nothing to endear him to his fellow pilots in an era when the subordination of self and emphasis on close team work were becoming the accepted essentials of air combat. Beurling spent more and more time alone, training his eyes to scan the sky with unerring acuity, developing his reflexes, and working out his theories of deflection shooting. He was only an adequate pilot, but nothing escaped his roving eyes

The War in the Air

and his gunnery was 'unbelievable,' according to his squadron gunnery officer.

In May 1942 Beurling got himself posted to Malta. Flying off an aircraft carrier in a Spitfire, at the very limit of its range, he arrived on the island with other reinforcements in early June. His new colleagues found him an odd, uncouth character. One of his pastimes was to throw morsels of meat on the ground, wait until they were covered with flies, and then stamp both meat and flies into the earth with the reflex epithet, "Goddamn screwballs!", which he applied to anything or anybody that irritated him (there were many of both) and which soon gave him his squadron sobriquet of 'Screwball' Beurling.

Three and half weeks passed before he registered his first victory over Malta, but then his score began to mount with fantastic speed. By July 14, when he was slightly wounded, he had claimed seven enemy machines; by October 14, when he was wounded again – more seriously, this time – and shot down into the sea, Beurling had twenty-nine 'kills' to his credit and had become the top-scoring Canadian of the war, collecting a commission he never wanted and four gallantry awards in the process. When he was posted back to Canada, as part of a public relations campaign to increase war production, he found himself a national hero. To the media and the public at least, he was now Flying Officer 'Buzz' Beurling – 'Buzz' sounded so much better than 'Screwball,' thought the PR experts.

Beurling transferred to the RCAF, which made no more fuss about his lack of educational qualifications. With the rank of flight lieutenant he returned to England and joined No. 403 Squadron RCAF, but he scored only two more victories before being taken off operations, perhaps because it was felt that he would continue to take chances until he was killed and the morale of lesser men would surely suffer if that should happen. His propaganda value as a war hero was now more important than his skill as a fighter pilot. His British wing commander, 'Johnnie' Johnson, reported the following conversation.

> "You know anything about this Mustang, Wingco?"
>
> "Not much," I said. "I hear one of the 83 Group wings is going to get them and they have a tremendous radius of action. I hear they can easily fly to Berlin and back."
>
> "Can they now?" exclaimed the Canadian. I could read his thoughts. Give him a long-range Mustang, fill it up with petrol each day and he'd either get himself killed or would finish up with more Huns than the rest of us put together.[4]

Beurling was finally taken off operations in January 1944. There were complaints that he went about the base throwing his hat in the air and shooting at it with his service revolver – one way of analysing and practising the principles of deflection shooting. Then there were threats of a court martial for low flying over station headquarters during a senior officers' conference. In May 1945, he was posted back to Canada, and in August he was released from the RCAF at his own request. After the war, lost and lonely in a world without air combat – "It's the only thing I can do well; it's the only thing I ever did [that] I really liked" – he joined the fledgling Israeli air force. But he saw no more of what he really liked. On May 20, 1948, he was killed in a crash near Rome while ferrying an aircraft to Israel.

By October 1942 British attempts at a strategic air offensive had been under way for almost three years, and for the first two of them it had been even less successful than the brief German offensive of 1940-41. The RAF efforts had begun in the winter of 1939-40 with four comparatively small-scale daylight raids – never more than fifty twin-engined aircraft – against the German fleet and naval bases. They resulted in virtually no damage to the enemy, while the attackers incurred losses of up to 50 per cent – a totally unacceptable figure. The failure of this day-bombing concept, with all its concurrent implications of precision strikes on factories and military facilities, had led the RAF – like the *Luftwaffe* – to adopt a desultory, capricious, and often wasteful technique of ill-coordinated night attacks. A Canadian pilot who participated in some of them recalls that

> during the one month [August 1941] we advanced from the junior crew [on the squadron] to the most senior.... I think one crew completed their tour and the rest were shot down.... Most of the time we were flying with no moon and it was difficult or impossible to recognize cities.... In those early days we could follow our own schedule and we would cross the Dutch coast after dark and try to cross back before daylight. That was the only restriction we had. We were given our target, we could pick our own route in.[5]

These raids did little significant damage. In mid-1941 the introduction of cameras linked to the bomb-release mechanism revealed that only one in five crews bombed within five miles of the assigned aiming point. Over the Ruhr, the most important target area but also the most smog-ridden, the ratio dropped to one in ten. Bomb loads were small, their high-explosive content was low, and a large proportion of them failed to explode at all.

Since the Canadian government had failed to arrange with the British for the creation of sufficient RCAF squadrons overseas – the result of having an air minister who was a charming drunk, and a chief of air staff who was also a jovial drinker and an undiscriminating anglophile to boot – many more Canadian aircrew were now being posted to RAF units. Meanwhile, the weight of the air war fell more and more heavily on Bomber Command. Though Canadians serving in it during 1939-40 had probably been outnumbered by their compatriots in the more glamorous Fighter Command, that

98 'Bombing up' a Halifax at an RCAF base in Yorkshire. The 4,000-pound 'canister' bomb of high explosive is accompanied by racks of small incendiaries – a typical bomb load once the policy of area bombing had been established.

ratio was soon reversed. The Canadian content of Bomber Command's RAF squadrons rose to more than a fifth of its total strength in 1944.

When the RCAF formed its first operational bombing squadron, No. 405, in early June 1941, the initial crews were drawn entirely from Canadians in the RAF. They were led by Wing Commander Pat Gilchrist, who had joined the RAF in 1935, completed an operational tour, and been awarded a DSO before he took over the command. The first operational flight of an RCAF bomber came on June 12, at 11:16 pm, when a twin-engined Vickers Wellington – the first of four, one of which returned early – rolled down an English runway. The next morning the three crews that completed their missions claimed to have dropped $4\frac{1}{2}$ tons of high explosive and another ton of incendiaries on railway marshalling yards at Schwerte, near Dortmund, "though results were difficult to assess owing to ground haze."

In the light of later findings regarding bombing accuracy, it seems statistically unlikely that they actually bombed Schwerte. However, by the end of the month thirty sorties had been flown for the loss of one aircraft and its crew. In July the number of sorties more than doubled – to seventy-nine, of which sixty-seven were considered 'successful' – for the loss of six aircraft.

One of the missing machines was Gilchrist's. Shot down over France, he parachuted to safety, evaded the Germans, returned to

189   *The War in the Air*

England *via* Switzerland, and then commanded RAF Coastal Command squadrons before transferring to the RCAF in 1945. He was promptly succeeded as squadron commander by another Canadian in the RAF, R.M. Fenwick-Williams. Not until February 1942, when John Fauquier took over the squadron, was an RCAF officer considered sufficiently experienced to be given command.

By the end of 1941, three additional RCAF bomber squadrons had been formed, each commanded by a Canadian from the RAF but with the majority of their personnel drawn from the RCAF. In 1942, which saw the formation of seven more Canadian squadrons, Bomber Command introduced four-engined 'heavies' capable of lifting bomb loads of up to ten tons each, the intricate concentration of the first 'thousand raid' on Cologne, an electronic navigation system called Gee; and élite Pathfinder crews to mark the target.

In the spring of 1942, when Bomber Command was assigned an innovative, single-minded commander, Sir Arthur Harris, who was dogmatically devoted to the idea of the 'strategic' bomber as a war-winning instrument, the tempo of bombing operations was stepped up and the objective of all this effort was clarified. Since it had proven impossible to hit precise targets, such as factories or power stations, at night, the aim would be to break German morale. What was euphemistically called 'area bombing' was formally approved, and the usual aiming points would be residential areas.

The proportion of high explosive used went down and that of incendiary materials went up, as Harris, with the enthusiastic backing of the chief of Air Staff, Sir Charles Portal, and of Prime Minister Winston Churchill, set about trying to raze German cities to the ground. Bombers were usually being loaded with one 4,000-pound, 'high capacity,' high-explosive bomb – a thin-skinned, drum-type canister, lacking any aerodynamic qualities, that simply tumbled through the air, since the precise location of the subsequent explosion was no longer important – and a mass of small incendiary bombs. The blast from the 4,000-pounder blew in doors, windows, and roofs over a wide area, creating effective drafts for the rain of incendiaries that accompanied and followed it.

Perhaps the point should be made here that although the Canadian government, the RCAF, and public opinion in Canada accepted the propriety of this 'terror bombing' (both Hitler's and Churchill's phrase for it), it was the British government and the RAF's air staff that were ultimately responsible. The latter formulated it and the former authorized it.

In 1941 everyone knew that the damage done to Germany had been negligible. A year later, it was estimated that 3 per cent of the built-up areas attacked had been devastated, and by the end of 1943, the estimate had risen to a highly optimistic 38 per cent. By December 1944 the claimed figure was 42 per cent. At the time this seemed a major contribution towards winning the war. One school of thought even held that bombing alone could bring victory, but hindsight tells us that British politicians and service chiefs consistently overestimated both the moral and economic damage inflicted. Germany's industrial production continued to rise more or less steadily until late 1944, when American precision daylight bombing (made practicable by the introduction of long-range fighter escorts) started it plunging irrevocably downwards.

John Fauquier dropped the first 4,000-pounder to be delivered by the Canadians, on Bremen, in January 1942, and "saw it burst with terrific results in the middle of town." Four nights later he and Fenwick-Williams each dropped another on the same target with very similar results. But the bomber offensive was still far from one-sided. Many crews never made the return trip at all, and among those that did there were many more that paid a heavy price. In the words of one combat report:

> Five bursts of cannon fire hit the plane. The pilot managed to evade the attackers and at 6,000 ft with the starboard engine coughing called on the crew to bale out but got no reply from them. He decided to try and carry on to base ... and arriving over England ... crash-landed. All the crew were found to be on board, though wounded. Sgt. (pilot) Farrow had a slight wound in the ankle.... Sgt. Millward had a cannon shell wound in the leg but it is hoped that it will not be necessary to amputate. Sgt. May and Sgt. Baker were so badly wounded that they died within 48 hours.[6]

Among one group of about fifty navigators who trained together in the early days of the BCATP, only five completed a first tour (usually thirty missions over Germany). Ten were shot down and became prisoners of war. The rest were killed.

The first German city to be virtually destroyed was Lübeck, a small Baltic port that handled the bulk of Red Cross shipments into and out of Germany. A medieval monument, with a tightly knit core of largely wooden houses, it appeared to the air staff an ideal opportunity for testing the new technique of area bombing, particularly since its position on the coast made it comparatively easy to find from the air. In March 1942 the experiment was made by nearly four hundred aircraft. A Canadian rear-gunner counted nearly a hundred major fires burning below as his Halifax turned for home, and the loom of those fires could still be seen when the bombers were seventy-five miles away. The centre of the city was burned out.

This attack resulted in German reprisals. Reinforced by two squadrons of bombers withdrawn from Sicily – an irrational move at the height of the campaign against Malta – a still puny *Luftwaffe* bombing force launched a series of so-called 'Baedeker' raids against Exeter, Bath, Norwich, and York. The first two raids caught the British by surprise, but on the last two the Germans lost heavily as

Fighter Command adjusted its night defences. British airborne radar had improved greatly since the early days and the first RCAF night-fighter squadron, No. 406, had a particularly successful time, destroying three enemy machines and claiming four more damaged.

The Germans had used only twenty-five twin-engined medium bombers for their attack on Exeter. But a month later, mustering every serviceable machine he could cobble together and combing the Operational Training Units for additional aircraft and crews, Harris launched 1,047 aircraft – many of them the new, heavy, four-engined machines – against Cologne and simply swamped German defences. Years later a Canadian pilot recalled the scene over the target that night.

We can see the black bursts of heavy flak, momentarily still, then whipping past the cabin as we leave them behind us at 180 mph. We can smell the cordite; if the burst is very close you can hear it; then it's time to move. For the most part, there is nothing to do amidst all the confusion but to hold Jake's course, grit the teeth, and sweat it out…. There were other aircraft around us as Ole gives me directions until the moment when he shouts, 'Bombs gone!' … As I drop a wing

99   This Lancaster of the RAF's No. 576 Squadron, whose crew included the usual quota of Canadians, staggered home from a raid so badly damaged that the rear turret fell off as the aircraft landed. The tail gunner's fate is not recorded.

to turn away, I get a full view of the target area. Immense fires
are raging now, and bomb flashes are practically incessant.[7]

In ninety minutes nine hundred bombers dropped nearly five hundred tons of high explosives and over a thousand tons of incendiaries
on the city centre. Only 39 aircraft were lost.

Two more 'thousand' raids (on Essen and Bremen) followed in
the next month, but the air staff found on those occasions that poor
weather and the use of so many inexperienced crews from training
units did not produce sufficient devastation to justify the effort
required to organize and launch them. Moreover, too many OTU
crews were lost, due to operational inexperience and the fact that they
were flying 'clapped out' aircraft which had already been relegated
from operational service to training duties. Great comfort was taken,
however, in the widespread enthusiasm for these gigantic raids that
was expressed by the media and the public. Their sponsor and organizer, Sir Arthur Harris, recorded (some time later) that

> [the] aim is the destruction of German cities, the killing of
> German workers and the disruption of civilized community
> life throughout Germany.
>
>   It should be emphasised that the destruction of houses,
> public utilities, transport and lives; the creation of a refugee
> problem on an unprecedented scale; and the breakdown of
> morale both at home and at the battle fronts by fear of

NORTH SEA

NORWAY

SWEDEN

IRELAND

DENMARK

BALTIC SEA

SIX GROUP BASES

ENGLAND

FRISIAN ISLANDS

Kiel

Wilhelmshaven

Hamburg

200 MILES

NETHERLANDS

Sterkrade
Gelsenkirchen
Wanne Eickel
Osnabruck

Munster

Hanover

Berlin

POLAND

English Channel

Calais

Boulogne

BELGIUM

Duisburg

Essen
Bochum

Dusseldorf

Cologne

Hagan

Castrop Rauxel

Dortmund

GERMANY

Elbe

Mons

Caen

Biennais

Chemnitz

Brest

Falaise

L'Isle Adam
(Bois de Cassan)

Mainz

Frankfurt

Lorient

Ludwigshaven

Mannheim

CZECHOSLOVAKIA

400 MILES

Rhine

Stuttgart

Bay of
Biscay

FRANCE

SWITZERLAND

AUSTRIA

HUN

600 MILES

YUGOSLA

**SIX (RCAF) GROUP
& 331 WING OPERATIONS
1939-1945**

ADRIATIC

ITALY

CORSICA

400 MILES

Formia

LEGEND

Bombing sorties over 1000 . . . . . ■

Bombing sorties 500-1000 . . . . . . ●

Bombing sorties 250-500 . . . . ▲

Bombing sorties 100-250
(Mediterranean only) . . . . ·

Mining sorties 350-400 . . . . . . ▦

Mining sorties 200-250 . . . . . . ▨

SARDINIA

Naples

Torre Annunziata

Salerno

Battipaglia

200 MILES

Messina

SICILY

Gerbini

ALGERIA

331 WING
BASES

MEDITERRANEAN
SEA

TUNISIA

The War in the Air

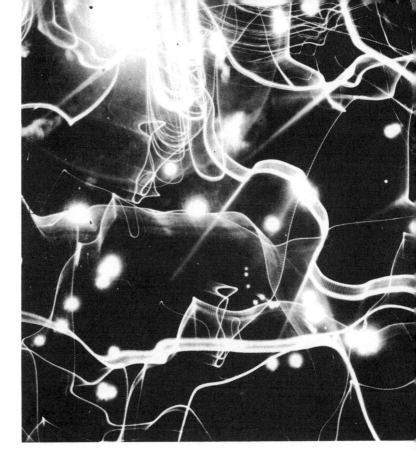

101 A bomb-aimer's view of the target, taken at 18,000 feet over Duisburg in May 1943. The intricate patterns of light are formed by searchlight beams, flak, sky markers, exploding bombs, and the glow of ground fires.

extended and intensified bombing are [the] accepted and intended aims of our bombing policy. They are not by-products of our attempts to hit factories.[8]

In Britain only the Archbishop of Canterbury, the Bishop of Chichester, and a parliamentary back-bencher, Independent Labourite Richard Stokes, among the politically prominent, raised the moral issue. In Canada, there was general approval of 'area bombing,' as it was euphemistically called.

For the rest of that year raids were continued on the old scale of less than five hundred aircraft per strike, but even when the bombing was concentrated, the air offensive did not have the effect it was sup-posed to have. German morale bore up surprisingly well. Meanwhile, Bomber Command's overall loss rate of nearly 4 per cent for 1942 was to be the highest of the air war. Statistically less than a third of every hundred crews could expect to survive a tour of thirty missions, although pilots sometimes flew home machines that should surely have crashed. The official report of a Wellington crew assigned to attack Duisburg in August described one such case.

The War in the Air

Whilst doing his bombing run on the target, this aircraft was attacked by an enemy fighter.... There were three large holes in the elevators, one in the port aileron, one large hole in the port tail fin, one huge rent at the intersection of the tail boom and the fuselage, another large hole in the bottom of the port engine nacelle, the top gunner's cupola was smashed and the magazines shot away from his guns, all port [fuel] tanks were riddled, the hydraulics shot away and the side of the fuselage seamed and scored with bullets.... Following the encounter the pilot attempted another run on the target and successfully unloaded his bombs.[9]

On the way back the port engine stopped and the aircraft staggered home on one engine to make a 'wheels-up' landing off the runway at the nearest English airfield.

Sir Arthur Harris was not to be distracted from his objective. Between February and August 1942, German production increased by 27 per cent for guns, 25 per cent for tanks, and 97 per cent for ammunition, but those figures were not known to the Allies at the time. In the same period, Bomber Command flew 21,000 night sorties, dropped 28,000 tons of bombs, and lost 852 aircraft.

Harris' command now included more than five hundred four-engined machines. By the end of the year, two more electronic navigation systems had been added to the Pathfinder technology – Oboe, a long-range, 'line of sight' navigation aid, and H2S, a radar navigation and target-finding device – together with the first of a whole range of visual target-indicator equipment. Although the tactical contest against German nightfighters and anti-aircraft guns saw first one side and then the other gaining a temporary advantage, the long-term balance was imperceptibly swinging in favour of the Allies by weight of numbers alone. The introduction of the 'bomber stream' (a carefully pre-arranged approach to the target area), the exploitation of diversionary tactics by other aircraft, and an ever-increasing concentration of the raiding force over the target in both time and space, all helped to swamp the defences where closer targets were concerned. But Harris' first attempt to destroy Berlin, a distant target, in the winter of 1942-43 had to be abandoned in the face of unacceptable losses.

Aside from the RCAF squadrons, nearly every Bomber Command crew included at least one Canadian. In the famed No. 617 ('Dambusters') Squadron, for example, there were 29 Canadians among the 133 airmen who flew in the spectacular low-level mission that smashed the Mohne and Eder dams in May 1943. Eighteen months later, when a combined force from Nos 617 and 9 Squadrons crippled the German battleship *Tirpitz* in a Norwegian fiord, 26 of the 195 flyers involved were Canadians.

There were now enough Canadian bomber squadrons in service to justify the formation of a specifically Canadian group. On January 1, 1943, No. 6 (RCAF) Group became operational under the command of Air Vice-Marshal G.E. Brookes. "The move [to form a Canadian group] was very unpopular with Canadian airmen," wrote a pilot who went to an RCAF squadron for his second tour, and a navigator noted that he had been far more humanely treated in the former. In the RAF, "if you were going to fly at night, someone would come in with a cup of tea and wake you up. On the Canadian squadron the way they woke you up was to put the sirens on."

On the other hand there seemed little chance for Canadians to gain higher command experience without their own group. The principle of posting senior RCAF officers to operational formations was accepted by the Air Ministry but resisted in the various commands, and Canadians posted into formations at senior levels were sometimes kept supernumerary for months. Only the creation of a Canadian group would ensure that Canadian airmen obtained some staff and command experience at group level.

This slight assertion of national identity at first proved a poor substitute for professional expertise and, inevitably, many mistakes were made in the early months of No. 6 Group's existence. Moreover, the group was initially equipped with Wellingtons and Halifaxes, and the former were becoming obsolescent, while the latter had a relatively low operational ceiling that left them particularly susceptible to flak. The first Lancaster would not to be taken on strength until August 1943. Although older aircraft were slowly replaced, many Halifaxes (the later versions somewhat improved by extensive modifications) were to remain in service with the group until the end of the war in Europe. (Contrary to popular belief, Bomber Command did not discriminate against 'colonial' squadrons in the allocation of aircraft: they were distributed on the rational principles of squadron seniority and common maintenance convenience.)

Finally, despite their common national origin, it took a long time to eliminate a lack of cohesion in the group as a whole, which represented various levels of experience. In mid-May 1943, three of the group's most experienced squadrons moved to North Africa, where they formed a Canadian wing under Group Captain C.R. Dunlap. From bases in Tunisia they participated in the interdiction bombing of Italy, attacking ports and railway facilities in support of Allied ground forces, before returning to No. 6 Group in November. When the last RCAF bomber squadron to be formed overseas was added to the group in September 1943, an excellent example of the difficulties of forming an effective Canadian formation was provided. Five experienced crews, most of whom had been in disciplinary trouble in their previous units – blamed mainly on high spirits and low flying – were posted in to form a nucleus; but three of the five very soon went miss-

ing on operations and the senior man left on the squadron with operational experience was a lowly pilot officer.

Understandably, then, during its first year of existence No. 6 Group was distinguished by its high percentage of both operational losses and training accidents, and by its low percentages of aircraft serviceability and of aircraft actually attacking the target. Losses in April 1943 reached the 5 per cent figure at which the RAF's director of bomber operations felt operational effectiveness might become "unacceptably low" if it were maintained over three months.

In May the loss rate touched 7 per cent, and in June it passed 7.2 per cent, figures at which the operations research scientists were proclaiming that any bomber force must certainly become "relatively ineffective." Between March 5 and June 24, 1943, the fledgling Canadian group lost over a hundred crews; a 'wastage' which meant that only twelve out of every hundred crews commencing a thirty-mission tour could expect to survive it.

In spite of its losses the group was still able to make a substantial contribution to the Allied air attacks on Hamburg in July. Seventy-two Canadian aircraft were among the 791 bombers that struck the city on July 24-25, when the target area "was left a mass of raging fires with dense black smoke rising to over 19,000 feet"; although of the 728 crews who claimed to have attacked the target, only 306 had in fact dropped their bombs within three miles of the aiming point. Two nights later 81 Canadian machines were among the 787 that returned to Hamburg to create the world's first 'firestorm.'

> As the many fires broke through the roofs of the burning buildings, a column of heated air rose more than two and a half miles high and one and a half miles in diameter.... The column was turbulent, and it was fed from its base by in-rushing cooler ground-surface air. One and a half miles from the fires the draught increased the wind velocity from eleven to thirty-three miles per hour. At the edge of the area the velocities must have been appreciably greater, as trees three feet in diameter were uprooted. In a short time the temperature reached ignition point for all combustibles, and the entire area was ablaze. In such fires complete burn out occurred; that is, no trace of combustible material remained, and only after two days were the areas cool enough to approach.[10]

In August 1943 came an attack on Peenemunde, the research and experimental station on the Baltic where the enemy was developing his rocket-powered 'V-weapons' – Bomber Command's first attempt at something like precision bombing by other than specially selected and trained crews since early 1942. Pathfinders – including the RCAF's No. 405 Squadron, which had joined them in April 1943 – played a major role, using H2S to find the target and then dropping coloured

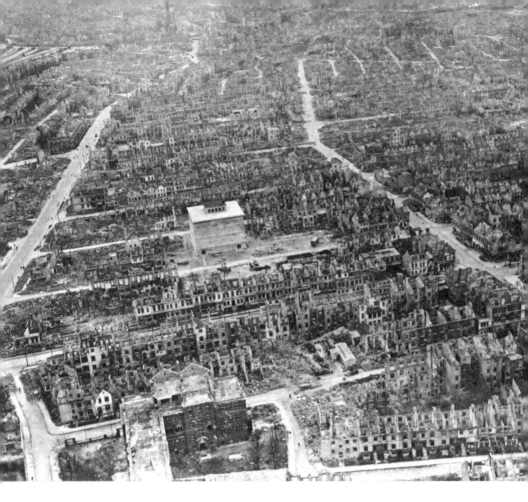

104 Bremen in August 1945.

visual markers to guide the main force on to it. Six hundred bombers were used, including sixty-three from No. 6 Group.

The Pathfinders' exploits were highlighted by the work of John Fauquier, now the commanding officer of No. 405 and, on this occasion, the associate master bomber, who helped control aircraft streaming over the target for the full forty-five minutes the raid lasted before dropping his own bombs. Extensive damage was inflicted and several important German scientists were killed. The development of the v-weapons project was set back severely, but the price was high. Overall losses were nearly 7 per cent and No. 6 Group lost nearly 16 per cent.

During the next three months the Canadians flew mostly against targets in the Ruhr and Rhineland, where the flak was heavy and nightfighters numerous but the comparatively short time spent over German territory reduced the chances of being shot down. "Our aircraft all reported in early this morning," one squadron diarist reported jubilantly, "as no losses on two consecutive nights is almost a record." Nevertheless, Canadian losses never dropped below $4^{1}/2$ per cent per month and, in October, were close to 6 per cent.

The War in the Air

Despite the resolution shown by the great majority of bomber crews, whenever particularly dangerous targets were assigned some crew members disabled equipment or reported imaginary faults in order to justify either not taking off or making an 'early return.' Although the percentage of Canadian machines designated service-able each day rose substantially during 1943, the number of crews failing to take off after manning their aircraft, and the number of early returns, also increased. When 115 machines were assigned to Berlin, 5 failed to take off and 11 returned early. On another occasion at the end of December, when 135 crews were ordered to the same very dan-gerous target, 6 failed to take off and 15 returned early. Even back in June, 75 per cent of the early returns had had their alleged malfunc-tions subsequently found to be "OK on test" and, by September, the number of failures attributed to "faulty crew manipulation" or subse-quently found "OK on test" was alleged to be "just as high as ever, if not higher" in the group's engineering reports.[11]

Air Vice-Marshal C.M. McEwen took command of the group in January 1944, when its fortunes were at their lowest ebb. On January 20, 147 Canadian aircraft were assigned to attack Berlin but 3 failed to take off, 17 returned early, and 9 were lost. The next night a raid on Magdeburg, in north-central Germany, was scheduled. Eleven out of 125 aircraft failed to take off, 12 returned early, and a horrendous 24 went missing.

Moreover, many crews who did press on apparently did not go where they were supposed to. Aircraft had long carried cameras trig-gered by the bomb release gear in order to photograph the targets they attacked and confirm their bombing accuracy, but during January there was "a large increase in the number of [camera] failures which could not definitely be explained," reported the group's photographic equipment staff. "The camera operated perfectly before take-off and afterwards."[12]

Discussing the morale problems of the Command as a whole, Air Vice-Marshal D.C.T. Bennett, the Pathfinder leader, observed that "a very large number of crews failed to carry out their attacks ... in their customary determined manner." It is hardly surprising that morale in the Canadian group, with its higher than average casualties, seemed to be slipping. During the second Battle of Berlin, Bomber Command's loss rate averaged 5.4 per cent, but the Canadians were enduring a rate of more than 6 per cent and in January their losses reached 7.3 per cent. In such circumstances only ten crews in a hundred would survive a tour.

However, in February 1944 No. 6 Group's loss rate was down by two percentage points; in March it fell dramatically again; and during April, when Bomber Command flew largely in support of the forth-coming invasion of France and far fewer missions were flown into Germany, it was down to 2 per cent, while the scale of operations con-tinued to increase sharply. In part, at least, this improvement was due

105 Survivors of the bombing of Mannheim.

to the increased emphasis their new commander put on training. Whenever they were not scheduled for operations, even the most experienced crews – such as they were – were required to fly cross-country training flights and fighter affiliation exercises, while ground crews were driven unmercifully towards higher standards of maintenance. All the RCAF squadrons were now equipped with Lancasters or the better kinds of Halifaxes, and a new unit, No. 415 Squadron, was added to the group from Coastal Command, giving it a total of fourteen squadrons.

From March to September, a period when Bomber Command was placed under the operational control of the Supreme Allied Commander, the American General D.D. Eisenhower, to support the invasion of northwest Europe, its primary objective was to support Operation *Overlord* by striking at targets in France and the Low Countries. Killing and wounding civilians was no longer desirable, since the civilians in question were generally French, Belgians, or

The War in the Air

106 Flight-Lieutenant Dick Audet, DFC and Bar, established an RAF/RCAF record that still stands – and is unlikely ever to fall – when he destroyed five enemy machines in five minutes. In less than a month of combat Audet was credited with 11 $^1/_2$ German aircraft. He was killed on March 3, 1945, when his Spitfire was hit by flak during a low-level sweep over northern Germany.

Dutch. The 4,000-pound canister-type 'blockbusters' and the large proportion of incendiaries disappeared from the bomb-bays, to be replaced with aerodynamically correct 2,000-pound bombs. During the previous year, American long-range escort fighters, accompanying Flying Fortresses on their daylight raids over Germany, had largely destroyed the *Luftwaffe*'s day fighter force and, at such short ranges, many raids could now be flown in daylight. Canals, railway marshalling yards, and repair facilities were the primary targets and they were totally destroyed one by one, while the towns and cities that bordered or surrounded them were left largely untouched. (Even so, however, several thousand French, Belgian, and Dutch civilians were 'collateral' casualties.)

After Allied troops landed in Normandy on June 6, 1944, the weight of Bomber Command was diverted from time to time to give immediate tactical support to ground forces engaged in 'set-piece' assaults. Some of these attacks were successful, some were not, and occasionally Allied troops were hit by their own bombers (see Chapter 7), but apparently the ground forces could never get too much of this heavy bomber tactical support. By and large, it worked wonders for troop morale.

The War in the Air

Another part of the bombing effort was turned against the launching ramps of the V-1 'flying bombs' that began to fall on London and southeastern England in June 1944. These sites, scattered along the Channel coast, were hard targets to find and harder still to damage, and the nearly 5,000 tons of high-explosive bombs that were aimed at them had little effect. However, most of the sites were overrun by Canadian ground forces before the Germans were able to develop a maximum effort from them.

Throughout Bomber Command loss rates dropped steeply, but in the Canadian case the drop was extreme. From sharing (with No. 4 Group) by far the worst record in the Command in January, they became, in May, the group with the lowest percentage of losses. This seems to have been mostly due to the switch to less well-defended *Overlord* targets over the summer, with the consequent reduction in losses permitting a body of expertise to be built up, and the extraordinarily heavy emphasis on continuous training of operational crews that Air Vice-Marshal McEwen insisted upon.

Losses were down to 1.6 per cent in June, the invasion month, when Pilot Officer A.C. Mynarski of No. 419 Squadron posthumously brought the Canadian group its only VC of the war. He was the mid-upper gunner of a Lancaster sent to bomb the railway marshalling yards at Cambrai, in northern France, a week after D-Day. When his aircraft was attacked by a German nightfighter and set on fire, the pilot ordered his crew to bail out and then jumped himself; but Mynarski, realizing that the rear gunner was trapped in his turret, struggled back through the burning fuselage to help him. As the bomber spiralled down, he fought to free his fellow gunner until his own clothing and parachute were also on fire. Only then, at the urging of the trapped man he was trying to save, did he make his way forward to an escape hatch and jump himself. He reached the ground safely but died from his burns soon afterwards. The man he had endeavoured to free miraculously survived the subsequent crash and was able to tell the story of Mynarski's valour.

In October Bomber Command was returned to the operational control of the Air Staff and Air Marshal Harris promptly reverted to the area bombing of German cities. Loss rates, which had fallen to 0.3 per cent in September, began to climb again, but the six-month breathing space they had been vouchsafed had worked wonders with No. 6 Group. It had been able to build up a cadre of experienced crews large enough to effect, by example and transmitted doctrine, the performance of the whole. At the end of 1944, McEwen was able to point out, in a summary of his tenure in command, that not only had the Canadians "sustained the lowest losses ... in the whole of Bomber Command" but also that "a study of the bomb plots shows the standard [of accuracy] to be well in the van of the command."[13] After

107 The charred corpses of two children, Hamburg.

The War in the Air

wrestling successfully with the various problems that had beset it during its first twelve months, the group began its third year in triumph.

In the early spring of 1945 the pace again quickened for the final all-out offensive against Germany. American daylight (and pin-point) attacks on synthetic fuel plants, which had begun during the previous summer, were playing havoc with the *Luftwaffe*'s fuel supplies; the German anti-aircraft defences were being overwhelmed as their communication networks were destroyed; and, with the enemy's day fighter force in desperate straits, Bomber Command turned increasingly to daylight attacks, reinforcing the American success. Night attacks and area bombing were not abandoned, however, and No. 6 Group contributed 66 aircraft to the notorious destruction of Dresden on a February night when the bulk of the Canadian planes were attacking the synthetic oil plant at Bohlen. Two Canadian aircraft were lost out of 183 that flew that night; between 30,000 and 50,000 Dresdeners – the exact number will never be known – were burnt or asphyxiated in the firestorm that engulfed the city.

By March 1945 it was clear that the end of the fighting in Europe could not be long delayed. Yet in the last two months of the war a large part of the cultural heritage of Europe was destroyed in order "to intensify the chaos behind the lines" in the course of Operation *Thunderclap*. On March 17-18 the beautiful Baroque city of Wurzburg was wiped out; on March 22 the medieval centre of Hildesheim was gutted. At the end of March, Winston Churchill, initially an enthusiastic supporter of *Thunderclap*, privately told his chiefs of staff "that the moment has come when the question of bombing German cities simply for the sake of increasing the terror, although under other pretexts, should be reviewed."[14]

Air Chief Marshal Sir Charles Portal responded that such attacks were no longer necessary, because "it is improbable that the full effects of further area attacks ... will have time to mature before hostilities cease. Moreover, the number of targets suitable for area bombing is now much reduced."[15] Nevertheless, on April 3-4 the thousand-year-old town of Nordhausen suffered the same fate; and on April 14 Potsdam was devastated. Institutional momentum appears to have overridden even prime ministerial and chief of staff conclusions.

There was, perhaps, more justification for the attack on Hitler's Bavarian retreat at Berchtesgaden on April 25 (even though Hitler was known to be in Berlin) when the Pathfinders of No. 405 Squadron RCAF led a raid by three hundred bombers. That same day the Canadian Pathfinders flew a second mission to mark two coastal defence batteries in the Frisian Islands for 192 No. 6 Group crews. Four of the aircraft did not return, but when the last Lancaster of No. 428 Squadron touched down at 8:30 p.m., No. 6 Group's last bombing operation of the war was over.

The War in the Air

Bomber Command's strategic air offensive was intended to win the war (or at the very least to shorten it significantly) by destroying production facilities, disrupting communications, and decisively crushing civilian morale. Although it produced vast physical destruction and the price paid in human lives was enormous, it failed to realize those objectives. However, it did keep some 700,000 Germans occupied in anti-aircraft duties and engaged, at its height, more than 10,000 heavy guns which might otherwise have been used against Allied ground forces.

When the war in Europe came to an end, Bomber Command had dropped – in round figures – nearly a million tons of bombs in the course of 365,000 sorties. No. 6 Group's contribution to that total included 126,000 tons in 41,000 sorties. The Command's casualties numbered 47,000 aircrew killed (over 8,200 of them Canadians) and 4,000 wounded.

Ironically, perhaps, many Canadians who had volunteered for aircrew duties in the belief that the air force offered a more individualized, more human environment than either the army or the navy had found themselves committed to a malevolent, technological, impersonal battle waged primarily against women and children. German casualties resulting directly from the Allied bombing offensives totalled more than 560,000 dead and 675,000 wounded, the majority being women and nearly 20 per cent children under sixteen. The British official historians have conjectured that the loss of German war production that resulted from all this may have amounted to 1.2 per cent in 1945, when the enemy's productive capacity was stretched to new limits and greater monthly tonnages were being dropped than ever before.[16]

The War in the Air

CHAPTER 9

Northern Italy and Northwest Europe, 1944-1945

Rome was the first European capital to be taken by the Allies on their march to Berlin. Its capture on June 4, 1943, freed the Vatican from the direct pressures of Fascist diplomacy and propaganda and heartened Catholics throughout the world. But with Rome in their hands, American strategists very soon lost what little interest they had ever had in the Italian campaign. They transferred their attention to the largely Franco-American landings (the Canadian-American First Special Service Force was also involved), which took place in the south of France on August 15. The British, however, were firmly committed to their Italian strategy, still dreaming of a breakout into Austria and the Balkans through the Ljubljana Gap in the eastern Alps. All through the long, hot summer of 1944 the Allied forces in Italy pushed doggedly north.

After the fall of Rome most of the Canadians in Italy went into army reserve for a well-earned rest and a re-structuring of the 5th Armoured Division, which had proved tactically unbalanced for effective deployment in the 'close' Italian countryside. Only the 1st Canadian Armoured Brigade accompanied the British spearheads in their advance from Rome to Florence. (According to General Leese, the Eighth Army's commander, it was "the most experienced armoured brigade in Italy and therefore in great demand.")

The Canadian Corps headquarters, on the other hand, was certainly not in demand: quietly overlooking his own responsibility for some of the problems that had beset the Canadians in the battle for Rome, Leese now argued that it was not really competent to handle a fluid battle at the corps level and suggested that the corps "be broken up and the divisions placed under command of a British corps."

When his views were transmitted to England, both General Crerar and Lieutenant General Ken Stuart, now the Canadian chief of staff there, objected to further fragmentation of the Army Overseas. Several command and staff changes were made, but discussions between Stuart (who flew out from England) and Leese, together with a reluctant vote of confidence that Stuart wrung from General Burns' two divisional commanders, Vokes and Hoffmeister, enabled Burns to keep his job for the time being.

For the men of the 1st and 5th Divisions, encamped in the Volturno valley north of Naples, life was pleasant enough. Training in the foothills and on the sun-baked Volturno flats was interspersed with short leaves in Naples and nearby coastal resorts. Ball games were played, teeth were fixed, and minds and bodies rested. At the end of July an inspection and investiture by 'General Collingwood' – who turned out to be King George VI travelling incognito – brought their idyll to an end and the next day the corps set off north to play its part in breaking the Gothic Line. After a brief sojourn in Florence, in the last week of August the Canadians found themselves back on the Adriatic coast, with the little town of Cattolica, some twenty miles ahead, as their objective.

The lessons of the Hitler Line had been well learned, and with the 1st Division leading as far as the Foglia River, where the 5th Armoured drew alongside so that the corps could attack on a two-division front, "the Canadians broke through the Gothic Line by finding a soft spot and going through," wrote Martha Gellhorn, the American war correspondent.

> It makes me ashamed to write that sentence because there is no soft place where there are mines and no soft places where there are Spandaus and no soft place where there are long 88mm guns, and if you have seen one tank burn with its crew shut inside it you will never believe that anything is soft again.[1]

The German Tenth Army's defences included 2,375 machine-gun posts, 479 anti-tank guns, mortar- and assault-gun positions, and 22 *Panzerturm* – tank turrets set in concrete – protected by 100,000 anti-tank and anti-personnel mines, 117,000 metres of wire obstacles, and 9,000 metres of anti-tank ditches.

An evening attack by the West Nova Scotia Regiment led them into one large minefield where the battalion reeled under a storm of fire from the enemy's automatic weapons, mortars, and artillery, trapped in exactly the sort of killing-ground the designers of the German defences had aimed to create. Next morning, in the pre-dawn twilight, the 'Van Doos' made an attempt to take the same German position. "The advance across the minefield was slow and laborious," wrote one of their company commanders.

> We had to follow a white tape which the engineers had unwound to mark where they had swept the path. Now and then, in the semi-darkness, we nearly stepped on a mine which they had lifted and left beside the tape in their anxiety to finish before daylight. Here and there, mutilated bodies still twitched in a final spasm. They were men of the other regiment who had attempted the assault the previous evening. Some wounded were still lying in the middle of the minefield after several stretcher-bearers had got themselves killed or wounded in trying to help them.[2]

Northern Italy and Northwest Europe, 1944-1945

108 A bulldozer was needed to drag this ³/₄-ton truck, and the 37-mm Bofors anti-aircraft gun it was towing, up the muddy bank of an Italian stream.

Once through the minefield the French Canadians burst into the machine-gun posts that covered it and that had wreaked such havoc among the West Novas the night before. "Firing from the hip, throwing grenades and howling like demons delivered from hell we charged the position, giving no quarter and asking none."

There were, however, some strong points that were less adamant than others – some of them softened-up by No. 417 Squadron RCAF, which had been converted from a fighter to a fighter-bomber squadron on June 22. The change had not proved to be a major chore: the Spitfires were fitted with a 500-pound bomb rack under each wing, the pilots were given two days to practise their new art on a raft anchored in a nearby lake, and operational flying resumed with a dive-bombing role added to their other responsibilities. This paucity of specialized training, combined with the Spitfire's inherent unsuitability for dive bombing, may have contributed to the loss of three pilots in five days at the beginning of July, but by the end of August they were flying as many as forty sorties a day from airstrips just behind the front.

Day after day, at the request of 'Rover' radio nets (forward air liaison officers operating on the ground from armoured cars, working in close co-operation with the front-line troops), they attacked gun emplacements, enemy headquarters, transport, and mortar pits with bombs and machine-gun fire. On September 3:

Northern Italy and Northwest Europe, 1944-1945

Eight aircraft airborne to carry out close support with Rover Jimmy. They were directed on to the Regimental HQ ... which they attacked at 17:15 hours scoring two hits beside house and 25 yds from small woods in which two small green tents were identified. Both sections then strafed the tented area. Intense light ack-ack from northeast and southwest of target.[3]

By then the Gothic Line was broken, the leading Canadians were north of Cattolica, and the enemy was in such disarray that a company of the motorized Westminster Regiment found a German truck, loaded with the first hot food it had seen in two days, driving right into their positions. They soon reported, with some frustration, that *Wehrmacht* cooking "was not a damn bit better than ours," but had more trouble convincing regimental headquarters that the German beer accompanying it tasted like "low grade spring water."

The Germans very quickly recovered their balance, however. The road northwards, through the Romagna, crossed a dozen rivers before debouching into the wide Lombardy plain, and they skilfully took advantage of the ground while Kesselring switched reserves from his western flank, where the Fifth U.S. Army had not yet closed with the formidable fragment of the Gothic Line that faced it across the lower Arno. Digging in on each river line in turn, the Germans put up a fierce resistance before slipping away – from the Conca to the Marano, from the Marano to the Ausa (it was mid-September and the weather was deteriorating now), from the Ausa to the Marecchia, the Marecchia to the Fiumichino, the Fiumichino to the Savio. There Private E.A. 'Smoky' Smith of the Seaforth Highlanders won Canada's third and last VC of the Mediterranean campaign before the winter rains settled in, the rivers rose, the roads turned to bogs, and the Eighth Army's momentum once again began to peter out. In a month the Canadians had endured nearly 4,000 battle casualties, while a further 1,500 men had gone down sick or suffering from battle fatigue.

The corps went into reserve at the end of October amid rumours – strengthened by the appointment of General McNaughton as minister of national defence on November 2 – that they were soon to be reunited with First Canadian Army. General Burns relinquished his appointment on November 5. He had exercised no more than an adequate control of the corps since the summer, and too many of his command relationships were still poisoned by earlier criticisms of his handling of operations on the road to Rome. "No one can be an impartial judge in his own case," Burns later observed, but "during the period of my command the corps had taken all objectives assigned to it, inflicting heavy losses on the enemy.... Though progress was not always as rapid as desirable, nevertheless, during our period of action we went further and faster than any other corps [in Italy]."[4] However, there seems little doubt that Burns was essentially a staff officer rather than a battlefield commander, and that his introverted personality worked against him in his relationships with both British superiors and Canadian subordinates.

The senior divisional commander, Chris Vokes, had expected to inherit Burns' appointment, although nearly everybody else realized that he had reached, if not passed, his ceiling at a divisional level. In the event, Charles Foulkes came from Holland to take command of the corps, while a disappointed Vokes moved to Holland, changing places with Major-General H.W. Foster of the 4th Armoured Division.

From a professional point of view the Canadians had come of age. Sicily had been a haphazard affair, southern Italy a chase. Ortona and the Hitler Line had been marred by technical failures in several respects. On the Gothic Line and in the Romagna, however, the Canadians were recognized as master craftsmen and, had they known of it at the time, they might have appreciated most of all the tribute of one of their most notable opponents, General von Vietinghoff, the commander of the German Tenth Army: "I am told that the 5th Canadian Armoured Division is excellent," he reported to Field Marshal Kesselring, "... though not strong in numbers, the Canadians are excellent soldiers."[5]

In December the Eighth Army – against the better judgement of its new commander, General Sir Richard McCreery – made one last try at a breakthrough into the Lombardy plain. The Canadians, in the lead again, ploughed forward to the Senio River (suffering a nasty set-back at the Lamone, *en route*), and compelled Kesselring to draw more forces from his western flank. Now the Germans were really desperate in their resistance. Another step backwards would have taken them beyond the river lines into open country where Allied armour might be deployed *en masse* to charge the Ljubljana Gap or to cut off their Fourteenth Army facing the Americans on the other side of the Apennines.

The Germans were aided by the weather and topography – the Senio's wide floodbanks stood forty feet above the plain, their outer slopes were steep, their inner slopes were stepped, and the winter current was fast – and they stopped the Eighth Army in its muddy, exhausted tracks. Northwest of Ravenna elements of the Canadian Corps, holding the northernmost outpost of the entire Italian front, settled into winter quarters.

More dramatic events were occurring in northwest Europe as the disabled German armies fell back across France. Bypassing Paris, General George Patton's Third U.S. Army spearheads had crossed the Meuse on the last day of August, while Courtney Hodges' First U.S. Army, after crossing the Seine northwest of the French capital, was also driving east at top speed. In front of Montgomery's 21st Army Group the Seine ran deeper and wider between very steep banks, and fresh German forces from the Pas de Calais were able to fight an effective

Northern Italy and Northwest Europe, 1944-1945

109 Winter in northern Italy. Battle-wise soldiers, like those of the Ontario Regiment, chose not to live in buildings, which were automatic targets for enemy mortar fire. Instead, from sandbags and tarpaulins, they built 'hoochies' against the back of their tanks and slept under the tanks themselves. This picture was taken on January 21, 1945.

rearguard action. Nevertheless, the British were in Amiens by the end of the month and their momentum carried them to Brussels on September 2 and to Antwerp the following day. There the advance guards were allowed to stop and rest.

If Field Marshal Montgomery (as he now was) had spurred them on to the shore of the Maas/Rhine estuary, only thirty miles to the north, he might have trapped the whole of the German Fifteenth Army, ensuring the early clearance of the Scheldt estuary, and opening the approaches to Antwerp by the end of the month. Pre-eminently a general of mass and matériel rather than manoeuvre, Montgomery of all people should have seen the importance of opening the greatest port of Europe when a million and a half men were having to be supplied through the now-distant, and much smaller, ports of Cherbourg and Le Havre. But he failed to press the pursuit over those last few miles, the Germans smartly reorganized their defences, and Antwerp's vital facilities were thereby denied to the invading armies until the end of November.

Following the Normandy breakout, the British and Canadian armies under Montgomery's command had switched positions, so that the latter now lay on the left flank of the Allied line. Thus First

Northern Italy and Northwest Europe, 1944-1945

110 The race across France: a Canadian artillery regiment rolls through the ruins of Falaise in August 1944.

Canadian Army's problems in crossing the Seine were greatest, their formations had suffered most in the Falaise battle, and they were left to deal with the German garrisons of the Channel fortresses – Le Havre, Dieppe, Boulogne, Calais, and Dunkirk – that punctuated their axis of advance and had been ordered by Hitler to hold out to the last.

Nor, perhaps, were they driven as hard as they should have been. On September 2, Montgomery had signalled General Crerar to "push on quickly," but Crerar's response was cautious to say the least. Le Havre fell to a combined assault by his I British Corps and the RAF's Bomber Command on September 12, and the Canadian commander then wrote to Montgomery that, "while the rapid fall of Le Havre has favourable potential influences, it is most important that the effect so gained should not be more than lost by an unsuccessful attack on the next objective, Boulogne. I therefore want Simonds to button things up properly, taking a little more time if necessary, in order to ensure a decisive assault."[6]

The 2nd Division triumphantly re-entered Dieppe – from the landward side, this time – without opposition on September 8, and once again Crerar managed to offend Montgomery when he chose to take the salute at a 'Victory' parade there, rather than attend a 21st

Northern Italy and Northwest Europe, 1944-1945

Army Group planning conference. If he had been a British, rather than Canadian, general, he might not have lasted much longer in command of one of the field marshal's armies.

Boulogne, the most important port between Le Havre and Antwerp, was defended more resolutely. Its capture was assigned to the 3rd Division (now commanded by Major-General Dan Spry, who had been promoted from a brigade in Italy), together with nine artillery regiments borrowed from neighbouring British formations, 750 heavy bombers of Bomber Command, and a substantial part of the Second Tactical Air Force. In ninety minutes on the morning of September 17, the aircraft dumped 3,232 tons of high explosive exactly on target and the artillery added every round they could fire to the bombardment. Then the armour moved in, although the extensive cratering impeded armoured vehicles, and over the next four days the German defences were battered down yard by yard.

The high point of the battle proved to be the capture of the so-called 'citadel,' a walled fortification perched on a limestone hill in the centre of the town that dates back to the thirteenth century. It fell to a singular combination of storybook tactics and modern technology, after a French civilian had shown an officer of the Stormont, Dundas and Glengarry Highlanders a secret tunnel leading into the fortress. The SDGs soon had a platoon in the tunnel and, at the same time, "Engineers in their armoured vehicles began to place petards against the portcullis. As the gate was blown in, the company commander and his platoon dealt the *coup de grâce* to the morale of the defenders by suddenly appearing in their midst, out of the tunnel. Scores of dirty white things immediately were seen fluttering from the walls in

111 When the Canadians re-entered Dieppe in September 1944, one of the first tasks assigned was the painting of the plain wooden crosses that marked the 855 graves in the Canadian cemetery.

112 A seemingly endless line of Sherman tanks of the Fort Garry Horse advancing across the South Beveland isthmus in October 1944 with flooded polders on one side and an embankment on the other.

token of surrender."[7] Only a beauteous and suitably grateful princess was needed to provide all the elements of a Hollywood epic.

Meanwhile Montgomery had belatedly realized the importance of the Scheldt estuary and again ordered General Crerar to move his army up as quickly as possible. Calais fell, on October 1, to an assault that lacked only the romantic aspects of the attack on Boulogne. The planned attack on Dunkirk was abandoned (it remained under siege – mostly by a Belgian brigade – until the end of the war in Europe, and the garrison did not capitulate until two days after the signing of the official German surrender) and First Canadian Army finally began to concentrate against the banks of the Scheldt.

In order to retain control of the estuary, the enemy held a pocket on the south shore, around Breskens, which was now supplied (by small boats and barges, under cover of darkness) from the island of Walcheren, on the north shore at the tip of the South Beveland peninsula. While the 3rd and 4th Divisions – Major-General Harry Foster had replaced George Kitching in command of the 4th Armoured on August 22 – began to crush the Breskens pocket in Operation *Switchback*, the 2nd Division started to push, painfully slowly, across the base of the Beveland isthmus on October 2. By that time General Crerar, suffering from persistent dysentery that had not responded to the usual medical treatments, had returned to England and the clearing of the Scheldt was left in the hands of Lieutenant-General Guy Simonds, as acting army commander, while Major-General Charles Foulkes temporarily led II Corps and Brigadier R.H. Keefler commanded the 2nd Division.

Under an umbrella of artillery fire and direct air support the Canadians could only inch forward and it took them three full weeks of vicious, bitter fighting to advance some seven miles and isolate the defenders of the Scheldt from landward re-supply. Much of the area consisted of flooded polders – sections of reclaimed land lying below sea level between breached dykes running more or less at right angles to each other. The Germans could burrow into a lateral dyke from the back, breaking only a small hole in the forward face through which to poke their automatic weapons, or in the top in order to align their mortars. The Canadians, on the other hand, were limited to narrow, exposed, and frequently mined lines of advance along the dykes, swept by German fire from a broad front. Mostly they stumbled and crawled along the sides of the dykes, between wind and water, eating, sleeping, fighting, and dying in sodden uniforms and squelching boots. This pattern was typical of much of the Scheldt fighting and more than neutralized any advantage of air support and vastly superior logistics the Canadians enjoyed.

The Black Watch of Canada, for example, experienced the most terrible day in its history – on Friday, October 13 – as it tried desperately to close a gap that was now little more than a mile wide. Their attack was launched early in the morning, but "by 1000 hours the leading company [still] lay on the start line, their ranks cruelly decimated by the withering fire," wrote the historian of the Toronto Scottish, some of whose machine guns and mortars had been assigned to provide fire support.

> The next company lined up and began to pass through. For two hours they too tried vainly to advance and a very small gain was made. The remaining companies then took their turn, each advancing a short distance at alarming cost. The gruelling battle carried on throughout the day and as evening fell the reformed companies were still pushing on yard by bloody yard. Every conceivable form of support was ordered up. Tanks were available but could not negotiate the flooded fields nor the narrow roads [along the top of the dykes].... Shortly before midnight the survivors reached their objective but were too few to hold it against a counterattack.[8]

All four of the Watch's rifle company commanders had been killed during the day. In three days the battalion had suffered 81 casualties. After two days' rest they had gone back into the line and, in two more days of envenomed fighting, lost another 183 men – more than a third of the unit and nearly all of its rifle companies gone in less than a week!

In the Breskens pocket, operations were equally difficult, although more use was made of close ground support by aircraft than on the north shore of the estuary. It was provided by Second Tactical Air Force's (2nd TAF) 84 Group, which had rocket-firing Typhoons, the most devastating airborne close-support weapons system of the war. Just south of Biervliet a company of the North Shores, which had already been accidentally shot up by Spitfires that morning, was being heavily mortared by the Germans when along came a flight of Typhoons. One of the North Shores recalled how

> the flight leader came down to about twenty feet from ground level to see who we were. I stood up and used pantomime to tell him about the enemy mortars back of the orchard and he was a bright lad. Away he went to look at the place and went back and picked up his flight and the mess they made of Jerry's mortar position was beautiful to behold.[9]

There were two kinds of Hawker Typhoon – the fighter-bomber variety, colloquially known as 'Bombphoons,' which each carried two 2,000-pound bombs, and those armed with eight 3-inch rocket projectiles (RPs) in which each warhead was equivalent in explosive power to a 6-inch shell. The former had greater hitting power, the latter were more accurate; the former were more effective against bridges and buildings, the latter against 'pinpoint' targets such as tanks and locomotives, while both had a devastating effect on troops' morale.

In the original planning for *Overlord*, No. 83 Group of 2nd TAF, which eventually contained thirteen RCAF squadrons, had been allocated to support First Canadian Army, assigned to lead the amphibious assault. That arrangement had been altered in February 1944, however, after Montgomery, doubting Canadian generalship, had switched First Canadian for Second British Army. Since No. 83 Group's training was far more advanced, it made sense for it to remain in support of the assaulting force, even though Canadian airmen would now be supporting British troops rather than their own comrades – leaving No. 84 Group (with no Canadian squadrons) to work with the 'follow up' Canadian army. All of the RCAF squadrons flew 'Bombphoons,' although there were, as usual, many Canadians in the RP Typhoon squadrons of the RAF.

From time to time, inevitably, there were accidents in which airmen strafed their own side, but in the battlefield balance of human lives (no more delicate scale exists) close air support was worth much more than it cost. The historian of the North Nova Scotia Regiment, recording an attack in the Breskens pocket in which one of its companies took fifty prisoners, wrote that "this attack might have been costly had it not been for an assault on the enemy by our aircraft – rocket firing Typhoons – immediately before the assault started.... [They] let go their rockets right on top of the artillery concentration and the enemy taken prisoner were obviously quite shaken by it all."[10] Not until November 2 was the pocket finally eliminated and an entry made in the 3rd Division log to that effect. Beside it somebody wrote "Thank God!" The division had suffered over two thousand casualties, something close to a quarter of them being fatal.

The South Beveland peninsula had been secured by October 31, but there remained the island of Walcheren at the end of the peninsula, garrisoned by some three thousand Germans well stocked with food and ammunition. Its batteries of heavy guns still commanded the mouth of the Scheldt. The capture of Walcheren was directed by First Canadian Army, but only the first stage of it was launched by Canadian troops. During the last day of October and the first of November, the 2nd Division, together with elements of the British 52nd (Lowland Scottish) Division, fought desperately to cross the 1,200-yard-long, straight and perfectly flat causeway joining the island to the Beveland peninsula.

The eventual honour of being 'first across' fell to B Company of the Calgary Highlanders, although they were forced back onto the causeway again and the final lodgement was established by Le Régiment de Maisonneuve. So desperate was the close-quarter fighting that the Germans were using 81-mm mortars at less than fifty yards' range and any kind of a headwind – or the slightest miscalculation – would have blown the bombs back on the mortar pits from which they had been launched.

On November 3 the 2nd Division was withdrawn from the battle, having lost 207 officers and 3,443 other ranks in a little over a month. Walcheren, its perimeter dyke breached and its centre flooded as a result of massive raids by Lancasters and Halifaxes of Bomber Command, was subsequently captured by British troops. A battalion of Cameronians from the 52nd Division, attacking from the peninsula, found an undefended ford just south of the causeway and sneaked across there without opposition. Commandos crossed the estuary in assault boats and landed on isolated sections of the perimeter dyke, fanning out to take the enemy batteries.

With the fall of Walcheren on November 8 and the subsequent opening of Antwerp, General Simonds received the enthusiastic congratulations of both Crerar and Montgomery, but in retrospect one may wonder whether the assault on the causeway was in the finest traditions of generalship. The amphibious attacks were clearly a better bet and many lives might have been saved had that approach been adopted from the beginning.

Practically every Allied aircraft in northwest Europe was now involved, from time to time and to some extent or other, in the direct support of the ground campaign. That meant that the bulk of the air casualties were a result of ground-based fire. In their air superiority role the fighters had very little to worry about, although the advent of enemy jet aircraft in the early fall must have given them a few moments' pause. However, on October 5, Spitfire pilots of the RCAF's No. 401 Squadron had convinced themselves that the new jets were not invulnerable, as they claimed the RAF/RCAF's first victory over a jet fighter – a Messerschmitt 262. No. 401's eventual total of 195 enemy

113

CHRISTMAS PREPARATIONS—A LA MODE.

aircraft destroyed was to make it the top-scoring RCAF squadron of the war.

As the ground forces closed on the Rhine, the responsibilities of the two tactical air groups were shifted. No. 84 Group, with its RP Typhoons, was made responsible for the whole of 21st Army Group's front west of the Rhine/Maas (i.e., close support of the front-line troops), while No. 83 Group concerned itself primarily with interdicting the enemy's lines of communication east of the river. Thus the Canadian fighter-bombers in No. 83 Group, now commanded by Group Captain Paul Davoud and flying out of Eindhoven, were usually striking into German territory, but did provide some close support from time to time, notably during the ill-fated Arnhem operation, in which, happily, Canadian ground forces were not directly involved.

The majority of No. 83 Group's missions were flown against transportation targets across the Rhine, with such success that the Germans even resorted to camouflaging their railway locomotives. But there was no way they could camouflage the smoke from their furnaces and steam from their boilers, or the lines and bridges that the trains ran on. By the end of October, when winter weather began to restrict flying operations, rail traffic across the Rhine had been virtually stopped and road traffic was being hammered unmercifully during the daylight hours.

In November, the Canadians found themselves manning a line along the Waal and Maas rivers. They fought no major battle during the three winter months but there was much nasty fighting in a minor key. The damp, penetrating cold, the mud, and the flooded ground also played their part in making the combat soldier's life miserable even when nobody was shooting at him. A subaltern in the North Nova Scotia Highlanders found himself

> living in caves and dugouts scooped out of the wooded hills.... There is a telephone in my dugout ...hooked up so I can communicate with company headquarters, a half mile back, or with our artillery forward observation post, a quarter of a mile on ahead of me. I often pick up the phone and listen in. The difference in voices. The people at HQ relaxed, unworried, loud (they shout over the phone), whistling, singing, joking, playing cards. The men at the observation post overlooking the enemy position whisper into the phone.... They try to end conversations as soon as possible, and seem to be talking with their heads pulled down into their greatcoats. This strange dialogue goes on intermittently all night.

Two weeks later he was

> back again in trenches, the December rain and hail, one day clear in four, two hours of windy sunshine a week, mud to the ankles. Some days we lie in the mud.... We eat twice a day, morning and night. Food is brought down a slippery path, mined along the fringes, under darkness and between scattered bursts of enemy fire, for they know our habits.[11]

Eight months earlier, a tentative suggestion by Ottawa that I Canadian Corps, in Italy, might be reunited with their comrades in northwest Europe when circumstances permitted, had failed to arouse any kind of positive response from the British. A more direct approach, made only ten days after General McNaughton assumed the portfolio of National Defence, initially proved no more successful; but over the turn of the year the Canadian pressure on London gradually became more persistent. When, at the end of January 1945, the Anglo-American combined chiefs of staff, meeting in Malta, finally decided on the transfer of more forces from Italy, it was promptly appreciated that "the Canadian divisions were the easiest to move quickly."

The first of them were in Holland by early March. General Foulkes' I Corps HQ became operational again on March 15 and, by

114 Wreckage left on the airfield at Eindhoven, Holland, after the *Luftwaffe*'s 'forlorn hope' attack on New Year's Day 1945.

April 3, the last of the Canadians from Italy had rejoined First Canadian Army. The largest Canadian combat force ever assembled now held the left flank of an Allied line that stretched from the Swiss mountains to the North Sea.

Meanwhile, the German counterattack in the Ardennes, which culminated in the 'Battle of the Bulge,' had little impact on the Canadian army. The enemy's last great aerial gamble, which followed a few days later, did leave its mark on the RCAF, however. On New Year's morning, when the *Luftwaffe* calculated that most of the Allied aircraft would be grounded and their crews nursing hangovers, eight hundred German fighters and fighter-bombers were launched against tactical airfields in a last-ditch attempt to inflict a major defeat on Allied air power. The enemy put every possible machine in the air, including his new jets and even some captured Mustangs and a Spitfire with *Luftwaffe* markings – one indication of its now desperate straits.

One hundred and forty-four Allied aircraft were destroyed and 84 damaged in the space of an hour and a half, but German losses turned out to be just about as high and the remnants of the *Luftwaffe* were far less capable of absorbing such punishment. Second TAF alone claimed 47 enemy aircraft destroyed, and nearly half of that total fell to the RCAF's No. 126 Wing, now commanded by Group Captain G.R. McGregor with Wing Commander 'Dal' Russel as his Wingco (Flying).

Eindhoven, where the Canadian Typhoon fighter-bomber and Spitfire reconnaissance wings were stationed, was hit particularly hard. A few planes had already taken off when the first wave of enemy aircraft came in, but eight were on the runway and five of them, togeth-

Northern Italy and Northwest Europe, 1944-1945

er with a considerable number of other machines that were parked in the vicinity, were destroyed and a great many more damaged.

When the Germans arrived at Evère, where Group Captain W.R. MacBrien's 127 Wing was based, four Spitfires were already in the air and claimed six of the attackers, but eleven Canadian machines were destroyed on the ground and a dozen more damaged. Wing Commander Johnnie Johnson, RAF, MacBrien's 'Wingco (Flying)' and the British Commonwealth's top-scoring fighter pilot, was watching No. 416 Squadron turn from the perimeter track on to the runway when the Germans arrived.

> From our reasonably safe position on the ground Bill [MacBrien] and I took stock of the attack. The enemy fighters strafed singly and in pairs. Our few light ack-ack guns had already ceased firing; later we found that the gunners had run out of ammunition. The enemy completely dominated the scene, and there was little we could do except shout with rage as our Spitfires burst into flames before our eyes.[12]

At the third Canadian base, Heesch, the story was very different. A large part of the McGregor-Russel wing was already airborne when the first Germans arrived, to bomb and strafe the runways without inflicting either casualties or damage. Then the Canadians already in the air pounced on them and, in the ensuing combat, claimed twenty-four enemy destroyed, three 'probables,' and seven damaged for the loss of only two Spitfires. Two of the Germans were claimed by Flight Lieutenant Dick Audet of 411 Squadron, who, two days earlier, had been credited with his first five victories, two Me 109s and three F-W 190s, in a fight that lasted less than five minutes – establishing an RAF/RCAF record that still stands and is unlikely ever to be beaten.

115 Amphibian 'Alligator' of the 3rd Canadian Infantry Division ploughing up the flooded Rhine near Nijmegen, Holland, in February 1945.

116 Kranenberg, Germany, was flooded when the Germans broke the dykes along the lower Rhine. The town was shelled and bombed, but the church spire remained standing.

Operations *Veritable* and *Blockbuster,* designed to clear the land between the Maas and the Rhine, began on February 8 with an attack by XXX British Corps (placed under First Canadian Army's command) that drove the enemy back some ten miles through the Reichwald forest. Initially Canadian participation was largely limited to General Spry's 3rd Division 'water rats,' working their way (in amphibious armoured vehicles) up the flooded Waal/Rhine flats until the widening of the front made it possible for General Simonds to deploy his other infantry division. The 2nd Division, now commanded by Major-General A.B. Matthews, a Toronto militiaman, was inserted into the line on February 14.

Two weeks later the weight of the whole operation was shifted to the left flank as the Canadians moved on to higher ground. The two infantry divisions now slogged their way forward into the heart of another forest, the Hochwald, while General Vokes' 4th Armoured Division first cleared the northern end of the vital Calcar-Uden ridge and then swung south, across the infantry's rear, to drive through the 'railway gap' that separated the Hochwald from the smaller Tuschenwald and Balbergerwald to the west. Now that they were fighting on German soil the opposition became quite fanatical and the Canadians were faced by hard-fighting paratroopers of *General* Alfred Schlemm's First German Parachute Army. They formed a core

TOURISTS IN THE HOCHWALD.

118 Closing the Rhine.
Canadian trucks and
armour struggle over a
muddy track through the
Hochwald in February
1945.

119 German refugees and prisoners of war move back through the Canadian lines, south of Calcar, Germany, at the end of February 1945.

around which gathered "old men and young boys who had hand grenades and old rifles and hearts full of hate."[13]

The Germans had concentrated (for them) an unusual amount of supporting firepower which had been pre-registered on every key crossroad or forest ridge, where, in the mist-shrouded woods, many shells exploded on impact with the tree-tops, creating 'air bursts' whose shrapnel often inflicted heavy casualties. The enemy's fire could not be neutralized to the usual extent by tactical air power, since the low cloud ceilings and very poor visibility inhibited close air support. During the whole course of this Battle of the Rhineland, close air support was impossible on nineteen of the twenty-one days' fighting.

The infantry's task was not made any easier by the occasional lack of adequate direction. "It was late afternoon before we finally got word to start ... and no one had given us any compass bearing to use," complained a company commander of the North Shores, in the fifth year of the war! "We simply had to enter a forest that contained many enemy strong-points and blunder through as best we could."[14] When they had finished blundering through the forest, however, two more heroes had won Victoria Crosses. Sergeant Aubrey Cosens of the Queen's Own Rifles, whose battalion had lost a hundred men, won his posthumously. Major F.A. Tilston of the Essex Scottish, which took 130 casualties, lost both his legs in winning his.

Northern Italy and Northwest Europe, 1944-1945

The armour also had its troubles, with their Sherman tanks bogging down in the shell-pocked, waterlogged ground or stalling on steep slopes. Moving up in preparation for driving out of the eastern end of the railway gap on February 28, two squadrons of the Canadian Grenadier Guards lost half their tanks before they even reached the start-line and, of those that crossed it, three out of ten "were almost immediately put out of action by five or six anti-tank guns firing from the right front."[15] Six hundred yards further on, four of the remaining seven were also disabled by German 88s. On the 27th and 28th, 4th Armoured Division lost more than a hundred tanks.

While the Canadians were storming the Hochwald and pushing southwards up the west bank of the Rhine, the Ninth U.S. Army was driving north against rather less formidable opposition. On March 10, opposite Wesel, the last German resistance west of the river was finally pinched out. Further south the Americans already had a toehold on the east bank, having captured a bridge at Remagen, halfway between Dusseldorf and Mainz, three days earlier. But the Remagen lodgement (and the one that General Patton established even further south on March 22) led only to the rolling, wooded hills of Hesse and Thuringia and the certainty of more of the close, brutal infantry fighting that overwhelmingly favoured the defence. Allied strategy demanded that the point of main effort be located further north,

120 In a railway yard in northern Germany a Canadian soldier waits for transport to take his prisoner away.

where there was the prospect of a breakout into the great North German plain and armoured columns would be able to make proper use of their speed, flexibility, and hitting power.

An amphibious crossing of the Rhine, between Emmerich and Wesel, took place on the night of March 23-24, preceded by the heaviest artillery bombardment of the war and a massive air bombardment. The Germans had been seriously weakened by their efforts to hold the west bank, a struggle that had cost them approximately 90,000 men on the First Canadian and Ninth U.S. Army fronts alone. Now the continuing bombardment stunned their forward defences and sealed off the selected zones, so that the actual crossing proved to be comparatively easy.

This assault was directed by Second British Army and carried out by XII and XXX Corps, the latter with the 3rd Canadian Infantry Division under its command for the occasion. Canadian involvement was supposed to be largely nominal – a graceful tribute to their doughty work in clearing the west bank – until a solid bridgehead had been established. The 3rd Division had landed with the British on D-Day and now its 9th (Highland) Brigade would cross the Rhine with them too. It was attached, appropriately enough, to XXX (British) Corps' 51st (Highland) Division, and the first Canadians across the Rhine were the men of the Highland Light Infantry of Canada. They arrived in front of Speldrop, a mile and a half away, just as a Scottish battalion had been forced out of it by a German counterattack. However, remnants of the Scots were fighting on, cut off and surrounded though they were.

The Canadians attacked in the late afternoon, supported by the fire of six field and two medium artillery regiments and two 7.2-inch siege batteries from the other bank of the Rhine. Still, it took two days to clear the village of its garrison of German paratroopers. "We began the house and barn clearing on the edge of the town," wrote one veteran infantryman. "Not many prisoners were taken, as, if they did not surrender before we started on a house, they never had the opportunity afterwards."[16]

With the bridgehead well established, XXX Corps began to develop its attack on a three-division front. The Canadians took the left flank, so that, having fought their way upstream along the west bank of the Rhine, they were now fighting their way downstream along the east bank. The Highland Light Infantry had been followed across the river by the North Nova Scotians, and they too drew a particularly unpleasant ticket in the lottery of battle. On March 25 they came up against elements of a *Panzer Grenadier* division that had been ordered to hold the key road junction at Bienen.

My platoon assaulted in a single extended wave. Ten tumbled down, nailed on the instant by fire from two or maybe three machine-guns.... The rest of us rolled or dropped into

121 Troops of the Black Watch of Canada crossing a makeshift bridge over the Regge River near Ommen, Holland, April 10, 1945.

122 A Sherman tank of the Fort Garry Horse surrounded by civilians in Rijssen, Holland, April 9, 1945.

a shallow ditch, hardly more than a trough six inches deep, at the bottom of the dyke. The Bren-gunners put their weapons to their shoulders but never got a shot away. (I saw them after the battle, both dead, one still holding the aiming position) ... A rifleman on my left took aim at a German weapon pit, and with a spasm collapsed on my arm. His face turned almost instantly a faint green and bore a simple smile.[17]

By nightfall the Maritimers held the southern part of the village. The battalion had lost 114 men – 43 killed – in taking it, however, and the following morning the Highland Light Infantry came back into the line to capture the northern half. As for the author of the quotation above, he, like many another brave soldier, had reached the limits of psychological endurance after seven months of more or less continuous front-line duty. Still unwounded after the battle, he made an effort to report to his commanding officer. "I hadn't any idea, apparently, of how far gone I was emotionally. Instead of furnishing a coherent account, I simply stood in front of him weeping inarticulately, unable to construct a sentence, even to force a single word out of my mouth." Two days later he was on his way back to England, a neuropsychiatric casualty of the war, like one in three or four of his fellow casualties.

The initial amphibious crossing had been quickly followed by an airborne landing of the British 6th and American 17th Airborne Divisions, the British force including the 1st Canadian Parachute Battalion. The Canadians encountered severe machine-gun and rifle

Northern Italy and Northwest Europe, 1944-1945

fire but, like other airborne units, took their objectives without delay or heavy casualties. During the fighting, however, one of the battalion's medical orderlies, Corporal F.G. Topham, won the fourth and last Victoria Cross to be awarded to a Canadian during the campaign for his courage and persistence in attending the wounded, despite being wounded himself. Three of the four Canadian VCs had been won on the banks of the Rhine within a month as the Germans fought for their own soil with a courage born of desperation.

By the end of March 1945 the 2nd Infantry and 4th Armoured Divisions had joined the 3rd Division on the east bank of the Rhine and all three formations were reunited under the command of II Canadian Corps. Storming north along the river, the Canadians had taken the Hoch Elten, a wooded ridge some three miles north of Emmbich, while, in the shattered town itself, Canadian engineers were constructing and floating across the Rhine a 1,400-foot-long pontoon bridge. The completion of this bridge, on April 1, gave Simonds' men their own lifeline to the west bank and an appropriate share of the torrent of equipment and matériel that was now pouring out of Antwerp.

I British Corps, which had been under General Crerar's command since the Normandy days of *Overlord*, now reverted to British control and Crerar was left with the two Canadian corps and a Polish armoured division. He launched the Italian veterans of General Foulkes' I Corps against the German Twenty-Fifth Army in western Holland, between the Rhine/Waal and Ijssel Rivers, and II Corps, together with the Polish armour, into the rich, open farmland between the Ijsselmeer and the Weser River. There was still some hard fighting to be endured, but German resistance was now rapidly collapsing and the sporadic opposition increasingly ill-coordinated. On April 11 the Americans reached the Elbe, by the 21st the British were in Hamburg, and three days later the Russians completed their encirclement of Berlin.

In his steel-and-concrete bunker deep under the heart of Berlin, just before 3:30 p.m. on the last day of April 1945, Adolf Hitler put a pistol barrel in his mouth and pulled the trigger. Four days later, at a few minutes to eight in the morning, a sharp-shooting rifleman of the Lake Superior Regiment, riding on a tank of the Canadian Grenadier Guards along a road just north of Oldenburg, "drilled the bicuspids of a German poised with a bazooka ready to fire."[18] It was, so far as can be ascertained, the last Canadian bullet of the war against Germany, for at eight o'clock exactly the cease-fire sounded in Europe.

By that time, Canadian ground forces had been fighting continuously for more than two years, either in Sicily and Italy or in northwest Europe. The ratio of battle casualties to the total numbers who became prisoners of war is a rough indicator of soldiers' morale over a period of time, and the Canadian ratio was the highest of all the Allied armies in the European campaigns. Their killed and wounded in Sicily and Italy totalled 24,885; in northwest Europe, 44,735. In Italy only 1,004 were taken prisoner; in northwest Europe, 1,864. Canadian soldiers had shown themselves to be as brave and tenacious as those of any nation and, in the case of other ranks and junior officers, as skilful as most. (Man for man, the Germans were probably the most combat-effective troops at the end of the war, as they had been at the beginning.)

The Canadian weakness lay in the paucity of talent at the higher levels of command – in one part, a reflection of the small number of professional officers in the pre-war service, and in another a reflection of their determination to keep key operational appointments in their own hands. Success at operational command levels normally requires both long and careful training and natural talent, but the small budget and low profile of the Canadian forces in pre-war days meant that young officers had had little opportunity to get the necessary training, while the small gene pool meant that, in the natural way of things, there was unlikely to be any significant degree of talent. General Maurice Pope (who was one of them and, moreover, one who did have considerable talents, albeit in a staff capacity) has since commented that "the Canadian military were not soldiers, although we had many experts on the King's Dress Regulations."[19]

In the first edition of this book we expressed the view that, "among Canadian divisional commanders and above, only Simonds, Vokes, and Hoffmeister could possibly be ranked as first-rate.... Many of the others were better staff officers than combat commanders." Twenty years of further study have led us to modify that judgement

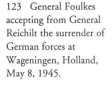

123 General Foulkes accepting from General Reichilt the surrender of German forces at Wageningen, Holland, May 8, 1945.

considerably, however. Hoffmeister, the militiaman who rose from infantry company commander to command the 5th Armoured Division (and was chosen to lead the Canadian ground force for the invasion of Japan until the dropping of two atomic bombs made that option redundant) retains his pre-eminent position, and was probably the only Canadian who could have reached his rank in the German army. Neither Simonds nor Vokes were nearly as good as they were painted, or as we thought them to be then – indeed, more recent research suggests that Simonds was certainly the most overrated of Canadian generals, while Vokes was no more than adequate.

On the other hand, two regulars who we earlier ignored, Dan Spry (who led the 3rd Infantry Division from mid-August 1944 until the last days of the northwest Europe campaign) and Harry Foster (who commanded the 4th Armoured Division from mid-August until the end of November 1944, and then the 1st Infantry Division until the conclusion of the war), seem to have been competent, and might have proved to have been more than that had they not been saddled with Simonds and Foulkes as corps commanders. The enigma still wrapped in mystery is E.L.M. Burns, who seems to have had all the talents necessary for high command except for that key element of charisma.

124 A Canadian corporal supervises two German prisoners stacking helmets and shell cases somewhere in northern Germany.

125 (ABOVE) Canadian
gunners display a copy of
the *Maple Leaf,* the
Canadian army news-
paper, announcing
Germany's surrender.

126 (RIGHT) Dutch
civilians celebrate the end
of the fighting in Europe
by climbing aboard
Canadian carriers in the
suburbs of Rotterdam.

Doctrinally, too many Canadian commanders mimicked the ponderous approach to battle commonly practised by their British exemplars and superiors and, even more than the latter, they thought small. Too little, too late, seemed to be their motto. Let the last word on them go to a regimental officer who served with the Loyal Edmonton Regiment. "Most seemed to insist on reinforcing failure.... They lacked imagination, they suffered from a rigidity that confounded the principles of fire and movement."[20]

Nevertheless, despite the failings of their generals and their comparatively small numbers, Canadian fighting men left a distinct imprint on the record of the war in Europe. Not perhaps as deep a one as their fathers had left a generation earlier, but enough to justify the adjective applied to them more than once by Field Marshal Montgomery – "magnificent."

CHAPTER 10

The War against Japan

Victory in Europe (VE-Day) came on May 5, 1945. The exuberance of the celebrations that marked the end of the war in Europe seems to have been, generally speaking, inversely proportional to the physical distance of the celebrants from the actual fighting. The great day was spent quietly by Canadians in Germany, gaily by those in Holland, boisterously in England and Canada – with the riotous exception of Halifax (described in the next chapter). The Queen's Own Rifles, still in action in front of Aurich until the last minutes of the war, noted in their diary that "there is no celebration but everybody is happy." In western Holland, where military operations had virtually ceased two weeks earlier, units of the 1st Division, pressing into Rotterdam to take the surrender of the German garrison, found themselves swamped with schnapps and pretty girls until their formations lost all coherence. In London, Canadians sang sentimental songs in Piccadilly Circus and stood on their heads atop the great stone lions that guard Nelson's Column in Trafalgar Square.

In one sense all these celebrations were premature, for Japan had not surrendered. But Japan had never been the threat that Germany had been. Despite the economic potential of its territorial acquisitions in China and southeast Asia, its eventual defeat had always been inevitable. The Japanese industrial base – the foundation of success in modern warfare – was very weak. In 1938, for example, Japan produced only seven million tons of crude steel and the United States, its prime enemy, more than ten times as much.

By 1944, Japanese production had actually decreased, while American production had risen by another five million tons. Moreover, Japan had no oil of its own. It had captured all the oilfields and rubber plantations of southeast Asia, yet in 1942 only 40 per cent of the output of the Dutch East Indies oilfields reached Japan; in 1943, only 15 per cent; in 1944, a mere 5 per cent; and in the last eight months of the war none at all evaded the American submarines blockading the Japanese homeland.

Canada played little direct part in weakening Japan's war potential before the end of the war in Europe. In March 1942, when the British needed another coastal reconnaissance squadron in southeast Asia, the RCAF's No. 413 Squadron, equipped with Consolidated Catalina flying boats, was sent to Ceylon from the United Kingdom, where it had been formed the previous July. It started its Far Eastern operations just a week after the arrival of the first aircraft in Ceylon. A Catalina searching for a Japanese fleet, including aircraft carriers, known to be prowling the Indian Ocean, found it some 350 miles

127 Canadian troops (wearing American helmets) file aboard an American transport at Nanaimo, B.C., bound for the invasion of Kiska.

south of the island. "We immediately coded a message and started transmission," the pilot has recorded, but Japanese fighters were already taking off.

> We were halfway through our required third transmission when a shell destroyed our wireless equipment.... Shells set fire to our internal tanks. We managed to get the fire out, and then another started and the aircraft began to break up. Due to our low altitude it was impossible to bail out, but I got the aircraft down on the water before the tail fell off.

An RAF air gunner, whose leg had been severed, went down with the aircraft. The rest of the crewmen swam clear of burning gasoline, pulling with them two of their comrades who were injured and unconscious but wearing 'Mae West' life-jackets. The fighters strafed them continuously, and the two men wearing life-jackets, who were unable to dive under the surface, were killed. The remaining six crewmen – all of them injured and three seriously wounded – were subse-

The War against Japan

128 Conditions were cramped aboard the troop transports that carried the 13th Canadian Infantry Brigade to Kiska.

quently recovered by a Japanese destroyer and spent the rest of the war in prison camps.

Their radioed warning had been picked up in Ceylon, however, and when strike forces from the carriers attacked Colombo next morning they were met by every fighter the British could put into the air. There were about nineteen Canadian Hurricane pilots serving with the RAF on the island and at least eight of them flew against the Japanese that day. They claimed two of the seven aircraft lost by the enemy, while one of them was shot down, happily without any personal injury.

In June 1942, Canada contributed one light-bomber and two fighter squadrons for defensive air patrols on the Alaska mainland when a Japanese strike force occupied Attu and Kiska, the westernmost islands of the thousand-mile-long, American-owned chain that loops out into the Pacific from the southern shores of Alaska. Some Canadian fighter pilots flew with their American allies on offensive patrols over the islands, and five of them died when an entire formation flew into the side of a fog-shrouded mountain on July 13, 1942. There was little military value in the Aleutians, and it was extraordinarily difficult to mount major operations around those cold, foggy, poorly charted, island fortresses. The Japanese were primarily trying to divert American attention and resources from the much more significant theatre of the south-central Pacific, and the issue of enemy occupation of American soil ensured their success.

In May 1943 the Americans retook Attu, using an entire division with massive air and naval fire support to confront the brigade of Japanese infantry that garrisoned it. In a short, small-scale, and exceptionally bloody campaign it took the Americans twenty days and nearly four thousand casualties – half as many again as the total number of Japanese on Attu – to destroy the enemy garrison.

An assault on Kiska followed. The 13th Canadian Infantry Brigade, from General George Pearkes' Western Command and partly composed of NRMA men – conscripts, whose service was constitutionally limited to the western hemisphere – together with the élite American-Canadian First Special Service Force (which, as we have seen, later fought in Italy and the south of France) joined some thirty thousand Americans scheduled to attack the island on August 15, 1943. Aircraft and ships pounded the barren muskeg and rock with bombs and gunfire for three weeks before the troops swarmed ashore, only to find that the enemy had left. "You are dancing the foolische order of Rousebelt," proclaimed a message crudely scrawled on an abandoned barrack wall. "We shall come again and kill Yank-joker."

The invaders inflicted a fair amount of damage on themselves without any assistance from the Japanese. Twenty Americans were killed by their own comrades as over-nervous patrols prowled the island in search of enemy soldiers who might have been dedicated to a suicidal last stand. Booby traps and mines left behind by the Japanese garrison killed four others. Fifty Americans were wounded – accidentally blown up or shot – during the first two months of Allied occupation. Among the Canadians, two were killed by booby traps and two in accidental explosions.

The islands were garrisoned until the end of the war. The Canadians stayed on Kiska exactly six months, filling in the time with fatigues, complaints about the lack of mail, and a protracted legal wrangle with National Defence Headquarters in Ottawa. Early in the war, servicemen serving outside the western hemisphere had been exempted from paying income tax. Now the Canadians on Kiska, who had suddenly become geography conscious, were quick to point out that longitude 177 degrees 30 minutes east – the hemispheric boundary – lay a mile or so east of their camp and appealed for a rebate of all taxes. Bureaucrats at Pacific Command headquarters responded by noting that the International Date Line, which generally followed the hemispheric boundary, jogged slightly in order to place the whole island in the western hemisphere for purposes of time – legally a dubious argument. The authorities in Ottawa argued more decisively that "the United States say the island is in the Western

129 On a British Columbia hillside an officer of the Royal Canadian Engineers, a sergeant, and the forest worker who discovered it inspect a Japanese 'balloon bomb' from a safe distance.

Hemisphere. There is no overriding authority to say that it is not, therefore Kiska must of necessity be where its owners say it is – in the Western Hemisphere."

The first direct attack on Canadian soil since the 1871 Fenian raid in Manitoba had occurred on June 20, 1942, only days after the Japanese occupation of Attu and Kiska. A Japanese submarine that had been patrolling off Seattle was ordered north to support the Aleutian assault and, in passing, chose to lob a few shells at the isolated lighthouse and radio station at Estevan Point on Vancouver Island. There were no casualties and very little damage was done. In the late fall of 1944, however, a potentially much more serious attack on North American territory was initiated by the Japanese. During the following winter, some nine thousand balloons – their gasbags made of mulberry bark paper – were launched from Japan. They carried high-explosive or incendiary bombloads of approximately fifty pounds each – usually four incendiary devices accounting for about two-thirds of the payload, together with an explosive 'core' designed to ignite and distribute the incendiaries over a twenty-yard radius.

They were carried across the Pacific at a height of twenty to thirty thousand feet by the prevailing winds, their makers hoping they

The War against Japan

would cause widespread forest fires as well as panic and confusion in western Canada and in the United States. However, their main value may have been to provide an offensive element to Japanese strategy on which Japanese public opinion – developing a defeatist tinge by 1944 – could focus.

Japanese sources have estimated that 10 per cent of the balloons should have reached North America, but in fact there are only 296 balloon incidents on record, 80 of them in Canada. The first to be reported in this country arrived on January 12, 1945, at Minton, Saskatchewan, with all but one of its bombs failing to function. The most easterly landing in Canada came near Nelson House, Manitoba, the most northerly at Canol Road, in the Northwest Territories, while British Columbia received more than half the Canadian total. Three of the balloons were shot down by the RCAF.

The initial reaction of both American and Canadian authorities was to impose a total security blanket on the presence of the balloon bombs, but a report from Alberta of schoolboys using a red hot poker to unsolder the connections from a bomb container soon necessitated restricted publicity. Police and servicemen were authorized to pass warnings by word of mouth to "any members of the public whom the authorities consider it desirable to be told of the balloon occurrences ... dependence must be placed on ranchers, trappers, H[udson's] B[ay] Posts, etc., passing word along of findings."

After a woman and five children were killed near Bly, Oregon, on May 5, the security net was further modified and newspapers were encouraged to publicize the existence of the balloons without mentioning either the total numbers reported or the government's fears that bacteriological warfare might be resorted to by this means.

> At this stage it is definitely considered that reference should not be made to the possibility of contaminated substance being carried ... and it is sufficient if information is given to the effect that persons should be kept away from balloon material because of possible danger from explosive missiles.[2]

Fears of anthrax in the Alberta cattle country, or typhoid on the Pacific watershed, proved groundless, however, and in April 1945 the Japanese abandoned the campaign, apparently assessing it (quite correctly) as an operational failure.

In contrast with this ineffectual undertaking against North America, an American strategic bombing assault on Japan created enormous havoc. In November 1944, B-29 Superfortresses operating from the Marianas – Saipan, Tinian, and Guam – began to raid Japan in force, using the same tactics that the United States Eighth Air Force had previously employed against Germany. The bombers were unsupported by long-range fighter escorts and made high-level attacks using primarily high-explosive bombs. These attacks inflicted considerable, but not vital, damage on the Japanese war potential and were accompanied by an unacceptable overall loss rate of 6 per cent, so that enthusiasm quickly began to flag.

There was a dramatic change, however, in February 1945 when General Curtis LeMay took command of the American bombing force. Applying the experience he had gained in the air war against Germany, LeMay decided to try low-level (7,000 ft) incendiary attacks by night. The first such raid, flown against Tokyo in early March 1945, resulted in the destruction by fire of fifteen square miles of the city, with an estimated 83,000 dead and 97,000 injured – a greater number of casualties than that later inflicted by either of the atomic bombs. LeMay's bombers then began the systematic destruction of urban Japan.

Benefitting from the fact that Japanese radar was comparatively unsophisticated and severely limited the effectiveness of their night-fighters, the American loss rate dipped to 1.4 per cent. In April P-47 escorts began to provide fighter cover and the Superfortresses could fly by day and night, their task being made even easier by the grave shortage of gasoline that increasingly handicapped the enemy's air defences. Then, on August 6, 1945, came the atomic bomb. Suddenly the enormous, complex, and intricate accumulation of men and material being assembled by the Allies for the invasion of Japan was no longer needed.

Planning for the assault on Japan had been under way for a long time. Even before the United States had entered the war, in the course of Anglo-American 'conversations' held during March 1941 in Washington, Britain and the United States had agreed that the defeat of Germany was their paramount concern. Only when Germany was defeated would Phase II of the war begin, and the full weight of the Allies be applied against the Japanese. The formulation of this strategy – and the ensuing debates over it – did not involve Canadians; grand strategy never did, unless Canadian sovereignty was involved in some way. But Mackenzie King accepted that Canada had an obligation to fight in the Pacific, although he cautiously argued that it would be "reasonable to take into account our four years of war to the Americans' two. Also we may be sure we will get little credit for anything we do, either on the part of the United States or Great Britain."

Early in 1944, Ottawa informed London and Washington that Canada's position as a Pacific power, as a member of the Commonwealth, and as an American nation, required its participation in the defeat of Japan. However, it was not made clear whether Ottawa felt Canada should work with the Americans or the British. C.G. Power, King's minister of national defence for air, later claimed that during the first eight months of 1944 "we were unable to formulate any definite plan of campaign against Japan." This was not entirely the Cabinet's fault, although King's obvious reluctance to enter into any kind of imperial commitment was partly to blame. Fearful of being labelled a tool of British imperialism, King refused to pledge Canadian resources to their campaign in southeast Asia – the only decision that could have been made quickly – and Canadian planning for Pacific operations could hardly begin until the Anglo-American relationship in that theatre had been settled. Meanwhile, King told Churchill that if operations were to take place in the North Pacific, then Canadian forces should serve there.

The British acknowledged that this would be acceptable on strategic, political, and administrative grounds. They still hoped, however, that Canada would join them in southeast Asia, as "British manpower will be severely strained." In July 1944, the British chiefs of staff put forward proposals for each of the Canadian services. The RCN might reinforce the British fleet, probably in the Bay of Bengal or the southwest Pacific, with the possibility of a later switch to the north since the Royal Navy still did not know whether or not the United States would accept a British fleet in the central Pacific. The RCAF could operate with the RAF, also in southeast Asia or the south-west Pacific, and the chiefs of staff suggested that an army be held ready in Canada for employment wherever required by the Americans.

King was not yet prepared to make any firm commitment, how-ever, arguing that Allied strategy should be determined first. He was also insistent that financial considerations be given priority. He sus-pected that his defence ministers "were pretty much set to make a very large contribution," but he himself was not and, as usual, he got his way. The Cabinet decided that only one division would be offered, while the navy proposals would be cut by 50 per cent and the air-force contribution substantially reduced. It was formally agreed that Canadian forces should "participate ... in operational theatres of direct interest to Canada as a North American nation, for example in the North or Central Pacific, rather than in more remote areas such as South-East Asia."[3] The exact contribution would be decided after the Quebec Conference of September 1944, code-named *Octagon*.

At *Octagon* the outlines of the British role in the Pacific were determined. It was also agreed that Canadian participation in the main operations against Japan would be acceptable "in principle," but no attempt was made to discuss the nature of the contribution. Although Mackenzie King wanted a Canadian presence in the Pacific, he remained totally opposed to operations by Canadians in southeast Asia. He claimed, probably quite rightly, that "no government in Canada once the European war was over could send its men to India, Burma and Singapore to fight with any forces and hope to get through a general election successfully." Convinced that the services and the defence ministers were scheming to commit Canadians to an 'imperial' war, he noted in his diary, on September 13, 1944, that in Cabinet he had had to "do most of the fighting myself to maintain

The War against Japan

what I would call the only tenable position which means keeping our forces for North or Central Pacific areas." The British influence there was, and would be, negligible; the American influence, overwhelming. With this purely political decision King unwittingly committed Canada and Canadians to the American way of war.

The dogmatic attitude of the prime minister makes it hard to understand how the RAF in southeast Asia came to be reinforced by two RCAF transport squadrons in October and November 1944. However, it will be recalled that the revised Article XV of the BCATP entitled Canada to thirty-five overseas squadrons – or three more than currently on the books. In May 1944 the British Air Ministry urged Ottawa to fill those slots with three more heavy-bomber squadrons and Air Minister Power quickly agreed – only to reverse his decision at the behest of Air Marshal Breadner, now stationed in London as the RCAF's senior officer overseas. Breadner pointed out that casualties were heaviest in bomber squadrons and recommended the creation of a light-bomber squadron and two transport squadrons instead.

The British had no need of light-bomber squadrons and agreement was finally reached on three medium-range transport units. The need was greatest in southeast Asia, and agreement was finally reached that two squadrons should be formed there "as soon as possible," on the clear understanding that they would be withdrawn as soon as the war in Europe ended, while a third would be formed in northwest Europe in early 1945. Meanwhile a Canadian Air Liaison Mission to India, condemning the conditions under which Canadians already there were serving, had suggested that "the RCAF not participate in the war in South-East Asia." The RCAF's right hand did not always know what its left hand was doing, however, and Nos 435 and 436 Squadrons began to form at Gujrat, north of Lahore, in what was then northwest India, in October 1944.

Whether at this stage Mackenzie King became aware of the RCAF's commitment is not clear but, in September 1944, Power cabled Breadner to arrange the withdrawal of No. 413 (Coastal Reconnaissance) Squadron in order to offset the formation of the two transport squadrons in India. Two months later, No. 413 was informed that it would shortly return to the United Kingdom for conversion to a bomber role and, in mid-January 1945, it embarked for England, although the two transport squadrons remained in southeast Asia until the end of the war against Japan. Before they left Burma, in September 1945, they had accumulated over 50,000 operational flying hours and delivered 46,000 tons of cargo and nearly 28,000 passengers to their various destinations.

Meanwhile, Canadian planning for Phase II (the war against Japan) was going ahead in Ottawa. In November 1944 the Cabinet approved a ground force of one division and ancillary troops for the Pacific. The United States rejected a suggestion that would have substituted an armoured for an infantry division (the armoured division would be smaller and easier to man) and the final agreement called for an infantry division, possibly reinforced with armour and some support troops. The Canadians would be organized on American lines and train in the United States to use American equipment and tactics – in short, be treated as an American unit. They would be used "as a follow-up in the main operation" – the invasion of Japan – and eventually be returned to Canada "in a priority consistent with that applied to other forces engaged in the Pacific war"; in other words, once again Canada's control of its soldiers would be significantly reduced.

Two months after the end of the war in Europe nearly 10,000 officers and 70,000 men had volunteered to join the Pacific Force (to be commanded by Hoffmeister). Of these only 2,796 officers and 36,386 men were found suitable in terms of service record, health, and age, but there were more than enough for immediate requirements and three months' reinforcements. The force began concentrating at nine stations across Canada in July 1945. American training teams came to Canada and Canadian instructors were sent south to be introduced to American methods and organization, while plans were put in hand to send the whole force to Camp Breckenridge, Kentucky, for further individual and unit training along American lines.

The RCN's major aim was to acquire more of the 'big ships' that would make them a 'balanced' fleet, instead of one that left them essentially a convoy escort force. The Pacific war seemed to provide a strong justification for doing so, but Mackenzie King was having none of it and the navy's Pacific planning was eventually reduced to encompass two cruisers, *Uganda* and *Ontario*, the *Prince Robert* (an anti-aircraft cruiser), two light fleet carriers (still under construction when the war ended), sixteeen destroyers, thirty-six frigates, and eight corvettes. However, only one of the cruisers, HMCS *Uganda*, ever saw combat service in the Pacific. Commissioned into the RCN in October 1944, she joined a British task force that was operating with the USN's Third Fleet's Fast Carrier Force in March 1945. This formation was supporting the American assault on Okinawa, and *Uganda*'s main task was as an anti-aircraft guard for the carriers; but at the end of July – just a couple of weeks before the war ended – she left the theatre because of a Cabinet policy decision that only volunteers would serve in the Pacific. A vote was taken, not enough of her crew volunteered to maintain a combat capability, and *Uganda* thus established the unique but dubious distinction of being the only Canadian unit that ever voted itself out of combat.

The RCAF also had ambitious plans for Phase II. There was a strong desire on the part of the air staff to field an integrated force under full Canadian command and control, but a combination of Cabinet reluctance to make major commitments and American pressure to make the RAF/RCAF contingents entirely self-supporting reduced their proposal, step by step, from a balanced force of twelve bomber, six fighter, three transport, and one air-sea rescue squadron to eight bomber and three transport squadrons. Eight squadrons of No. 6 Group flew from the United Kingdom to Canada in June 1945 for re-training and the thirty days' leave granted to all volunteers for the Pacific.

They were to return to Britain for conversion to Avro Lincoln aircraft in September, and the first two squadrons were scheduled to arrive in Okinawa in December 1945. When the other six arrived, a Canadian group was to be formed and, eventually, the contingent would total fifteen thousand men. However, these plans were abruptly halted by the two atomic bombs dropped on Hiroshima and Nagasaki on August 6 and 9, 1945. On August 10 an Imperial Conference in Tokyo decided to sue for peace; on August 14 all hostilities ended; and on September 2 the Japanese formally surrendered.

On August 9 – at almost the same moment that the second atomic bomb was falling on Nagasaki – a Canadian pilot in the Royal Navy's Fleet Air Arm, Lieutenant Robert Hampton Gray, was leading a flight of Corsair fighter-bombers from HMS *Formidable* against a number of Japanese ships at Onagawa Wan, on the northern island of Honshu. Having already led very similar strikes against five Narvik-class destroyers in a Norwegian fiord a year before, and against a Japanese destroyer in the Inland Sea just a few days earlier (an attack that won him the Distinguished Service Cross), 'Ham' Gray knew what to do and did it unflinchingly.

Flyers astern of Gray saw him go into a run aimed at one of the destroyers. As his plane swung onto an attacking course, a cone of fire from ships and shore batteries centred upon it. A first hit registered; then a second. A moment later streamers of flame flickered astern of the aircraft, which still held steadily to its course. Weaving and ablaze it bore down to within fifty yards of the destroyer before its bombs were released. One struck directly amidships; a second fell on, or close alongside, the target, which sank almost immediately; but before it disappeared Gray's riddled plane had dived into the waters of the bay. Three months later, as Canada settled to the calmer routines and more uncertain problems of peace, the *London Gazette* announced the posthumous award of a Victoria Cross to Gray for his "brilliant fighting spirit and most inspiring leadership."

Canadians played only a minor part in the design and production of the atomic bombs that ended the war against Japan. In the summer of 1939 experiments at Columbia University – the culmination of thirty years of theorizing and experimentation in Europe and America – indicated the possibility that uranium might be used to liberate a million times as much energy as any known chemical explosive. The

246   *The War against Japan*

130 The Eldorado Mine camp at Port Radium, N.W.T., on the eastern shore of Great Bear Lake. This photograph was taken in 1937 when radium was extracted from pitchblende for use in cancer therapy and uranium was an unimportant by-product of the refining process.

war seemed imminent in Europe, and Albert Einstein, probably the best-known scientist in the world at that time, wrote his now-famous letter to President Roosevelt, reporting that "it may become possible to set up a nuclear chain reaction in a large mass of uranium by which vast amounts of power ... would be generated.... This new phenomenon would also lead to the construction of bombs."

From that moment the race was on to unlock the secrets of nuclear fission, and uranium acquired unusual importance. It was not a common element but, in the form of uranium oxide, it was a by-product of radium extraction. Radium, the basis of cancer therapy in the 1930s, came from pitchblende, and a rich deposit of pitchblende had been worked by Eldorado Gold Mines on the eastern shore of Great Bear Lake in the Northwest Territories since 1933. The ore was transported to Port Hope, on Lake Ontario, where the largest refinery of its kind in North America (and probably the largest in the world) was turning out radium at $30,000 a gram – and uranium oxide, as a by-product, for nothing.

In 1940 economic difficulties connected with the expansion of Canada's war industry had led Eldorado to close down its mining operations in the North, although the Port Hope refinery was still extracting radium from accumulated stocks of ore. Suddenly, however, a new market appeared in the early spring of 1942 when the possibility of atomic bombs began to acquire practical military significance. Vast quantities of uranium were needed. With the prospect of a large American contract in sight, Eldorado reopened the mine, which was in production again by August 1942. However, before that time control of it had been taken from Eldorado. On June 15, Mackenzie King recorded in his diary "an interview with Malcolm MacDonald [British high commissioner in Ottawa] and two scientists

The War against Japan

from England about the acquisition of some property in Canada, so as to prevent competition in price on a mineral much needed in connection with the manufacture of explosives." The Canadian government had promptly bought a majority interest in Eldorado.

One product of uranium fission is a number of relatively fast-moving neutrons. In order for an uncontrolled chain reaction (i.e., a nuclear explosion) to occur, these neutrons must initiate fission of other atoms by bombarding them in turn. But since such fission is brought about most readily through the impact of comparatively slow-moving neutrons, it is necessary to introduce some medium that will moderate the speed of the emitted neutrons. In 1942 two possibilities seemed to offer promise as moderators: graphite and so-called 'heavy water,' or deuterium oxide.

For the large-scale production of heavy water, heavy hydrogen offered a convenient starting-point. Again, Canada had a built-in advantage, for heavy hydrogen was a by-product of the production process employed in the manufacture of ammonia and the largest ammonia producer on the continent was in Trail, B.C. During the summer of 1942, the United States contracted for additional facilities at Trail as well as at three other plants in West Virginia, Indiana, and Alabama. The Trail plant was first into production by six months, but heavy water in the required quantities did not become available until the middle of 1944.

Long before that time, however, Canada had been eased out of the apparent mainstream of nuclear research. As the likelihood of an atomic bomb became more and more probable, the Americans began to take an increasingly exclusionary approach to the matter. In January 1943, they decided unilaterally to "restrict our interchange [of all scientific information] by the application of the principle that we are to have complete interchange on design and construction of new equipment only if the recipient of the information is in a position to take advantage of it in this war."[4] This ruling effectively barred both Britain and Canada from all American nuclear know-how, including that related to post-war applications, since neither boasted the economic and industrial potential that would have permitted them to manufacture atomic bombs in the foreseeable future.*

Using the extant Canadian resource and research capability, a small Anglo-Canadian program of research into the use of heavy water as a neutron moderator in the fission of uranium had begun in

---

*Bearing in mind the relative magnitude of the Commonwealth commitment against international aggression, both before and after the United States entered the war, their attitude can hardly be described as generous. On the other hand, the post-war Gouzenko revelations in Canada and the convictions for espionage of Allan Nunn May, Klaus Fuchs, and Bruno Ponticorvo (all of whom had worked on British atomic research teams) suggest that, from a security point of view, these precautions had considerable justification.

131 Louis Slotin working on the University of Chicago's cyclotron.

Montreal during 1942, however, and the scientists there continued to provide some input into the American project. Canadian research expanded to Chalk River, Ontario, in the summer of 1944, where the facilities required for the operation of a nuclear pile were conveniently available. By that time American research had confirmed the adequacy of much cheaper graphite as a moderator for wartime purposes, but the work in Montreal and Chalk River had paradoxically laid a basis for Canadian eminence in that post-war field of nuclear industrialization in which the Americans had hoped to reign supreme.

Meanwhile Canadian uranium continued to fuel laboratories and workshops of atomic bomb technology in the United States, and individual Canadian and British scientists were employed in the highly compartmentalized and strictly censored project that the Americans code-named *Manhattan District*. One of the Canadians was Walter Zinn, who assisted Enrico Fermi in establishing the world's first nuclear chain reaction at the University of Chicago on December 2, 1942. Another was Louis Slotin, a wiry young man from Winnipeg who had helped to build the University of Chicago's cyclotron ('atom-smasher') in 1938. After working with Fermi and Zinn at Chicago, Slotin went to Oak Ridge, Tennessee, to help build the first plutonium reactor. When that project was accomplished he moved to Los Alamos to play a major part in the construction of the first bomb.

Although he had a doctorate in biochemistry and a mind quite capable of appreciating the esoteric principles of nuclear physics, Slotin worked on the practical application of atomic theory rather than in the realm of theory itself. The creation of a 'critical'

The War against Japan

mass of uranium or plutonium that might result in a nuclear explosion could only be roughly determined by theoretical calculation at that time. But precision and certainty were essential in building the bomb, and Louis Slotin and Luis W. Alvarez, a Californian, were the scientists who ascertained, by practical experiments, the exact quantities that would bring about 'criticality.' Slotin's approach was pragmatic to an extreme. Carrying out adjustments with an ordinary screwdriver, he brought two hemispheres of plutonium closer and closer together while, with his ear cocked to the ticking of a Geiger counter, he measured the rising criticality of the neutron count.

There was no danger of a nuclear explosion unless the hemispheres were to be brought together with extreme rapidity – i.e., by means of conventional high-explosive charges driving them violently together – but there was the risk of a more moderate chain reaction that would bring about an uncontrolled burst of radiation deadly to any living thing it contacted. Slotin's object was to stop just short of the critical point at which a chain reaction would begin and then ease the hemispheres apart again. If he reached, or passed, that point – measured in fractions of a millimetre – then a deadly burst of radiation would be released. Slotin called this process "tickling the dragon's tail."

American security regulations and Slotin's 'foreign' citizenship combined to prevent his being posted to the South Pacific to assemble the bombs that would be used against Japan. Alvarez went instead. The Canadian remained at Los Alamos and built the explosive mechanism of the experimental *Trinity* bomb that exploded at Alamogordo, New Mexico, at ten minutes past five in the morning of July 16, 1945. Even the scientists were astonished at the power of the explosion. Dr. Robert Oppenheimer, a key figure in the bomb's design, clinging to a pillar in the control room five and a half miles away as the whole structure rocked, and watching the sinister mushroom cloud form, was reminded of the words of Sri Krishna in the sacred Hindu epic, *The Bhagavadgita*, "I am become Death, the shatterer of worlds."

On May 21, 1946, while working on the post-war testing program, Slotin tickled the dragon's tail once too often. His screwdriver slipped, the hemispheres came too close, and the mass of plutonium became critical. The laboratory was instantly filled with a dazzling bluish glare and the neutron-counter 'blew' as the radiation level soared right off the scale in a fraction of a second. Instead of freezing or flinching, Slotin tore the hemispheres apart with his hands, told his colleagues to stand still, and sketched on a blackboard each man's position so that doctors would be able to calculate accurately the degree of radiation to which they had been exposed. For him, who had been closest and who had actually touched the hemispheres, there could be no hope: after nine days of agony, Louis Slotin died. His body, packed in a lead-lined coffin, was brought back to Winnipeg by a USAAF airplane. The *Winnipeg Free Press* reported that three thousand people attended his funeral. None of them knew the cause or precise circumstances of his death, for the techniques of manufacturing atomic bombs were still 'Top Secret.'

CHAPTER 11

The Home Front

The population of Canada between 1939 and 1945 varied between eleven and twelve million, and well over two million of them made a direct contribution to the war, either in uniform or by working in industry, government, or on associated tasks. This amounted to total mobilization of the Home Front, because virtually everyone else in the population was either a dependant or, like farmers, foresters, fishermen, or miners, unavailable for 'essential' war work. The War Measures Act, originally brought in during the First World War, came into effect once again, and, as in any belligerent nation, total mobilization was accompanied by arbitrary government and propaganda, while censorship became commonplace. "These were the tools of totalitarianism," two Canadian historians of warfare and society have have remarked.[1]

To avoid the permanent replacement of democratic with totalitarian government, which would be likely to follow any serious weakening of society caused by the strains of war, the government had to minimize the basic weaknesses and emphasize the strengths of the community, providing a solid foundation on which to build when the war was over. The central concern was manpower. The Cabinet's constant preoccupation was to keep the size of the armed forces within reasonable bounds because compulsory military service overseas would arouse bitter opposition, particularly in Quebec.[2]

Even for those who did not subscribe to the isolationist position, there were important differences with the rest of the country in language and culture that impeded active contributions to a war effort dominated by English Canadians. Though the fall of France in 1940 provoked a surge of sympathy for that country among the Québécois, that was tempered by a broader indifference to European events, and was not exploited with any success.

In March 1939, and again in September, Mackenzie King had promised that there would be no conscription for service overseas. In October 1939 the federal Liberals were able to take that message to Quebec during a provincial election. Premier Maurice Duplessis' attack on federal war policies, which he said would undermine provincial autonomy and bring about assimilation, would amount to a provincial rejection of those policies if he was re-elected. King's Quebec-based Cabinet ministers – C.G. Power, P.J.A. Cardin, and Ernest Lapointe – announced that they would resign if Duplessis won, thus leaving King with a Cabinet that would almost certainly be pro-conscriptionist. Adélard Godbout's Liberals defeated Maurice Duplessis and the Union Nationale party, however, thus ensuring that there would be no formal

132 An anti-conscrip-
tion rally in Montreal,
March 1939.

opposition to King's war policies. But the promise that overseas conscription would not be implemented was resented by many anglo-
phones in the Cabinet, in Parliament, and in the country as a whole,
particularly in the armed forces.

Shortly after King's great victory in the general election of 1940
– the government was returned with 181 seats – the National
Resources Mobilization Act, or NRMA, which authorized conscription
for home defence, was passed by Parliament in June 1940. Single men
and childless widowers between 21 and 45 were required to register
for military service, but the mayor of Montreal, Camillien Houde –
who had figured so prominently in the 1939 royal visit and had
attained the status of a French Canadian folk hero – publicly stated
his intention not to register and urged others to join him in disobey-
ing the law. He was interned under the War Measures Act until 1944.

The first three groups of young men called up, beginning in
October 1940, had to spend thirty days in training – a too-brief exercise that, since it produced no trained soldiers, occupied instructors
and equipment that could have been better used elsewhere.
Nonetheless, it was the first step towards a more active involvement
of the population in the war effort. In February 1941, the system was
altered to require four-month periods of enlistment and, after April
1941, NRMA men were required to serve for the duration of the war.
Later nicknamed "zombies" by the General Service men who had volunteered for overseas service, these conscripts had an unenviable reputation in the armed forces and in most of the country. The fact

253

remains, however, that their existence released volunteers for overseas and also provided military defence that sometimes – as at Kiska in 1943 – was more than a token contribution. Moreover, NRMA service was no disgrace in many of the rural communities the men came from, not only in French Canada but in some other parts of the country as well.

By the summer of 1941, General McNaughton, in England, and staff officers of the three services, in Ottawa, had begun to worry that to maintain an army that now comprised four divisions, and to continue the expansion of the navy, and most particularly the RCAF, would require more men and women than the population could provide without full conscription. There was no doubt that hard fighting lay ahead. The question was, to what extent should Canada be committed? Two divisions were already in England, serving as a garrison and training for the invasion of Europe; two others were preparing to join them, but there was no prospect of large-scale fighting. At a time when the navy and air force were engaged in active operations against the enemy, there was a growing feeling that Canadian soldiers should also be involved.

With that in mind, McNaughton, in July 1941, warned C.G. Power, the associate minister of national defence for air, that "before embarking on new adventures ... we should be certain that we will be in a position to carry out ... the military commitments already undertaken." But as those commitments would create a need for replacements once the army was in combat, any additional military undertaking might easily bring about the very thing Mackenzie King feared: a reinforcement crisis.

For the moment the manpower question was more one of principle than need. The Canadian army – except for the two battalions that went to Hong Kong – did not see action until the summer of 1942 at Dieppe. What worried many people – described by General Pope, soon to become vice-chief of the general staff, as "over-zealous and impatient spirits, principally in Ontario" - was that, unlike Canadians, every British (and subsequently every American) serviceman could be sent to serve in any theatre. Why should Canada restrict its conscripted troops to service at home?

For most French Canadians the question was beside the point. They showed their feelings in the national plebiscite of April 1942 on the question: "Are you in favour of releasing the Government from any obligations arising out of any past commitments restricting the methods of raising men for military service?" Four-fifths of French-Canadian voters opposed any change to the NRMA. On the other hand the national result – two to one in favour of overseas service for NRMA men – virtually forced the government to introduce into Parliament an amendment to the act removing the prohibition on overseas service. Mackenzie King was attacked by both wings of his Cabinet. Public Works Minister P.J.A. Cardin resigned because he felt that the government had gone too far. Defence Minister J.L. Ralston tendered his resignation (he was talked out of it for the time being) because the government would not go far enough. He objected because King still insisted that overseas conscription could not be *implemented* without a vote of confidence from Parliament. The amendment passed, however, and in spite of King's notorious compromise formula - "not necessarily conscription but conscription if necessary" - it was nothing less than a violation of his 1939 pledge, particularly in the eyes of Quebec.

One can sympathize with both sides in this situation. King had to some extent painted himself into a corner by trying to cater to opposite opinions. Each decision he made, though apparently essential at the time, had moved the country inexorably towards "conscription if necessary." The possibility always existed for meeting manpower demands with volunteer forces, but it depended on a sympathetic understanding of French-Canadian attitudes and language requirements, and on the co-ordination of recruiting programs in all three services.

134 By March 1942 the campaign to vote *Non* in the plebiscite brought out anti-conscription demonstrators. But this photograph shows little evidence of animosity when a group of BCATP trainees crossed the demonstrators' path in Montreal.

In June 1941, an army staff analysis indicated that enlistment figures in Quebec were much higher than at a comparable period of the First Word War. (There was no way of calculating exactly how many recruits were of French-speaking origin.) Nevertheless, Ottawa concluded that the French-Canadian response could still be improved upon, not only by a more imaginative approach to recruiting, but also by providing more appropriate conditions of service. Recruiting should take into account that when a French Canadian volunteered he might have to accept a certain loss of face in his own community. Gabrielle Roy captured the situation well in her 1947 novel, *The Tin Flute*, when a young soldier tries to explain to his family and friends why he joined the army:

> "But Ma Philibert," he said trying to soothe her, "if your neighbour's house was burning, you'd go and help him, wouldn't you?"
>
> "The devil I would."
>
> Boisvert snorted. "Ugh! We have our share of burning houses right here. And plenty of troubles of our own. You don't have to go so far away to find 'em."
>
> "I know," said Emmanuel. "I didn't enlist to save Poland either, believe me."
>
> "Then why did you?" demanded Boisvert, nonplussed....

The Home Front

"Has it never occurred to you," he asked, "that sometimes a man helps himself when he helps others?"

"The hell he does," replied Boisvert. "These days it's
every man for himself."[3]

It was discouraging for a volunteer to find not only that his
motives were likely to be misunderstood at home but that he did not
stand an even chance of being accepted in a fighting capacity unless
he spoke English. Of fifty-five thousand French-Canadian volunteers
in the army, more than half served in anglophone units. Only the
'Van Doos,' Le Régiment de la Chaudière, Le Régiment de
Maisonneuve, Les Fusiliers de Mont-Royal, Le 4e régiment de l'ar-
tillerie, and three medical units were entirely French speaking. Nine
English-speaking units had from 30 to 65 per cent French-Canadian
content; forty-four had from 5 to 25 per cent.

There were no francophone units in the navy. The addition of
French-speaking ships or units would have added a massive administrative and training burden to the undermanned and overwhelmingly anglophone staffs in naval bases and training schools. When a
nation with such an enormous length of coast had only seen fit to
support a minute naval service prior to 1939, it is hardly surprising
that its composition did not reflect the English-French make-up of
the population. It was an unfortunate situation, but one for which no
remedy existed when there was not even a small nucleus of fully
trained French-speaking personnel to train ships' companies, let alone
take ships to sea in the face of the enemy. The RCN did institute special English-language training but, in spite of this and in spite of the
fact that numerous French-Canadian officers and men served with
great distinction, it is true that owing to language problems a great
many francophones were only considered suitable to serve as stewards
or as seamen without technical specialization.

The air force was the most difficult service for a French Canadian
to enter. It was more particular about documentation than the other
services and the RCAF did not open a recruiting centre in Montreal
until the summer of 1941. To join, a recruit had to produce birth and
marriage certificates, educational diplomas, and two letters of reference. Quebeckers of rural origin, in particular, ran into difficulty here
because their Christian names took various forms, birth and bap-
tismal certificates often gave different names, and the recruiters were
thoroughly baffled. Nevertheless, in 1942 the RCAF reluctantly formed
No. 425 (Alouette) Squadron, equipped with Halifax bombers and
attached to Bomber Command of the RAF, as a French-Canadian
unit. It was not easy to find a francophone squadron commander, but
by 1942 there were three hundred French-speaking Canadians in the
unit, forming 50 per cent of the aircrew and 90 per cent of the ground
crew. This, however, was still not enough to compensate for the obsta-

cles to entry and advancement in the RCAF for most French Canadians.

In all three services, prejudice played its part in varying degrees. On some bases not only was English the working language, but the speaking of French was forbidden. Quebec, then, was an obvious centre of resistance to the military manpower policy eventually settled upon. But it was not just resistance that led to shortcomings in the volunteer system. There was also the problem of uncontrolled competition for recruits among the three services.

Each service was able to recruit freely those Category 'A' men whose physiques, psyches, and mental abilities made them suitable for front-line duties, but the air force got the lion's share. There was a great demand for aircrew and this coincided with the spontaneous desire of a very large proportion of the country's youth to join the RCAF. Flying offered a much more acceptable way of fighting the war than clumping through the mud as an infantryman or riding through it in a tank. The cockpit of a Spitfire held more attractions than the bridge or engineroom of a corvette. The romance of 'the wild blue yonder,' and the prospect of an environment less inimical to the individual than the earthbound army and navy, brought patriotic youngsters flocking to enlist as aircrew. The ultimate result of this enthusiastic response was excessive recruiting by the RCAF at the expense of the army. However, the extraordinary success of the BCATP, which trained aircrew for the RCAF while providing a large-scale military commitment at home (and one which involved comparatively few casualties), made it easy for the Cabinet to acquiesce in this lopsided distribution of resources.

Because of the fluctuation in demand, the large proportion of men who had to drop out of training for various reasons, and the lengths of time it took to train aircrew to an operational standard (not less than nine months), the BCATP found it necessary to build up a very substantial pool of aircrew candidates who could be fed into the training stream as required. The ups and downs experienced by the RCAF in meeting its aircrew quotas are well illustrated by the revisions in age qualifications for pilot training. In April 1940, all aircrew candidates were required to have passed their eighteenth birthday and pilot applicants were not to have reached their twenty-eighth.

By September 1941, as the strategic bombing offensive against Germany began to increase in tempo, a falling off in enlistments brought a lowering of the minimum age to $17^1/2$ and a raising of the maximum to 33 (35 with special permission). In August 1943, the minimum age for aircrew enlistment was reduced to 17, and the 17-year-olds were placed in a 'holding pattern.' They could not begin flying training until their eighteenth birthday and, in the meantime, were either sent on leave without pay or given pre-aircrew academic training. They returned to basic service training at $17^1/2$ and six months later were fed into the aircrew training stream. This early enrollment reflected the RCAF's determination to take the 'cream of the crop' and also emphasized the attraction the air force held for Canadian youth. In the third quarter of 1943, boys of 18 or under accounted for 50 per cent of the total aircrew intake.

The constant need for replacing training failures was always a problem, particularly with pilots, and great efforts were made to keep the failure rates as low as possible. The first difficulty arose over selection procedures. How was aircrew potential to be assessed? Physical failings were easy to spot and it was possible to make fairly accurate judgements of mental stability, but intellectual capabilities were harder to pin down. At first, selection procedures relied on education levels – only junior matriculants or higher were eligible. Then an 'ability to learn' test was devised and in 1942 an improved version of it, known as the 'classification' test, was introduced. It supplied a much better assessment of flying potential, but failure rates remained high at elementary flying training schools: between June 1943 and March 1944 they were just over 30 per cent. One student pilot reported that at the start of the course

> my instructor mentioned that I would be given, like everybody else, eight – and only eight – hours of instruction, by which time I would be expected to go solo.... One or two needed that extra hour denied by service regulations and this I thought was a great pity, for who knows what talent was likely to be relegated to lesser service [sic] by this very stringent rule.[4]

Another problem was created when men (especially potential pilots) were reluctant to apply for aircrew training for fear of failing. The inspector-general of the RCAF noted in July 1943 that the selection and training of pilots "has become so systemized and mechanical that the fact that we are dealing with human beings has been lost sight of."[5]

Failures were replaced by recruits from the 'pool,' which also included a number of ground crew who had volunteered for aircrew training. In the early days of the BCATP, the RCAF had made a deliberate policy of recruiting for ground crew – in far greater numbers than necessary to meet aircrew requirements – tradesmen who were medically fit for aircrew. In March 1943, the air force, although it refused to give up its skilled technicians, conceded that the army had been deprived of an important source of recruits. When the army agreed to refer to the air force all its recruits who were medically qualified for aircrew, the RCAF agreed to stop enlisting men for ground duty who were fit for overseas service for the army. It further promised to try to direct aircrew who failed to graduate into the army. By February 1945, however, only thirty-eight rejected airmen had transferred – nearly eleven thousand had been kept in the RCAF and assigned to ground duties.

135 Among the countless schools created by the BCATP was No. 1 RCAF Officers' Training School, set up as a 'finishing school' for officers. Chubby Power is taking the salute at the opening of the school at Domaine d'Estrel, Que., on July 31, 1943. The officer behind him on his right (at the end of the line) is Air Marshal L.S. Breadner, chief of Air Staff.

Ironically, just as the two services reached agreement after eighteen months of undignified scrambling for men, and just as the casualty rate in Bomber Command began to drop dramatically, the British suddenly discovered that instead of a shortage of aircrew they had an embarrassingly large surplus, especially of pilots, scattered in remote parts of the world and previously overlooked. A scaling down of the BCATP began in November 1943 and developed rapidly in the new year. The enlistment of 17-year-olds was discontinued, and the upper age limit for all aircrew was lowered to 28. After February 1944, only a token number of new candidates were taken in because a large reserve of trainees had been built up over the previous two years – in September there were still 5,400 of them.

This surplus was in sharp contrast to the shortages that became apparent in the Canadian army at the same time. Although the army had been industriously trying to convert Home Defence conscripts (zombies) to General Service status, and although it objected to the RCAF's competition for recruits, the general staff was singularly slow in recognizing that a reinforcement crisis was brewing. In December 1943, while the 1st Division was fighting its way into Ortona, Brigadier A.W. Beament, in charge of the Canadian reinforcement system in Italy, raised a danger signal: battle losses in the infantry were running at a rate higher than expected. General Stuart, who as chief

The Home Front

of staff in Ottawa had been responsible for the expansion of the army, and was now chief of staff at Canadian Military Headquarters in London, did not believe the wastage would continue at such a high rate. He preferred to rely upon British figures from the Western Desert and Tunisia in 1942 and 1943 – and planned for replacements accordingly.

On March 14 1944, Stuart issued instructions that no important communication on reinforcements was to be sent out from CMHQ in London without being approved by him. Although during the next three months a number of staff officers raised the spectre of infantry shortages in internal correspondence, CMHQ sent no reports to Ottawa that might suggest there was a reinforcement problem. Defence Minister Ralston's military advisers in Ottawa were therefore in no position to offer him conflicting advice. On June 7, the day after D-Day, the adjutant-general told him that "I concur in Gen. Stuart's opinions.... I can state with confidence that from our present resources we will meet our commitment for 1944."[6]

His optimism was transitory. Efforts to provide replacements from artillery, engineer, and armoured corps units (all of which were incurring fewer casualties than expected) brought in about four thousand men to the infantry but, with the high casualty rates that prevailed in northwest Europe, there was still a deficiency of nearly two thousand in II Canadian Corps by the end of August 1944.

In mid-September, what had previously been a matter of internal urgency assumed the proportions of a full-scale crisis. Conn Smythe, a former hockey star turned Toronto sports promoter, and now a major convalescing from a wound received in France, told the Toronto press on September 18 that the level of training of infantry replacements in Europe was unacceptably low. He claimed that "large numbers of unnecessary casualties result from this greenness, both to the rookie and to the older soldiers who have the added task of trying to look after the newcomers as well as themselves," and suggested that "the relatives of the lads in the fighting zone should ensure no further casualties are caused to their own flesh and blood by the failure to send overseas reinforcements now available in large numbers in Canada."[7]

The furore that Smythe's statement aroused sent Ralston, who had been a First World War infantryman, scuttling off to Europe to see for himself. He found the training to be satisfactory (many a veteran disagreed with him) in both Italy and Holland; but wherever he went the infantry was shorthanded and, at CMHQ in London, staff officers doubted whether they could maintain even the present flow of reinforcements. Reporting that Stuart "had painted too rosy a picture" in August, Ralston argued vehemently for conscripted service overseas.

The ensuing Cabinet meetings considered every possible alternative. However, there was no consensus. A substantial minority that included Angus L. Macdonald, T.A. Crerar, J.L. Ilsley, and, eventually, C.D. Howe hewed resolutely to the conscriptionist line. Discussions might have continued forever when Mackenzie King suddenly began to interpret events in terms of a conspiracy to unseat him as prime minister. His reaction was dramatic. Early on the morning of November 1, he discussed the issue with General McNaughton, whom he had previously been considering as the next governor general. McNaughton did not see conscription as inevitable and "agreed that the Canadian Army was not needed for the winning of the war."[8] That was enough for King: he promptly dismissed Ralston, using the resignation letter that the latter had drafted in 1942, and McNaughton was sworn in as minister of national defence the following day. The conscription crisis was still unsolved, but the circumstances in which it would henceforth be considered had altered radically.

When General McNaughton had first discussed the problem with King he had been somewhat out of touch with military matters, having been on indefinite leave since his return from England. However, a quick survey of the manpower situation as presented by his new staff convinced him that there was indeed an urgent need for some fifteen thousand additional General Service men. He ordered a new campaign to persuade the conscripts to volunteer for General Service – the NRMA men were the most obvious source for sufficiently trained infantry – but it was not pushed too enthusiastically by some of his pro-conscriptionist regional and district commanders, who had their own ideas about what should be done. The widespread belief among General Service men that only conscription for overseas could meet national requirements, because NRMA men would respond to no other incentive, is well represented in reports on army morale in the Pacific Command. 'Zombies' there were frequently contrasted with 'REAL CANADIANS' who were doing the fighting. A staff officer summarized the situation in 1944:

> The general G[eneral] S[ervice] complaint is why people like these be allowed to live in this country and derive benefits from the efforts of Canadians, who are fighting and helping win the war so that this country may remain free. When the peace has been won this will be a great country, and why should these spineless jellyfish be allowed to progress with the country when they have not had the courage to help her in times of trouble?[9]

Attitudes like this no doubt had the effect of stiffening the resistance of NRMA men to General Service. As the officer in question went on to say, the zombies, when asked why they would not volunteer,

> state that they do not owe the country anything, that during the 'Depression Years' the country didn't care whether they

were alive or not, but now it is at war they are wanted. When it is pointed out that there are plenty of men O/S [overseas] who were just as badly off as they were, they merely state, "If they want to be suckers, we aren't."[10]

The comparative failure of the campaign converted McNaughton, albeit reluctantly, to the conscriptionist position. His conversion was reinforced too by the resignation of the commander of the Winnipeg district, who considered it impossible to adhere to the prime minister's policy. "If the Commanders, one after the other, began to resign, the whole military machine would run down, begin to disintegrate and there would be no controlling the situation," he told the prime minister on the 22nd. This news came as a blow to King. The war was so close to being won. But as he groped for a course of action, he suddenly recollected that he had always claimed that if conscription was necessary it would be enforced. Now conscription surely was necessary, both to find reinforcements for the front and to prevent the collapse of the military machine. (Thoughts of a military revolt also crossed his paranoic mind.)

That night he told the Cabinet of his decision to introduce overseas conscription. It was a decision that he reached none too soon, since, unknown to him, most of his key English-speaking ministers had been meeting that day; and a group that included Howe, Ilsley, Crerar, and Macdonald had decided to submit their resignations if conscription were not enforced. "It was apparent to me," King wrote in his diary, "that it was only a matter of days before there would be no government in Canada." Among the opponents of conscription, only C.G. Power, the alcoholic anglophone Quebecker who was associate minister of national defence for air, resigned. The King government thus survived its biggest crisis.

When conscription was brought in, there were no civil disturbances comparable to those in Quebec in 1917, but among NRMA units there were some incidents of mutiny and rioting. At Terrace, in British Columbia, the situation became serious for a few days, but eventually the troops responded to the very moderate disciplinary measures imposed by General Pearkes' staff, who understood that the trouble had been caused by a mere handful of men. Some 13,000 NRMA soldiers eventually went overseas, but only 2,463 ever served in field units in Europe – a number that made the whole conscription exercise seem rather artificial in the end. They suffered 313 battle casualties, of which 69 were fatal, and, in the words of the official historian, "there were no complaints of their performance in action."

The conscription issue was, indeed, an artificial one. Even before large numbers of reinforcements were needed, Canadian military leaders consistently underestimated infantry replacement rates because they were relying on British figures, although Canadian needs proved to be higher. Whether the Canadians fought harder, were

The Home Front

assigned the most difficult tasks, were more careless or less well trained, those losses can hardly be attributed primarily to the 'greenness' of their reserves since their casualties had been peculiarly high all along. And the casualties alone are not enough to explain the reinforcement problem. It was also a result of inflexibility in the Canadian military organization.

The Americans, for example, coped with their shortages much more effectively than the Canadians by reorganizing the formations available in the field. In the European theatre, less than 4 per cent of American troops were assigned to headquarters duties compared to the Canadian 13.6 per cent. The Canadians might also have emulated the example of General Patton, who in September 1944, finding that his army was nine thousand riflemen under strength, lopped an arbitrary 5 per cent off the establishments of his various subordinate headquarters. "This has produced loud wails from all the section chiefs, who declared they could not run their offices," he recalled. "As a matter of fact, even the 10 per cent cut which we subsequently made had no adverse effect [on fighting efficiency]."

Energetic remustering, cuts in headquarters personnel, the combing out of 'lines of communication' establishments, and, if necessary, a reduction in fighting strengths could surely have seen the Canadians through. The Army Overseas was never more than fifteen thousand men short, and even then there were over forty thousand General Service men medically fit for infantry (Canadian standards were uncommonly high) languishing in Canada, with perhaps fifteen thousand more in the United Kingdom. However, the failure to use them may be explained in part by General Burns' curt comment to Ralston that "the troops would not feel that the government and country was supporting them wholeheartedly ... if ... it allowed them [the NRMA men] to sit comfortably in Canada." There were many Canadians, in and out of uniform, who were determined that the burden should be equally shared.

Conscription for service overseas was not the only problem encountered in the deployment of manpower. Rapid industrialization and the modernization and expansion of existing industry created – especially after late 1941 – an insatiable demand for workers. Anticipating future needs, the government had formed the National Labour Supply Council in June 1940 and set up an Inter-Departmental Committee on Labour Co-ordination in October of that year. The Committee's report, twelve months later, revealed that competition existed "between the armed forces and industry, between war and non-war industries and among industrial concerns generally." So the Cabinet set up a Manpower Committee and brought in National Selective Service.

King tabled the necessary Orders in Council on March 24, 1942, emphasizing measures to encourage women to join the labour force.

In July 1941, the army had created the Canadian Women's Army Corps, and the air force formed the Canadian Women's Auxiliary Air Force, later changed to the Royal Canadian Air Force (Women's Division). A year later the navy brought in the Women's Royal Canadian Naval Service. By the end of the war, these three services had increased to a strength of 21,624, 17,085, and 6,781 women respectively. Another 4,518 women were in the medical and nursing services. They helped to release men for other duties and performed some tasks that men could not have done so well. Similarly there was a rapid increase of women in industry.

Although at the peak period there were a million women in all kinds of employment compared with 638,000 in 1939, women could not provide the complete answer to manpower shortages in industry. It was necessary, in January 1943, to impose new National Selective Service civilian regulations that resulted in the compulsory transfer of about 127,000 principally male workers from low- to high-priority industries over the following two-and-a-half years. Men in the armed forces were given special leave to bring in the harvests – a severe disruption to both training and morale in many units – and some military personnel were released to work in the coal-mining and lumber industries. One way or another, over a million Canadians eventually joined the industrial work force.

Nevertheless, war was straining national resources to the limit and, in the process, was uncovering some of the weaknesses in the Canadian social structure. In wartime the pace of living speeds up, change occurs at a faster rate, and what in peacetime might be unacceptable behaviour becomes tolerated. Racism, for example, is usually frowned on in polite society, but a war against another race or nation almost fosters it. Not surprisingly in the circumstances, therefore, the nastiness of war made one segment of the Canadian population suffer some of the miseries shared by the millions of displaced persons who formed the human debris of the war in Europe.

Japanese immigrants had begun to arrive on the west coast more than half a century before Japan's attack on Pearl Harbor.[11] By 1942 people of Japanese descent living in British Columbia numbered 22,000, of which the majority – over 13,000 – were Canadian born (Nisei) and therefore citizens of Canada, 3,223 were naturalized Canadians, and 5,564 were Japanese nationals (Issei), most of whom had resided in Canada for a generation and 2,000 of whom were women. A law-abiding, industrious people, the vast majority were successful fishermen or market gardeners, while a few had branched out into the business world and were running small shops or taxi services that, for the most part, served their own communities. They lived in Vancouver, in various communities along the southern British Columbian coast, and on farms in the lower Fraser and Okanagan valleys.

136 Expropriated Japanese-Canadian fishing vessels, December 1941.

The attitudes of Caucasian Canadians to these resident Japanese were heavily influenced by generalized anti-Oriental feelings that were particularly strong in British Columbia (and on the Pacific coast of the United States), where immigration of Chinese and Indians, as well as Japanese, had been opposed and feared for over half a century. The sinister image of a 'Yellow Peril,' which conveyed a threatened extinction of the white race by Orientals, had frequently found its way into published diatribes in the early part of this century, and this kind of racism was not absent from the agitation – often stirred up by politicians as an easy crowd-pleaser – that came to a climax after the bombing of Pearl Harbor when war hysteria on the west coast gave a new meaning to the 'peril' of the Japanese presence.

The industry and efficiency of the Japanese had made them highly competitive in a depressed labour market and suggested to the business community that they might easily become serious rivals at higher economic levels. Attempts were made in the 1920s to remove them from the fishing industry by reducing the number of licences issued; naturalized and native-born citizens were denied the vote on the pretext that those who had Canadian citizenship but had retained their Japanese citizenship (a matter that they had no choice about, since the Japanese government insisted that they could not renounce it) were untrustworthy; and the possibility of 'repatriating' or compulsorily expelling them was intermittently discussed. The few voices that were raised in protest against this – among them those of the *Vancouver Province* and the Co-operative Commonwealth Federation (one of the founding elements of the New Democratic Party) - were largely dismissed. In fact, in the federal election of 1935, anti-Japanese propaganda against the CCF was widely used by the Liberals. For example, the slogan "Look behind the solicitor for a CCF candidate, and you will see an Oriental leering over his shoulder with an

The Home Front

137 Japanese-Canadians in Vancouver begin the journey to the interior of British Columbia and three years of internment.

eye on you and your daughter" was heard on radio broadcasts in Vancouver.[12]

With Japan's attack on Pearl Harbor, in December 1941, and Canada's subsequent declaration of war, anti-Japanese interests in British Columbia were provided with a golden opportunity to deal with the 'problem' that obsessed them. Action began with the arrest and internment of thirty-eight Japanese who were already on RCMP dossiers as potential subversives; some 1,200 fishing boats were impounded; and registration of all persons of Japanese origin, regardless of citizenship, was required. There was a probably groundless, but firmly held, belief that the attack on Pearl Harbor had been aided by a Japanese fifth column in Hawaii (where none of the large population of Japanese descent was ever interned, although the Americans did evacuate nearly all people of Japanese ancestry from their own west coast); there was talk of invasion – the possibility of which General Maurice Pope rightly thought absurd – and of the need to protect national security from acts of treachery.

At meetings in Ottawa with British Columbian politicians on January 8 and 9, 1942, the army point of view was expressed by Pope: "I cannot see that they constitute the slightest menace to national security." The RCMP was satisfied that it had interned the few Japanese

The Home Front

138 The community kitchen of the camp at Slocan City, B.C., about 1943.

who were possibly dangerous and the RCN saw no problem, since all Japanese fishermen had been removed from the sea. The politicians, who represented and largely shared their constituents' widespread fear and distrust of all people of Japanese origin, objected strongly to this attitude, however. General Pope has reported a conversation with one of them: "Sadly he said that for years his people had been telling themselves that war with Japan would afford them a heaven-sent opportunity to rid themselves of the Japanese economic menace for evermore. And now after a period of some weeks nothing had been done. Not a word did they say about national security."[13]

When the evacuation of all male Japanese nationals between 18 and 45 (some 1,700) was announced on January 14, west coast politicians, their party organizations, and various regional pressure groups launched a campaign to have all resident Japanese Canadians interned. On February 26, 1942 – bending to the pressures of the local majority that were either irrational or self-seeking, and to some expressed fears that riots might ensue if all Japanese Canadians were not removed from the coast – the Cabinet announced a mass evacuation under the War Measures Act, which gave it sweeping powers that included "arrest, detention, exclusion and deportation" and that could be enforced without constitutional challenge in the absence of a Charter of Rights.

The Home Front

Over the next eight months a clumsy and sometimes callous handling of the evacuation brought much hardship and degradation to nearly twenty thousand hapless people. They were sent by special trains to the interior valleys of British Columbia, most of them being housed in hastily constructed shacks in the vicinity of the Slocan valley. Until these huts were put up, many of them were housed in tents or under the leaking roof of a dilapidated hockey rink. In addition, there were psychological hardships. The majority of these men and women were citizens but were being treated differently from all other citizens (most of those of German and Italian descent merely had to report regularly to the Registrar of Enemy Aliens). They were members of a tightly knit cultural community that was unexpectedly splintered by external forces totally beyond its control. Family groups had already been broken up by the initial evacuation of adult males.

When some of the men, temporarily housed in the Vancouver Immigration Building, refused to board trains without their families, force had to be used to bring them to order. "We worried about what would happen to the women and children," one of them has recorded.

> We said "After we know that our families are safe and well looked-after then we will go anywhere."... But when we resisted the police came and took us one by one.... My wife was sent to Slocan, to Lemon Creek, along with my daughter and my sister. My daughter was still small, less than a year old ... they had to put up tents for temporary housing. Later they started building cabins – two families to each cabin. It was cold and they had no heat, they used to put the lantern underneath the bed for warmth.[14]

Those men who refused to accept passively the injustice of the evacuation, and in many cases of being separated from families, were sent to internment camps in northern Ontario, where the conditions were even worse.

> There were nothing we could do, so we gave up. I was in that camp for four years. When it got cold the temperature went down to as much as 60° below. We lived in huts with no insulation. Even if we had the stove burning the insides of the windows would all be frosted up, really white. I had to lie in bed with everything on that I had.... At one time there were 720 people there, all men, and a lot of them were old people. We were treated just like prisoners of war.... We were allowed one card and one letter a week from our families, but those letters were all censored.... I used to wonder how my family was getting along, I only heard from them occasionally.[15]

In the spring of 1945 the federal government offered the Japanese a choice between settling "east of the Rockies" or repatriation to Japan. (By the end of the war some 7,000 had taken the opportunity offered to them of leaving the internment camps to perform various kinds of labour in other parts of Canada.) Over 10,000 initially chose repatriation, well aware that they were expected to relinquish any claims to Canadian nationality. Their decision was based on fifty years of prejudice, the 1942 evacuation, and the current plan for postwar resettlement outside of British Columbia, which portended the same prejudiced treatment that had marked their life in Canada to the present. Some 4,700 later sought to change their decision and remain in Canada, but in 1946 nearly 4,000 did return to Japan. Those who remained spread across the land with memories that became less bitter as the years passed, in spite of the fact that reparations for property that had been sold without consent were often far less than the value of the property. Citizens of Japanese descent were finally granted the franchise, federally in June 1948 and in British Columbia in March 1949.

Spawned out of the democratic process, the events in British Columbia and even aspects of the conscription problem represented the sorts of evils the democracies were fighting to destroy. Two kinds of military service put the equality of Canadians into question and led to a potentially nation-splitting crisis, yet they resulted from what the prime minister perceived as the necessities of the war situation and the requirements of national unity. Evacuation of the Japanese was a fundamental violation of individual freedom, but in the final analysis it was also the expression of the will of the majority in British Columbia. The times exposed the flaws of human nature more readily than usual. Mackenzie King, his ministers, and many leading personalities deserve criticism for failing to anticipate and cope appropriately with both problems.

The Cabinet, however, did compensate for its mistakes in those areas by an excellent pragmatic grasp of social and economic requirements. Under its direction, war-nourished industrial and economic growth brought desperately needed improvements in the standard of living. From the very beginning of hostilities, social and economic matters were seen as an aspect, not just of the war effort, but also of reconstruction after the war. Armed with the bitter experience of twenty years, Canadian leaders were determined to prevent a repetition of the high prices and inflation of the First World War, the postwar rehabilitation problems of the 1920s, and the Depression of the 1930s. On December 8, 1939, Ian Mackenzie, minister of pensions and national health, became chairman of the Cabinet Committee on Demobilization and Re-establishment. It slowly started the machinery for what became an excellent rehabilitation program, and Mackenzie took advantage of the prime minister's interest in social reform to propose the introduction of unemployment and health insurance. The principal obstacle to such reforms in the past had been the difficulty of obtaining the approval of the provinces for enacting such federal legislation. The time was now ripe, Mackenzie argued, to propose such reforms and, in the case of unemployment insurance, the Cabinet agreed. Eight of the nine provinces had Liberal governments and, as the prime minister pointed out, the current prospect of economic gain afforded precisely the conditions needed to start building up financial reserves for an unemployment insurance program. Ralston, Ilsley, and Howe – who then held the Finance, National Revenue, and Transport portfolios respectively – opposed the measure vigorously because they thought the money was needed to finance the war,[16] but they were unable to overcome King's advocacy of the reform in Cabinet. Thus, in August 1940, unemployment insurance became law – the first step in introducing a national social security program.

Mackenzie, encouraged by his victory, expanded his interests beyond rehabilitation and persuaded the prime minister to approve the establishment of a Committee on Reconstruction in February 1941. Chaired by Principal F. Cyril James of McGill University, it was designed to chart a course in line with Mackenzie's own interpretation of social security, based on the prime minister's 1918 book, *Industry and Humanity*, and, as the latter told a House of Commons committee, the inspiration of a British Liberal, the young Lloyd George. Out of the James Committee's work came the Marsh Report, entitled *Report on Social Security for Canada*, and published in March 1943. It was prepared in less than a month by Leonard C. Marsh (a young British-born economist who held social welfare views similar to those espoused by the CCF) as Canada's response to the famous Beveridge Report of December 1942, the blueprint for Britain's post-war society.

Like Beveridge, Marsh advocated family allowances, health insurance, and funeral benefits. He went beyond Beveridge in recommending a post-war guaranteed employment program that would cost one billion dollars. Marsh in fact was advocating a social-security scheme that involved protection against unemployment, sickness, and old age. It was seen by many in the press, and in Ottawa, as wild-eyed radicalism. Nonetheless, the social-security expenditures would 'prime the pump' and thus help avoid a post-war depression.

Even before the Marsh Report, the James Committee had come out in favour of a Ministry of Economic Planning and in support of a national health insurance scheme that had been maturing for years. The government's Economic Advisory Committee – consisting of Deputy Minister of Finance Clifford Clark, W.A. Mackintosh, an economist from Queen's University, Graham Towers, governor of the Bank of Canada, Donald Gordon, and Norman Robertson – opposed these recommendations and advised Mackenzie King to restore the responsibility for reconstruction planning to the existing departments of government.

139 Propaganda is only one of the purposes of the graphics in this scene at a Quebec lumber camp, May 1942.

By this time, moreover, King had developed reservations about James and his committee, who were becoming too radical for his tastes, and now he withdrew his earlier support. In September 1943, he told the Liberal caucus – nervous about CCF gains in the polls and in the Ontario provincial election of August 1943, when it had become the Official Opposition – that it was appropriate "to have everything in readiness for the moment the war was over, to improve conditions, but we should not forget until that moment came that the supreme duty of the Government and everyone in the country was for the men at the front and the winning of the war."[17]

The Home Front

YOU SERVE by SAVING

Buy WAR SAVINGS CERTIFICATES

WAR SAVINGS STAMPS 25¢

$5 FOR $4 $10 FOR $8 $25 FOR $20 $50 FOR $40 $100 FOR $80

140 This poster was widely used and had several texts.

King's doubts about the commitment of public funds to social security were alleviated in subsequent months – particularly when his secretary, J.W. Pickersgill, Ian Mackenzie, and his new Quebec lieutenant, Louis St Laurent (who had joined the Cabinet after the death of Ernest Lapointe in November 1941), persuaded him of the political and economic advantages of the program. They reminded him of the impressive swing towards the CCF, the strength of labour as a political force, and the likelihood that it would have to be appeased by offering security to workers. Economic czar C.D. Howe emphasized the need to maintain full production after the war and supported a pension system for workers as well as health insurance, although he opposed family allowances, claiming that they would encourage idleness. St Laurent's justification suggested, on the contrary, that there would be a positive link between family allowances and industrial production.

The Home Front

There can be no doubt that the father of a large family has burdens that are more onerous than those of a single man or even the head of a small family; he requires more but there can be no system under which an employer could be required to pay him more, because that would make it more difficult, if not impossible, for him to get any work at all.[18]

In 1944 and 1945, therefore, the Cabinet, overcoming the opposition of some ministers to certain aspects of the reconstruction program, brought in legislation for farm-improvement loans, an agricultural and fisheries support program, the Industrial Development Bank, the National Housing Act, the Veteran's Insurance Act, the Export Credit Insurance Act, and that most potent of political weapons, family allowances. These measures would help re-elect the Liberal government in June 1945.

At the same time the government was engaged in a vigorous battle against inflation. During the 1914-18 war, costs had increased with great speed, leading to demands for increased wages and long, costly strikes. The Cabinet was determined to avoid making the same mistake in this war, and thus it had created the Wartime Prices and Trade Board (WPTB) on September 3, 1939, with sweeping powers to control the price, supply, and distribution of the necessities of life, although in its first two years it played a limited role.

The Cabinet first intervened in the economy in December 1940, imposing a form of wage control on war industries, while the WPTB imposed partial price controls on rents, coal, sugar, timber, steel, milk, and other essentials. However, by the fall of 1941 stronger measures were necessary to deal with a sudden, sustained spurt in the cost of living, and the government imposed a total freeze on wages and prices. The need to maintain production, of course, meant continuing exports – a need already expressed in mutual aid and one that demanded energetic measures for preserving the industrial capacity that had been built up by the war.

In October 1941 the WPTB, under Donald Gordon, became at a stroke one of the most powerful agencies in the land, intruding into every aspect of life. Rules and regulations abounded, and Canadians at home were at last faced with the reality of total war. Permission was required to change jobs, to be promoted, to get gasoline for an automobile, and coupons were necessary to purchase meat. Despite the controls and the bureaucracy, the policy was a success. The consumer price index increased by less than a point between 1943 and 1945. The cost of living index rose from 101.5 in 1939 to 120.4 in 1945, and most of that increase took place before the wage and price controls of October 1941. By contrast, the average annual income of Canadians rose from $975 at the beginning of the war to $1,538 in 1945. People were generally better off than they had been for years, with more real income in their pockets, with unemployment insur-

-TO VICTORY

141

ance as a cushion against lay-offs, and, by the end of the war, with family allowances.

Above all, war-induced prosperity brought jobs. In 1939 more than 10 per cent of the labour force were out of work. By mid-1941 this rate had been cut in half, and by 1943 Canada reached full employment. As a result, labour unrest was not a major source of social disruption during the war. There were strikes – major ones on occasion – but even in vital war industries the disturbances were seldom serious enough to warrant unusual precautions for maintaining public order. At the Aluminium Company of Canada, in Arvida and

The Home Front

Shawinigan Falls, troops were called out to protect the plants from possible sabotage, once in July 1941 and once in November 1943.

The trouble on the second occasion seems to have stemmed as much from the efforts of the American Federation of Labour to move in on the National Catholic Syndicate, as from the desire to imitate steel workers and coal-miners, who had been striking throughout Quebec, by going out to win concessions from the employer. There were no riots and no untoward behaviour reported by the military. Most of those incidents that did occur took place in pleasant summer weather. "Thirty or forty below zero seems a little too much to face," reported an observer at Arvida in November 1943. "Trouble will occur as soon as the weather turns for the better."[19]

The unions grumbled that controls on wages stopped them from making headway at a time when their role was vital. But, in fact, the war gave Canadian unionism an extraordinary boost and total membership almost doubled from 359,000 in 1939 to 711,000 in 1945. Many labour leaders remained grateful to the Liberal government and showed their support at election time, something that had the effect of weakening the CCF, which was desperately trying to forge firm alliances with the labour movement.

Full stomachs and full employment are not necessarily the only measure of a healthy society. A 1943 pamphlet issued by the left-leaning Workers' Educational Association, and entitled 'The Permanent War of Homo the Sap,' tried to warn its readers, through satire, that once the war was over wartime prosperity and social benefits could easily disappear. In peace there would be "no strangling government interference, no bossy political bureaucrats, no confiscating and ruinous taxation, no shortage of necessary materials, no ham-stringing priorities," and the consequence was likely to be a return to the bad old Depression days when impoverished rugged individualism replaced government control. The pamphleteer was fortunately proved wrong, partly because, as the opinion polls revealed, so many Canadians thought as he did and influenced King's reconstruction policy, partly because the satirist's picture was overdrawn – life may have been trying sometimes, but it was not totally constricting.

Nevertheless, the controls were there and for the first time since the Great War the government managed the flow of information. To co-ordinate the dissemination of propaganda and to measure the state of opinion in the country the government established the Wartime Information Board, headed (as of 1942) by John Grierson. Through its offices the government was able to influence the interpretation of the war in the press and on the radio (there was, of course, no television), distribute and co-ordinate the dissemination of war propaganda, and conduct public opinion polls. Propaganda went hand in glove with censorship. Directives in the handbook called *Radio Broadcasting*

143 Premier King –
"We can't have any criticism of my war effort."

1940

Toronto Telegram

Censorship, issued in October 1941, stated that the object of censorship was

> to prevent the enemy, so far as may be possible, from obtaining naval, military, air, economic, or other information, of a nature inimical to the national interest.
>
> It is also the business of censorship to prevent the dissemination of news or talks which might cause dissatisfaction amongst the civil population, injuriously affect the morale of the armed forces, or prejudice His Majesty's relations with foreign powers.[20]

144 One of the first security posters, issued about 1940 by the Directorate of Public Information, Ottawa.

The Home Front

CARELESS TALK BRINGS TRAGEDY IN WARTIME

The Home Front

There was to be no indication or speculation on such things as the movement of troops, the progress of the BCATP from month to month, or the establishment and activities of prisoner-of-war or internment camps.

At a Round Table Conference of the Canadian Institute of International Affairs, held in May 1941, the elements of 'democratic' propaganda were summarized. It was expected "to have the groundwork of truth" and should "evoke wherever possible an emotional response." Within that framework, stress was to be laid on developing:

1. A pride in Canada and in her achievements of the past and present....
2. Confidence in Canadian institutions....
3. A burning conviction that freedom is essential....
4. A realization, both emotionally and intellectually, of the consequences of defeat....
5. The identification of every individual with a nation at war in the common cause....
6. A sense of personal responsibility on the part of every individual to do his share to ensure that democracy works as the best policy.
7. Equality of sacrifice.
8. A sanguine confidence in our victory. This demands staying power (as a long war seems inevitable) and a cheery, serene, buoyant spirit.[21]

The popularity of films made the cinema a powerful focus of propaganda. Newsreels confronted viewers with many events of the war as they actually happened and feature films, produced by studios in the United States and England, not only entertained people, but affected their emotions and bolstered their feelings of patriotism. They dealt with loyal families suffering bravely under war conditions, families living without their men, war-service experiences, and successful military operations. *Dangerous Moonlight* (1940), unashamedly sentimental, presented the heroic but futile Polish stand against German armed might to the romantic strains of the Warsaw Concerto, which became extremely popular, and left audiences with a message of inevitable victory.

Noël Coward was both the writer and star of *In Which We Serve* (1942); in a thinly disguised portrait of Lord Louis Mountbatten, he embodied the British naval tradition – and the English class system – in which nobility, decency, and bravery were bound to prevail in the long run, in spite of the enemy's apparent material superiority. *One of Our Aircraft Is Missing* (1942) did for British airmen what the Coward film did for British sailors. In the romantic *Mrs. Miniver* (1942) noble behaviour in a family context survived bombings, the evacuation of Dunkirk, and personal tragedy. This Hollywood depiction of wartime England had enormous popularity in North America, less in Britain.

Desert Victory (1943) and *Tunisian Victory* (1943), about the British successes in North Africa, both made by the British Army Kinematography Unit, and *Target for Tonight* (1943), about the strategic bombing offensive, used a documentary approach to give apparently realistic portrayals of the growing armed might of the Allies. In such quality films the enemy was, for the most part, a faceless entity, but a host of second-rate Hollywood productions made German and Japanese characters either unredeemably villainous or figures of fun – somewhat unsophisticated animations of the ideas expressed in the political cartoons of the day.

In Canada, to counteract the prevailing dominance of Hollywood and to co-ordinate all government film activity, the National Film Board had been set up under John Grierson in 1939. The talented film-makers he acquired were to make the NFB internationally known in the field of propaganda during the war. The immensely popular American newsreel *The March of Time* had its Canadian counterparts in the *Canada Carries On* series, released once a month from 1940 (until 1960), and *World in Action* (1942-45).

Film was a relatively new propaganda weapon but posters had been used at least since the French Revolution, and various Canadian propaganda agencies – the Wartime Information Board, the information services of the army, navy, and air force, the Red Cross – seized upon this cheap and effective means of communicating with the public. About five hundred designs (of which over three hundred are in the National War Museum) vary in subject from rather conventional invitations to buy war bonds, through dramatic appeals to patriotism by means of arresting imagery, to sober warnings ("Careless Talk Brings Tragedy in Wartime").

Radio, which probably had an even more devoted audience than television today, was mainly escapist, with predominantly American programming. Newscasts, however, provided the most immediate and vivid contact with the realities of war and were listened to avidly. Among the Canadian correspondents, Matthew Halton and Marcel Ouimet gave on-the-spot reports of fighting at the front and of air raids over England, often including the sounds of the events themselves.

The written reports of war correspondents such as Peter Stursberg and Charles Lynch, illustrated with the photographs of Ken Bell and others, brought the war (with a strong Canadian slant) to readers of newspapers. Indeed, newspapers devoted almost all their space to some aspect of war activities. One woman later recalled how they bombarded the public with war propaganda to a point of near saturation.

> The newspapers, they were just propaganda sheets. My goodness, on the front pages, war, war, war, and in the insides, how to cook cheaper, how to do Victory Gardens,

145 Food rationing was never severe. Montreal, May 27, 1942.

why we should have car pools, buy Victory Bonds and tell our friends they were traitors if they didn't load up on them too....

You remember those Sunday supplements, they were jammed with war stuff. How to cook cabbage, make cabbage rolls, and then drink the cabbage juice. Or carrots. Swiss chard. Spinach. Did they think we didn't know that stuff, like how to make a dollar do the price of ten? You'd think the idiots in their big offices in Toronto and Ottawa didn't know about the Depression we just went through — ten years of nothing.[22]

One Home Front episode at the end of the war dramatized the consequences of a misguided application of controls on a frustrated, pent-up community. On VE-Day, May 8, 1945, Halifax was closed

146 Looters swarming in and out of the Hollis Street liquor store, Halifax, May 8, 1945.

down – nothing had been done to handle the spontaneous outburst of joy that was certain to mark the German surrender. There were some seven thousand soldiers and seventeen thousand sailors in the area, most of whom felt they had been victimized and abused by local establishments and had grown to hate the city. When the servicemen mingled with civilians on the streets, a jovial street party turned into a destructive rampage that spilled over into Dartmouth on the other side of the harbour. Liquor stores were broken open and 65,000 bottles of spirits and over 100,000 quarts of beer were soon exacerbating the situation. An orgy of vandalism followed, with 564 business firms suffering damage to their premises (mostly broken windows, but some arson) and 207 shops actually looted. Some of the latter were virtually destroyed before order was restored.

Other riots, though less severe ones, occurred elsewhere in Canada: there was bitterness just below the surface of life on the Home Front about the system that had given Canada ten years of nagging concern for sons, brothers, and fathers overseas, for the wounded, maimed, and prisoners of war. And there were blacker emotions evoked by loss through death, by horror at the atrocities revealed in Hitler's concentration camps, by a fear still lurking in the minds of many that peace might bring depression upon the land again. But it would be wrong to suggest that negative feelings were uppermost when the war ended. It was, on the whole, a time of high optimism, a moment for belief in a future where, in spite of all dangers, individual freedom could flourish and the relative prosperity at home would continue unabated. There was pride in the nation's accomplishments and in the sense that Canada had a new and important place in the world.

The Home Front

147, 148 More looting
in Halifax on VE-Day,
and the results of looting.

The more than a million men and women in the armed forces had come from a profoundly innocent generation that had been confined to a world of sharply limited horizons. Only the rich, who could afford to travel, or the unemployed, who were often obliged to look for jobs far from home, had seen much beyond their own provincial surroundings. Now, for more than five years they had been crossing from one end of the country to the other; many had gone overseas and some to the ends of the earth. Most had tested themselves successfully in unfamiliar and trying circumstances. Away from homes and families for years at a time, rubbing shoulders with strangers and subjected to varying degrees of stress, they had discovered that they had unique regional qualities – not only French and English, but also Maritimers, 'Upper Canadians,' westerners, and British Columbians. The war brought self-confidence and new awareness of national identity. It also brought some political radicalization as contacts were made between different social classes and with people from other Allied nations.

149   Sailors celebrating in Ottawa on VJ-Day.

The general election of June 1945 – with the CCF vote probably mainly responsible for cutting down government seats to 125, compared to 181 in 1940 – reflected the new national mood. Though the

The Home Front

overseas service vote was apathetic, it went strongly in favour of the CCF. The prime minister, who did not enjoy universal popularity, was cordially disliked in the armed forces overseas because of his approach to conscription. (Indeed, the service vote defeated him in his own riding of Prince Albert.) The total military vote, however, resulted in a narrow government plurality of 118,070 over the CCF's 109,670, leaving the Conservatives far behind.

Canadians supported the government because it had prevented inflation and satisfied widespread desires for social security. The Tories accused King of bribing the voters with the baby bonus, but he could claim that his majority proved the success of his wartime policies. The Second World War had changed Canadians and altered their consciousness of themselves, their society, and their role in the world – perhaps even more than in 1918. King recognized this. His government's constant attention to reconstruction after 1944 allowed Canada to make a successful transition to post-war conditions. When the war against Japan ended and peace finally came, in August 1945, the ominous implications of Nagasaki and Hiroshima did not pass unnoticed. But in Canada prosperity seemed assured, confidence reigned supreme, and hope for individual happiness was unlimited.

Epilogue

Canada was very far from being ready for a large-scale war in 1939 and its efforts often fell short of requirements. One does not build an efficient war machine in only a few years without a great deal of experience or, failing that, an enormous industrial and economic base like that of the United States. Initially, Canadian industry was unable to cope with the unprecedented amounts and standards of production that were required, and it was slow in getting into high gear – though it ultimately did so, to great effect. The army went through agonies of command problems and performed less well than the public realized or some historians are willing to accept. The navy also experienced terrible growing pains when large-scale expansions began in 1940, and until 1943 it was unable to hold its own in the war at sea. Nor was the air force able to provide overseas formations of greater than wing strength until 1943, and it never did succeed in fighting as an independent command.

It has to be admitted that, in the final analysis, Canada's effort was not essential to winning the war. Nonetheless, the country did its utmost, and that was more than enough to win the respect of other nations and to earn for Canada a place in world affairs of a totally unprecedented kind. Its provision of raw materials and munitions was an important contribution to Britain's survival. The extremely generous financial assistance to Britain, especially in the form of mutual aid, was crucial in relieving that country's dollar shortage. To convoy some 43,000 ships, amounting to more than 235 million deadweight tons, across the Atlantic was a great strategic triumph of the war, and one in which Canadian ships and aircraft played a major part, especially after 1943. The training of 153,000 aircrew out of a total of 239,761 engaged in British and Commonwealth flying operations was, quite simply, a decisive contribution to obtaining command of the air – an essential prerequisite to victory that would have taken much longer to achieve without the Canadian contribution.

The production in Canada of more than 815,000 motor vehicles (including most of those used by the British Eighth Army) was an industrial coup. The impressive growth of the aircraft industry made Canada important in that field, and the building of about a thousand ships was an enormous achievement for an industry that had been moribund at the beginning of the war, even though the number was a drop in the bucket beside British and American figures.

The war effort can also be measured in terms of sacrifice. Casualties were not so appalling as in the Great War, but the Canadian men and women who lost their lives represented the supreme gesture a nation can make in support of its ideals and its allies: 22,917 in the army, 17,101 in the air force, and 2,024 in the navy.

At the war's end Canadians felt their part in the war effort had been beyond compare. Men and women returned from overseas to joyful receptions, even to cheering crowds and cascading tickertape.

> Back to Ottawa on a train crowded with returning soldiers. Train after train travels across Canada from east to west laden with them, dropping them off by threes and fours at small towns and in their hundreds at the big cities. The train windows are crowded with their sunburned, excited faces. They lean out in their shirt-sleeves, whistling at the girls at the station platforms, making unflattering jokes about Mackenzie King. We passed through one little station where there were a few mugwumps standing about on the platform staring bemusedly at the train and a group of soldiers on the train began themselves to cheer. "Hurray! Give the boys a welcome." The stations are crowded with them striding about self-consciously – men of the world – having proved something about themselves that is plainly to be seen in their sun-paled divisional patches and the ribbons on their chests – the 1939-43 Star, the Africa Star, the France and Germany award, the Voluntary Service Ribbon.[1]

For many of those who travelled across the country to their homes, Canada was

> still only half-real, familiar, and yet, because so unchanged, curiously foreign and a little frightening. The endless flow again of evergreens, log-flecked lakes, violently rushing rivers and little wooden stations knotted with people in strange variegated clothes, civilians looking bored, even a little resentful, or filled with childish noisiness.[2]

The government made generous preparations for returning soldiers, sailors, and airmen. There would be the best of medical care for the wounded and maimed, grants for education, land grants for farmers, clothing allowances for all, hefty cash settlements. Only a rich country could have provided such largesse, and Canada was rich in 1945. The wealth that the land had produced in the war years, the hard work on the home front and overseas, the government's planning for the peace and its economic and social policies had been geared not to permit the blight of depression to settle on the country once again.

The war made Canadians nationalistic and gave them confidence in themselves and their country. There was still loyalty to the British tie among English Canadians, but it was now somewhat different in cast. In 1939 England had been a great power, but in 1945 it was a debtor state, owing billions to Canada and ravaged by the war's efforts. The loyalty now was more nostalgic in tone than it had been

150 Two Canadian soldiers outside Nijmegen read a farewell message from their commander before starting for home.

Epilogue

PERSONAL MESSAGE
FROM
THE ARMY COMMANDER

Here is wishing you a satisfactory and speedy journey home. and that you find happiness at the end of it.

You go back with your share of the magnificent reputation earned by the Canadians in every operation in which they have participated in this war. A fine reputation is a possession beyond price. Maintain it — for the sake of all of us, past and present — in the days ahead.

I know that you will get a great welcome on your return. See to it that those Canadian units and drafts, which follow after you, get just as good a welcome home when they, also, get back.

Good luck to each one, of you — and thanks for everything.

(H.D.G. Crerar) General.

151 Prime Minister Mackenzie King at the San Francisco Conference, 1945. Norman Robertson, under-secretary of state for external affairs, is seated behind him with his hand to his head.

before the war. Attitudes towards the United States had also changed. The Americans who had built the Alaska Highway were sometimes referred to as an "army of occupation" only half-jokingly. But the Roosevelt administration had helped Canada mightily during the war, co-operating in North American defence as a result of the Ogdensburg Agreement and accepting Canadian economic aspirations with the Hyde Park Declaration. Gratitude, therefore, was perhaps dominant over suspicion. That, too, was different from 1939.

In 1939 Canada had been wracked by the Depression, dispirited, out of work. But in 1945 it was booming, its factories working at top speed. And, incredibly, the nation had become a power in the world, with the third-largest navy, the fourth-largest air force, and an army of almost seven divisions, five of which (and two independent armoured brigades) were overseas, where they had earned the respect of both enemy and Allied observers for their fighting qualities. For a country of eleven million people this was an astonishing achievement.

This new power was reflected in the way other nations regarded Canada. 'Canada' and 'Canadians' had become household words in countries where Canadians had fought, especially in Holland. As one of the few countries that had emerged with its territory unscathed by war, as an industrial and agricultural producer, and as a rich land, Canada was sought after by the less fortunate. Canadian aid, money, know-how, and technology were in demand, and the government and people were generous in providing what was required. Canadian diplomats and officials abroad received more respect than they had ever known. Their confidence was reflected in the way they argued for Canadian positions and approaches to world problems.

As early as 1943 Lester Pearson, as a member of the Canadian legation in Washington, had made the point that Canada was now irretrievably committed to international collective security: "a bomb dropped on a Chinese village," he said, "echoes across the St Lawrence."[3] Mackenzie King, in August 1944, had argued in the House of Commons that the directing bodies of future international organizations, and particularly the United Nations, should consist of "those countries which have the most to contribute to the maintenance of the peace of the world."[4] He and his advisers believed Canada had played a sufficiently prominent role in the war to earn a recognized place in the United Nations as a near-great power. This was an application of the so-called functional principle as defined by the prime minister in the House of Commons in July 1943, according to which "representation on international bodies should not be restricted to the largest, nor extended to all states, but should be on the basis of the contribution the state has to make."[5]

On that basis, Canada could claim a major role in civil air transport, for example, or in questions concerning food and raw material production, and possibly even in security matters. There were difficulties in establishing ready acceptance of this principle by the superpowers during the war and at the creation of the United Nations in 1945. Nevertheless at the war's end, instead of being the rather insignificant state the world had known in 1939, Canada had established its right to the status of 'middle power.' It had come out of the shadows.

Notes

1: THE EVE OF WAR

1 Public Record Office [PRO] London, Cab 23/88, Cabinet Conclusion 34(37)5, June 16, 1937, quoted in J.L. Granatstein, *Canada's War: The Politics of the Mackenzie King Government 1939-1945* (Toronto, 1975), p. 2.

2 C.P. Stacey, *The Arts of War and Peace 1914-1945* [Historical Documents of Canada, Vol. V], (Toronto, 1972), pp. 492-3.

3 Sir Maurice Hankey to Sir George Pearce, January 2, 1935, PRO, Cab 63/81.

4 Hankey, "Impressions of Canadian Defence Policy," ibid.

5 Ian Mackenzie Papers, File X-4, quoted in C.P. Stacey, *Six Years of War* (Ottawa, 1955), p. 14.

6 Charles Ritchie, *The Siren Years: A Canadian Diplomat Abroad 1937-1945* (Toronto, 1974), p. 96.

7 Mackenzie King Diary, June 15, 1939.

8 J.W. Wheeler-Bennett, *King George VI* (London, 1959), p. 379.

2: AN UNMILITARY PEOPLE

1 Secretary of State for Dominion Affairs to Secretary of State for External Affairs, September 6, 1939, quoted in C.P. Stacey, *Arms, Men and Governments: The War Policies of Canada, 1939-1945* (Ottawa, 1970), Appendix 'C'.

2 We are grateful to Professor J.L. Granatstein for the substance of this passage, which depends upon his interpretation in *Canada's War* (Toronto, 1975).

3 P. Stratford (ed.), *André Laurendeau: Witness for Quebec* (Toronto, 1973), pp. 23-4.

4 L.B. Pearson, *Mike: The Memoirs of the Rt. Hon. Lester B. Pearson*, Vol. I: *1897-1948* (Toronto, 1972), pp. 138-9.

5 King Diary, September 12, 1939.

6 G.R. Stevens, *A City Goes to War* (Brampton, Ont., 1964), pp. 177-8; D.J. Goodspeed, *Battle Royal* (Toronto, 1962), pp. 355-6; T.H. Raddall, *West Novas: A History of the West Nova Scotia Regiment* (Toronto, 1947), pp. 24-5.

7 C.P. Stacey, *Six Years of War* (Ottawa, 1955), p. 63.

8 Memorandum by Loring Christie, June 19, 1939, in J.A. Munro (ed.), *Documents on Canadian External Relations*, Vol. VI: *1936-1939* (Ottawa, 1972), pp. 209-10.

9 Stacey, *Arms, Men and Governments*, p. 20.

10 Barry Broadfoot, *Ten Lost Years 1929-1939: Memories of Canadians Who Survived the Depression* (Toronto, 1973), p. 373.

11 Subtitle of G.F.G. Stanley, *Canada's Soldiers* (Toronto, 1954; rev. 1960).

12 Humphrey Carver, *Compassionate Landscape* (Toronto, 1975), pp. 63-4.

3: THE SINEWS OF WAR

1 Stacey, *Arms, Men and Governments*, Appendix 'C'.

2 C.B.A. Behrens, *Merchant Shipping and the Demands of War* (London, 1955), pp. 7-9, 35, 45, 55, 188.

3 Granatstein, *Canada's War*, p. 49.

4 Stacey, *Arms, Men and Governments*, p. 25.

5 BCATP Agreement, December 17, 1939, in ibid., Appendix 'D'.

6 Harold Balfour, *Wings over Westminster* (London, 1973), p. 117.

7 Brereton Greenhous *et al.*, *The Crucible of War* (Toronto, 1994), ch. 1.

8 R.J. Hammond, *Food* (U.K. Civil Series, London, 1951), Vol. I, p. 69; W.N. Medlicott, *The Economic Blockade* (U.K. Civil Series, London, 1952), Vol. I, pp. 315, 372-3, 541.

9 Maurice Pope, *Soldiers and Politicians* (Toronto, 1962), p. 165.

10 J.L. Granatstein and R.D. Cuff, *Canadian American Relations in Wartime: From the Great War to the Cold War* (Toronto, 1975), pp. 69-92.

11 Howe Papers, File S-5(1), Howe to J.L. Ilsley, July 21, 1941, quoted in Granatstein, *Canada's War*, p. 188.

12 F.M. Smith (ed.), "History of the British Admiralty Technical Mission in Canada," p. 48, in Directorate of History [DHist], Department of National Defence [DND].

4: THE ATLANTIC BRIDGE

1 W.S. Churchill, *Their Finest Hour* (Boston, 1949), p. 598.

2 Gilbert Tucker, *The Naval Service of Canada*, Vol. II (Ottawa, 1952), pp. 31-2.

3 Barry Broadfoot, *Six War Years 1939-1945: Memories of Canadians at Home and Abroad* (Toronto, 1974), p. 174.

4 Alan Easton, *50 North: An Atlantic Battleground* (Toronto, 1963), p. 15.

5 "NHS 8000-HMCS *Chambly*," DHist, DND.

6 Murray to Capt. R.E. Reid, October 15, 1941, in National Archives of Canada [NAC], RG 24, Vol. 11979/51-15.

7 Wolfgang Frank, *Die Wolfe und der Admiral: Triumph and Tragik der U-Boote* (Hamburg, 1954), p. 303; S.W. Roskill, *The War at Sea 1939-1945*, Vol. I (London, 1956), p. 96.

8 Memorandum dated January 5, 1943, Admiralty file M.015473/42. Quoted in Historical Records Office, Canadian Naval Mission Overseas, "Canadian Participation in North Atlantic Convoy Operations June 1941 to December 1943," November 27, 1945, in DHist, Kardex 122.013 (D2), DND.

9 Easton, *50 North*, p. 99.

10 Ibid., p. 166.

11 J.A. Boutilier (ed.), *The RCN in Retrospect 1910-1968* (Vancouver, 1982), p. 186.

12 RCN Monthly Report No 31, August 1944.

13 Douglas to Air Marshal L.S. Breadner, June 25, 1944, in DHist, Kardex R/57/162, DND.

14 Roskill, *The War at Sea 1939-1945*, Vol. III, Pt II (London, 1961), p. 286.

5: THE ARMY OVERSEAS, 1940-1943

1 G.W.L. Nicholson, *The Gunners of Canada*, Vol. II: *1919-1967* (Toronto, 1972), p. 55.

2 Farley Mowat, *The Regiment* (Toronto, 1955), p. 26.

3 L.B. Pearson, *Mike*, Vol. I: *1897-1948* (Toronto, 1972), p. 168.

4 First Brigade War Diary, NAC.

5 John Swettenham, *McNaughton*, Vol. 2: *1939-1943* (Toronto, 1969), p. 110.

6 R. Macleod and D. Kelly (eds), *Time Unguarded: The Ironside Diaries 1937-1940* (New York, 1962), p. 242.

7 Stacey, *Six Years of War*, pp. 440-3, 448.

8 Ibid., p. 486.

9 Private information.

10 B.L. Villa, *Unauthorized Action: Mountbatten and the Dieppe Raid* (Toronto, 1989), p. 3.

11 J. Campbell, *Dieppe Revisited: A Documentary Investigation* (London, 1993), ch. 5.

12 "Miscellaneous Reports on Dieppe Raid," DHist Kardex 593(D3), DND.

13 Private information.

14 "Miscellaneous Reports on Dieppe Raid," DHist Kardex 594, DND.

15 "Miscellaneous Reports on Dieppe Raid," DHist Kardex 594.013(D17), DND.

16 Lucien Dumais, *Un Canadien français à Dieppe* (Paris, 1963), pp. 143-4. [Author's translation.]

17 W. Reyburn, *Glorious Chapter: The Canadians at Dieppe* (Toronto, 1943), p. 113.

6: SICILY AND SOUTHERN ITALY

1 Arthur Bryant, *The Turn of the Tide, 1939-1943* (London, 1957), p. 596.

2 C.M. Johnson, *Action with the Seaforths* (New York, 1954), p. 145.

3 G.W.L. Nicholson, *The Canadians in Italy, 1943-1945* (Ottawa, 1956), p. 178.

4 Viscount Montgomery of Alamein, *Memoirs* (London, 1958), p. 184.

5 Arthur Bryant, *Triumph in the West, 1943-1946* (London, 1959), p. 278.

6 Charles Comfort, *Artist at War* (Toronto, 1956), p. 38.

7 Stacey, *Arms, Men and Governments*, p. 232.

8 Waldo Smith, *What Time the Tempest* (Toronto, 1953), p. 181.

9 Stevens, *A City Goes to War*, p. 274.

10 A. Kesselring, *The Memoirs of Field Marshal Kesselring* (London, 1953), p. 192.

11 A.E. Powley, *Broadcasts from the Front* (Toronto, 1975), p. 62.

12 Raddall, *West Novas*, p. 169.

13 R.H. Roy, *The Seaforth Highlanders of Canada, 1919-1965* (Vancouver, 1969), p. 292.

14 Johnson, *Action with the Seaforths*, p. 305.

15 John Windsor, *Blind Date* (Sidney, B.C., 1962), pp. 47-8.

7: OPERATION *OVERLORD*

1 A.V. Sellwood, *Dynamite for Hire* (London, 1956), p. 129.

2 Quoted in John Winton (ed.), *The War at Sea 1939-1945* (London, 1967), p. 336.

3 Eric Luxton, *1st Battalion, The Regina Rifle Regiment, 1939-1946* (Regina, 1946), p. 34.

4 R.M. Hickey, *The Scarlet Dawn* (Campbellton, N.B., 1949), pp. 194-5.

5 Warren Tute, *D Day* (London, 1974), p. 209.

6 C.P. Stacey, *The Victory Campaign* (Ottawa, 1960), p. 133.

7 Cornelius Ryan, *The Longest Day* (New York, 1959), p. 246.

8 Quoted in H. Essame and E. Belfield, *The Battle for Normandy* (London, 1965), p. 85.

9 Ibid., p. 89.

10 No. 404 Squadron Operational Record Book, DHist, DND.

11 D.E. Harker, *The British Columbia Regiment 1939-1945* (Vancouver, 1950), p. 17.

12 W.R. Bird, *The North Shore (New Brunswick) Regiment, 1939-1945* (Fredericton, N.B., 1963), p. 263.

13 Quoted in Alexander McKee, *Caen: Anvil of Victory* (London, 1964), pp. 336-7.

14 R.L. Rogers *History of the Lincoln and Welland Regiment* (Montreal, 1954), p. 153.

15 No. 439 Squadron Operational Record Book, DHist, DND.

16 A. Fortescue Duguid, *A History of the Canadian Grenadier Guards, 1760-1964* (Montreal, 1965), p. 281.

8: THE WAR IN THE AIR

1 See H.A. Halliday, *No. 242 Squadron, The Canadian Years* (Stittsville, Ont., 1981).

2 J.A. Kent, "The Battle of Britain: Extracts from a Personal Diary," *The Polish Airman's Weekly Review*, June 1957.

3 Greenhous *et al.*, *The Crucible of War 1939-1945*, p. 212.

4 J.E. Johnson, *Wing Leader* (New York, 1957), p. 166.

5 DHist biographical files, DND.

6 Quoted in *The RCAF Overseas: The First Four Years* (Toronto, 1944), pp. 164-5.

7 Jerrold Morris, *Canadian Artists and Airmen 1940-45* (Toronto, n.d.), p. 89.

8 Quoted in Greenhous *et al.*, *The Crucible of War 1939-1945*, p. 725.

9 DHist biographical files, DND.

10 Quoted in Hans Rumpf, *The Bombing of Germany* (London, 1963), p. 94.

11 Six Group Monthly Engineering Reports, DHist Kardex 181.005 (D2001), DND.

12 Six Group Monthly Photographic Summaries, DHist Kardex 181.009 (D4253), DND.

13 Six Group Monthly Operational Summaries, DHist Kardex 181.005 (D2002), DND.

14 Greenhous *et al.*, *The Crucible of War 1939-1945*, p. 862.

15 Ibid.

16 Sir Charles Webster and N. Frankland, *The Strategic Air Offensive Against Germany 1939-45* (London, 1961), Vol. IV, p. 482.

9: NORTHERN ITALY AND NORTHWEST EUROPE, 1944-1945

1 Martha Gellhorn, *The Face of War* (London, 1967), p. 125.

2 J-G. Poulin, *969 Heures d'Enfer* (Québec, 1946), p. 40.

3 No. 417 Squadron Operational Record Book, DHist DND.

4 E.L.M. Burns, *General Mud* (Toronto, 1970), p. 220.

5 Quoted in G.W.L. Nicholson, *The Canadians in Italy, 1943-1945* (Ottawa, 1956), p. 564.

6 Quoted in C.P. Stacey, *The Victory Campaign* (Ottawa, 1960), p. 337.

7 W. Boss, *The Stormont, Dundas and Glengarry Highlanders 1783-1951* (Ottawa, 1952), p. 217.

8 D.W. Grant, *'Carry On': The History of the Toronto Scottish Regiment (MG) 1939-1945* (n.p., 1949), p. 106.

9 Bird, *The North Shore (New Brunswick) Regiment*, p. 447.

10 W.R. Bird, *No Retreating Footsteps: The Story of the North Nova Scotia Highlanders* (Kentville, N.S., n.d.), p. 257.

11 Donald Pearce, *Journal of a War* (Toronto, 1965), pp. 102, 113.

12 Johnson, *Wing Leader*, p. 271.

13 R.W. Thompson, *The Battle for the Rhineland* (London, 1955, p. 209.

14 Bird, *The North Shore (New Brunswick) Regiment*, p. 523.

15 Duguid, *A History of the Canadian Grenadier Guards*, p. 322.

16 J.F. Bartlett, *1st Battalion, The Highland Light Infantry of Canada* (Galt, Ont., 1951), p. 107.

17 Pearce, *Journal of a War*, p. 164.

18 Battalion War Diary, May 5, 1945, in RG 24, National Archives of Canada.

19 Pope interview, July 7, 1977, DHist biographical files, DND.

20 Quoted in S.R.G. Brown, "The Loyal Edmonton Regiment At War, 1939-1945," unpublished thesis at Wilfrid Laurier University, Waterloo, Ontario, p. 78.

10: THE WAR AGAINST JAPAN

1 Quoted in T.W. Melnyk, *Canadian Flying Operations in South East Asia, 1941-1945* (Ottawa, 1976), p. 29.

2 General Staff Historical Report No. 28, p. 8, DHist, DND.

3 Stacey, *Arms, Men and Governments*, p. 58.

4 J.B. Conant [scientific adviser to President Roosevelt], to C.J. Mackenzie [president of National Research Council of Canada], quoted in Wilfred Eggleston, *Canada's Nuclear Story* (Toronto, 1965), p. 65.

11: THE HOME FRONT

1 S.F. Wise and R.A. Preston, *Men in Arms* (New York, 1971), p. 304.

2 Stratford (ed.), *André Laurendeau: Witness for Quebec*, pp. 23-4.

3 Gabrielle Roy, *The Tin Flute* (1947; New Canadian Library ed., 1958), pp. 33-4.

4 Richard Gentil, *Trained to Intrude* (London, 1974), p. 44.

5 Croil to Power, July 28, 1943, in RG 24, Vol. 3262, HQ 232-3-11, NAC.

6 Stacey, *Arms, Men and Governments*, p. 433.

7 Ibid., p. 440.

8 Mackenzie King diary, Oct. 31, 1944, quoted in ibid., p. 455.

9 DHist Kardex 322.009 (D217), DND.

10 Ibid.

11 The following discussion has been based in part on information contained in Ken Adachi, *The Enemy That Never Was: A History of the Japanese Canadians* (Toronto, 1976).

12 Ibid., p. 82.

13 Pope, *Soldiers and Politicians*, p. 177.

14 Daphne Marlatt, *Stevenston Recollected* (Victoria, 1975), p. 66.

15 Ibid.

16 J.W. Pickersgill, *The Mackenzie King Record, Vol. I: 1939-4* (Toronto, 1960), p. 61.

17 Ibid., p. 580.

18 "Memorandum on Post-War Policies," November 18, 1943, in Mackenzie King Papers, J 4, File 39-06, C 257111-18, NAC.

19 DHist Kardex 142.81A (D14), DND.

20 *Radio Broadcasting Censorship: Handbook Consolidation of Directives* (Ottawa, 1941), p. 5.

21 G.C. Andrews, *Canada at War: A Report of a Round Table held by the Canadian Institute of International Affairs at its 8th Annual Conference, Kingston, Ont., May 1941* (Toronto, 1941), pp. 11-14.

22 Broadfoot, *Six War Years 1939-45*, pp. 31-32.

EPILOGUE

1 Ritchie, *The Siren Years*, p. 207.

2 Earle Birney, *Turvey* (Toronto, 1963), p. 277.

3 Quoted in James Eayrs, *In Defence of Canada*, Vol. 3: *Peacemaking and Deterrence* (Toronto, 1972), p. 35.

4 Canada, House of Commons Debates, August 4, 1944, quoted in R.A. Mackay (ed.), *Canadian Foreign Policy, 1945-1954: Selected Speeches and Documents* (Toronto, 1971), p. 4.

5 Canada, House of Commons Debates, July 9, 1943, in ibid., p. 3.

Bibliography

Readers interested in learning more about Canada's part in the war might examine any or all of the published works cited in the preceding Notes. Such studies may be rounded out with selections from the following list.

Canada's strategic assets – the relative security of its geographic position in a European and, later, a Pacific war; the economic significance of its proximity to the United States and of its natural resources and industrial capacity; the political implications of membership in the British Commonwealth – are the subject of discussion in various volumes in the British official history of the Second World War, especially *North American Supply* (London, 1955) by H. Duncan Hall and *Studies of Overseas Supply* (London, 1956) by Hall and C.C. Wrigley. One official American volume, *Military Relations between the United States and Canada, 1939-1945* (Washington, 1959) by Stanley W. Dziuban, examines sympathetically the 'triangle versus partnership' question.

Robert Rumilly propounds the widely accepted view that the war emphasized the basic division between French and English Canadians in his *Histoire de la Province de Québec*, tomes XXXVIII-XLI (Montreal, 1968-69) and his colourful, two-volume, biography, *Maurice Duplessis et son temps* (Montreal, 1973). Conrad Black, *Duplessis*, (Toronto, 1977) complements Rumilly's work in English. Norman Hillmer *et al.*, (eds), *On Guard for Thee* (Ottawa, 1988) is a collection of essays that examine the wider implications of ethnicity and the Canadian state in the Second World War.

Pro-conscription forces found their chief spokesman in the Conservative leader Arthur Meighen, whose biographer, Roger Graham, devotes considerable attention to conscription in his *Arthur Meighen*, Vol. III: *No Surrender* (Toronto, 1965). The most comprehensive and balanced work on this subject, however, is *Broken Promises: A History of Conscription in Canada* (Toronto, 1977) by J.L. Granatstein and the late J.M. Hitsman. General E.L.M. Burns, in a rather technical but still readable study, *Manpower and the Canadian Army* (Toronto, 1966), demonstrates that administrative weaknesses were at the root of the army's manpower shortage. Surprisingly, there is still no adequate full-length account of the impact of the war on the economy. *History of the Department of Munitions and Supply: Canada in the Second World War* (Ottawa, 1950) by J. de N. Kennedy contains data that have not been published elsewhere, but it is not a full treatment of the subject and is a difficult book to use. It shows the need for official accounts, by professional historians, of the civil as well as the military aspects of national affairs. There are useful chapters in Robert Bothwell, Ian Drummond, and John English, *Canada, 1900-1945* (Toronto, 1987) and in J.M. Bliss, *Northern Enterprise* (Toronto, 1987). Robert Bothwell and William Kilbourn have written the biography of Canada's wartime economic czar, *C.D. Howe* (Toronto, 1979), and Bothwell has also penned the history of *Eldorado: Canada's National Uranium Company* (Toronto, 1984).

On the military side, histories of army units dealing, either entirely or in large part, with their experiences in the Second World War, are plentiful. Their quality varies widely, but anyone interested in following the adventures of a local regiment should be able to find its story through the public library system. Those concerned simply with examining the ethos of a typical fighting unit cannot do better than look at Farley Mowat's entertaining story of the Hastings and Prince Edward Regiment, entitled simply *The Regiment* (Toronto, 1955).

Campaign studies include the rigorous and generally incisive work by J.A. English, *The Canadian Army and the Normandy Campaign: A Study in Failure* (New York, 1991), and Jeffery Williams' more conventional and broader account, *The Long Left Flank: The Hard Fought Way to the Reich, 1944-1945* (London, 1988). *Not in Vain* (Toronto, 1973) by Ken Bell and C.P. Stacey offers a reflective, essentially pictorial, retrospect of the Canadian experience in northwest Europe. Denis and Shelagh Whitaker, *Tug of War* (Toronto, 1984), dealing with Canadian operations in the Scheldt estuary, and *Rhineland* (Toronto, 1989) and *Normandy: The Canadian Summer* (Montreal, 1994) by W.J. McAndrew, M. Whitby, and D. Graves provide good overviews of those campaigns. (A useful book for travellers is Terry Copp's *A Canadian's Guide to the Battlefields of Normandy* (Waterloo, 1994).

Daniel Dancocks, *The D-Day Dodgers* (Toronto, 1991) presents a popular account of Canadians in the largely neglected Italian campaign. For an illuminating view of the strains of battle in Italy and northwest Europe, see Terry Copp and Bill McAndrew, *Battle Exhaustion: Psychiatrists and the Canadian Army, 1939-1945* (Montreal, 1990). The literature on Dieppe is voluminous and increasingly contentious; Brereton Greenhous, *Dieppe, Dieppe* (Montreal 1993) provides a recent, highly critical overview.

Since the first edition of this book was published, many first-person accounts have appeared, particularly by veterans of Sicily and Italy. Prominent among them are Farley Mowat, *My Father's Son: Memories of War and Peace* (Toronto, 1992), Fred Cedarburg, *The Long Road Home* (Toronto, 1984), and C. Sydney Frost, *Once a Patricia* (St. Catharines, Ont., 1988), all concerned with the Italian campaign. Senior officers' memoirs include J.V. Allard (with Serge Bernier), *The Memoirs of General Jean V. Allard* (Vancouver, 1987); Howard Graham, *Citizen and Soldier* (Toronto, 1987); and George Kitching, *Mud and Green Fields* (Langley, B.C., 1986). J.L. Granatstein, *The Generals* (Toronto, 1993) is a collective biography that reviews the personalities and politics of some – but not all – of the army's higher commanders.

The navy and air force have, until recently, been less well served. Joseph Schull's excellent popular account, *The Far Distant Ships* (Ottawa, 1952 and, in reprint, Toronto, 1987), discreetly passes over the less successful phases of Canada's war at sea. Marc Milner's *North Atlantic Run* (Toronto, 1985) is the best account of the RCN's convoy operations. Michael Hadley, *U-Boats Against Canada* (Montreal 1985) is a sound study of German submarine warfare in Canadian waters. James Boutilier (ed.), *The RCN in Retrospect, 1910-1965* (Vancouver, 1982) and W.A.B. Douglas (ed.), *The RCN in Transition, 1910-1985* (Vancouver, 1988) are collections of essays that include important new material on the Second World War. Tony German, *The Sea*

Is at Her Gates (Toronto, 1990), a popular history of the RCN from its origins to recent times, provides a good survey of wartime activities. J.D.F. Kealy and E.C. Russell have written *A History of Canadian Naval Aviation, 1918-1962* (Ottawa, 1965).

Naval unit histories are rather fewer in number, and generally less well written, than the army's regimental histories. William Sclater's *Haida* (Toronto, 1946) competently tells the story of a Canadian destroyer and gives some colour to the wartime navy, as does James Lamb, *The Corvette Navy: True Stories from Canada's Atlantic War* (Toronto, 1977). Of first-person accounts, Hal Lawrence, *A Bloody War* (Toronto, 1979) is among the most memorable. The flavour of the lower deck is preserved in Frank Curry, *War at Sea: A Canadian Seaman on the North Atlantic* (Toronto, 1990).

Volume II of the official history of the RCAF, *The Creation of a National Air Force* (Toronto, 1986) tells the story of the North Atlantic convoys, the defence of Canada's coasts, and the Aleutian campaign, from an air perspective; but neither it, nor Volume III, recounts the history of the thousands of Canadians who served with the RAF from 1939 to 1945. Carl Christie's *Ocean Ridge* (Toronto, 1995) recounts the full story of the RAF's Ferry Command. However, Larry Milberry and Hugh Halliday, in *The Royal Canadian Air Force at War, 1939-1945* (Toronto, 1990) provide a good overview. A fine selection of first-person narratives, spanning the whole range of air operations, are to be found in Hedley Everard, *A Mouse in My Pocket* (Picton, Ont., 1988); M. Lavigne and J.F. Edwards, *Kittyhawk Pilot* (Battleford, Sask., 1983); Dave Mackintosh, *Terror in the Starboard Seat* (Toronto, 1980); Bill Olmstead, *Blue Skies* (Toronto, 1987); Douglas Alcorn and Raymond Souster, *From Hell to Breakfast* (Toronto, 1980); Murray Peden, *A Thousand Shall Fall* (Stittsville, Ont., 1981); and Walter Thompson, *Lancaster to Berlin* (Toronto, 1986).

Two of several studies on women in the armed forces deserve special mention. They are G.W.L. Nicholson, *Canada's Nursing Sisters* (Toronto, 1975) and Ruth Roach Pearson, *"They're Still Women, After All"* (Toronto, 1986).

Index

Aberhart, William, 13, 19
Abruzzi, Italy, 143
Afrika Korps, 185
Agira, Sicily, 138
Alaska, 237-40
Aldershot, England, 105
Alençon, 169
Aleutians, 238, 240
Alexander, Field Marshal Sir Harold, 137, 149
Alvarez, Luis, 250
American forces. *See* U.S. forces
Amiens, France, 213
Anderson, Major-General T.V., 28, 29
Anglo-Canadian Inter-Governmental Inspection Board (later Inspection Board of the United Kingdom and Canada), 51
Angus, Flying Officer A.B., 179
Antwerp, Belgium, 213, 219
Anzio, Italy, 149, 155
Ardennes, Belgium/France, 106, 222
Argentan, France, 171
Argentia, Nfld, 75
Arielli Ridge, 148
Armies, Allied: 1st U.S., 208, 212; 2nd British, 157, 169; 3rd U.S., 171, 208; 5th U.S., 131, 141, 142, 151; 7th U.S., 133; 8th British, 52, 140, 149, 208, 212; 9th U.S., 227, 229. *See also* British army; British Expeditionary Force (BEF); U.S. Army; U.S. Army Air Force
Armies, Canadian: 1st Canadian, 116, 132, 157, 169-70, 171, 208, 211, 218, 222. *See also* Canadian army
Armies, German: 1st Parachute, 224; 7th, 169; 10th, 209, 212; 14th, 212; 25th, 231. *See also* German forces
Army Groups: 12th U.S., 157; 21st British, 157, 212
Army, Navy and Air Supply Committee, 15
Arnhem, Netherlands, 218
Arques-la-Bataille, France, 120
Arromanches, France, 169
Asdic, 33, 67, 79

ATFERO. *See* Atlantic Ferry Organization
Atlantic Ferry Organization (ATFERO), 84-9
Atomic Bomb, 246-51; Canadian research on, 247-8, 250-1
Attu Island, Aleutians, 238-40
Audet, Flight Lieutenant Dick, 203, 223
Aurich, Germany, 236
Australia, 15, 37, 43, 59, 114
Austria, 12, 208
Auxiliary Active Air Force, 35
Avranches, France, 171

Badaglio, *Mareschal* Pietro, 138
Bader, Group Captain Douglas, 180
Baie de la Seine, 156
Baillie-Grohman, Rear Admiral T., 129
Balbergewald forest, Germany, 224
Balfour, Harold, 43
Balkans, 185, 208
Balloon bombs, 240-1
Bangalore torpedoes, 122-3
'Barber Pole,' Group, 82
Basic Defence Plans for North America, 47, 48
Battle of Britain, 110, 170, 182-5
Battle of the Atlantic, 62-104 *passim;* protecting supply routes, 65-6, 72, 92-5, 97-8; Intelligence and, 80, 82-5, 101; convoys, 63, 66, 72, 74, 76, 84; Allied naval forces, 63, 69, 75, 76, 82, 90, 92, 94, 97-8; Air support, 63, 72, 74, 78-9, 89-90, 96, 98-9, 101-2; on the North American seaboard, 76-9; ferrying aircraft, 84-9; Escort Groups, 81-2, 90, 97-8; European coastal warfare and, 99-104
'Battle of the Bulge,' 222
Battle of the Rhineland, 224-3
Bay of Biscay, 69, 91, 97, 99
BCATP. *See* British Commonwealth Air Training Plan
Beament, Brigadier A.W., 260
Beatty, Sir Edward, 84
Beaverbrook, Lord, 84
BEF. *See* British Expeditionary Force
Beinen, 229
Bell, Ken, 281

Bennett, Air Vice-Marshal D.C.T., 84, 201
Bennett, R.B., 131
Berchtesgaden, Germany, 206
Bergen, Norway, 180
Berlin, Germany, 110, 131, 201, 206, 208, 231
Beurling, Flight Lieutenant George Frederick, 186-8
Beveridge Report, 271
Biervliet, Netherlands, 218
Blackader, Brigadier K.G., 174
'Black Pit,' 78, 89
Bletchley Park, 83, 101
Blockbuster, Operation, 224
'Bloody Sunday,' 14
Böhlen, Germany, 206
Boomer, Flying Officer Ken, 181
Botwood, Nfld, 72
Boulogne, France, 120, 294-5
Bourassa, Henri, 16, 25, 282
Bowhill, Air Marshal Sir F.W., 88
Bradley, General Omar, 157
Brand, Commander Eric, 82
Breadner, Air Marshal L.S., 43, 244, 260
Bremen, Germany, 191, 193
Breskens, Netherlands, 216, 217
Brest, France, 108-9
Brigades, Canadian: 1st Armoured, (originally 1st Army Tank), 132, 136, 141, 143-4, 150, 208; 1st Infantry, 107, 109, 125, 136; 2nd Armoured, 172; 2nd Infantry, 152; 3rd Infantry, 142; 4th Armoured, 171; 7th Infantry, 161; 9th (Highland) Infantry, 162, 229; 13th Infantry, 238-40
Britain: and Canada, 13, 14-15, 20, 23, 30, 31, 35, 37, 40-5, 28; and the U.S., 13, 18, 19, 45, 49-50, 69, 75-6, 248; declares war, 21; Canadian forces in, 27; and the BCATP, 36-7, 42-4; mobilization, 40, 41; economy, 45-6, 49, 287
British Admiralty, 23, 31, 32, 54, 63, 67, 80, 107; Technical Mission, 53-4
British Air Ministry, 23, 37, 40
British army, 23, 28, 45, 107; in Norway, 106; in France, 107-9, 170-1, 212-3; in Hong Kong, 111-6; in Sicily, 33-9; in Italy, 139-41, 142, 149-55; in north-